The Country of the Blind

A MEMOIR AT THE END OF SIGHT

Andrew Leland

PENGUIN PRESS NEW YORK 2023

PENGUIN PRESS
An imprint of Penguin Random House LLC
penguinrandomhouse.com

As discussed in chapter 5, describing images is an important practice for inclusion and access in the arts (and elsewhere). To that end, a description of the dust jacket and author photo of this book appears on pages 324–25, after the Notes on Sources.

LIBRARY OF CONGRESS CATALOGING-IN-PUBLICATION DATA
Names: Leland, Andrew, author.
Title: The country of the blind: a memoir at the end of sight / Andrew Leland.
Description: New York: Penguin Press, 2023. |
Includes bibliographical references and index.
Identifiers: LCCN 2022051325 (print) | LCCN 2022051326 (ebook) |
ISBN 9781984881427 (hardcover) | ISBN 9781984881434 (ebook)
Subjects: LCSH: Leland, Andrew. | Blind—United States—Biography. |
People with visual disabilities—United States—Biography.
Classification: LCC HV1792.L453 A3 2023 (print) | LCC HV1792.L453 (ebook) |
DDC 362.4/1092—dc23/eng/20230513
LC record available at https://lccn.loc.gov/2022051325
LC ebook record available at https://lccn.loc.gov/2022051326

Printed in the United States of America
1st Printing

Designed by Alexis Farabaugh

For Lily and Oscar

What so clearly appears as an end is better understood as
a beginning whose innermost meaning we cannot yet grasp.
Our present is emphatically, and not merely logically, the
suspense between a no-longer and a not-yet.

Hannah Arendt, *Men in Dark Times*

The splinter in your eye is the best magnifying glass.

Theodor Adorno, *Minima Moralia:
Reflections from Damaged Life*

Contents

PART III

Structured Discovery

Author's Note

I've changed the names of a handful of nonpublic figures to protect their privacy.

Introduction: The End Begins

I'm going blind as I write this. It feels less dramatic than it sounds. The words aren't disappearing as I type. I'm sitting comfortably in the sunroom. The sun is rising like it's supposed to. I can plainly see Lily sitting next to me, reading in her striped pajamas. The visible world is disappearing, but it's not in a hurry. It feels at once catastrophic and commonplace—like reading an article about civilization's imminent collapse from the climate crisis, then setting the article down and going for a pleasant bike ride through a mild spring morning.

There's no cure for retinitis pigmentosa (RP), the condition I was diagnosed with more than twenty years ago, so I usually see my eye specialist every other year. At these visits, I go through a full day of tests, but these just track the decline. At the end of the day, we have a short conversation about the someday promise of stem cell or gene therapy. During my last visit, she showed me an illustration of how much vision I had left. It reminded me of ice cubes melting in hot water: two small, wobbly ovals in the center, and two skinny shapes floating along the sides. The wobbly ovals represented the central vision I still had, and the strips were my peripheral vision. I had about 6 percent of what a fully sighted person sees. My doctor frowned graciously as she gestured at the skinny french fry shapes. "When those go," she said in her medical deadpan, neither cheerful nor grim, "your mobility will become more limited. Those two strips of residual peripheral vision are what you're using to get around."

Describing what I can't see is surprisingly difficult, mostly because my brain adapts to it so quickly. I have severe tunnel vision, but what I see doesn't look like a tunnel; the walls of the enclosure aren't visible. I have the strongest sense of the contours of my blindness in periods when my vision changes—when suddenly there are things I don't see that I ought to, that I saw until recently. I bump into furniture in my house that hasn't moved in years. I'll put a cup down for a moment and it disappears. I'll painstakingly rake the wobbly ovals and slender french fries of my residual vision across the table's surface again and again, and when I finally find the cup, it's standing blamelessly in what even a few weeks ago I would have described as "plain sight." It's still in plain sight—it's just that my sight is growing less and less plain.

RP is painless, if you don't count the bruises that accumulate from violent encounters with inanimate objects, like chairs that haven't been pushed in all the way or cabinet doors that have been left to hang open. The most painful part so far has been the not-knowing. I live much of my life these days in a speculative mode, like a science-fiction writer who looks at the present and tries to imagine the future. As I cook dinner, or walk my son, Oscar, home from school, or find my way from the airport to a train station in an unfamiliar city, I ask myself: What will this be like when I can't see? I perceive everything with this paradoxical double vision: through sighted eyes, and through blind ones. While most futures are difficult to see, shrouded as they are beneath the fog of contingency, mine is doubly difficult to visualize. The crystal ball remains clouded over.

But I can't just accept blindness as a visual death sentence. The blinder I get, the more curiosity I feel about the world of blindness and what possibilities might exist there. So I went out in search of that world, to find a more accurate image of what might be waiting for me.

• • •

Blindness is a radically distinct way of being in the world. Humans are so fundamentally visual in their understanding and experience that blindness requires its own domain. The early science-fiction writer H. G. Wells's short story "The Country of the Blind" takes this idea literally, imagining a civilization of blind men and women who live without any knowledge or need of the sighted world, in a hidden mountain valley. One day an explorer called Nunez, separated from his expedition in a rockslide, ends up falling into this forgotten valley. There he discovers the fabled country of the blind, which has existed without sight for fifteen generations. Every person he meets was born blind, just like their parents and grandparents and great-grandparents before them. They don't even understand the concept of sight; their language has no word for *see*. As he comes to terms with his situation, Nunez proceeds with supreme confidence, repeating the old proverb to himself like a mantra: "In the Country of the Blind, the One-Eyed Man is King."

I find myself approaching blindness a bit like Nunez, as an accidental, curious, and sometimes wary visitor to this strange and often beautiful country. For now, I still feel like an outsider. My partial sight sets me at a remove from those who can't access all the visual information that I do; I'll never be native to blindness, the way that those born blind are. My brain developed visually, and learning blind skills, from reading with my fingers and ears to drawing mental maps of my city, requires a radical shift in the way I relate to the world around me. But unlike Wells's character, who escapes in the end, I'm here to stay, slowly becoming a naturalized citizen.

There's a common set of questions a blind person is almost guaranteed to hear if they spend enough time in public, at least in the US. Strangers will turn to them on buses or sidewalks, and ask, *How do you eat? Who dresses you? Can you sign your own checks?* Questions like these, which suggest that the world of blindness is an infant's world, where a blind person can't even put on a shirt or bring a fork to his mouth without sighted assistance, are infuriating. They exacerbate the painful difference that the experience of disability carries—no one else is being asked how she accomplishes the most basic tasks of daily living as she waits in line for her breakfast burrito. But for someone like me, who still feels like a tourist in the country of the blind, wondering when I might actually move here, these questions have some urgency: I need to know how I will live, and what kind of blind person I'll be. How will I travel independently? How will I write, and read, and work? How will I watch movies, or appreciate art? How will I experience my son's journey from little kid to teenager as a blind father?

This book isn't merely the account of my own experience of vision loss, though; it's the chronicle of an intentional journey I took into the greater world of blindness. Writing it has pulled me deeper into blindness than I otherwise would have gone at this stage in my retinal degeneration. As I lose more and more vision, I feel a new motivation to temper my speculations and fears with knowledge and direct experience. Over the last few years, I traveled around the country, exploring every place I could think of where blindness intersects with contemporary life.

Blind people don't benefit from the sort of large, well-established institutions that Deaf communities have built. Part of this may be because hearing blind people don't face the same barriers to verbal communication that Deaf people do, and so they never needed to develop a distinct shared language. Language is the most important feature in the formation of a community, and sign language is no exception. In the US, the signing community is as linguistically and culturally rich as any other language community. Many Deaf students describe their arrival at schools like Gallaudet, the world's first fully Deaf-centric university in Washington, DC, as a revelation. Having spent their childhoods feeling isolated from hearing families and peers, suddenly they're plunged into a world of Deaf culture and language, where they no longer need accommodations to eavesdrop on a conversation or attend a lecture.

Still, I found pockets of concentrated blind life. In Florida, I attended the national convention of the largest blindness organization in the US, wandering among thousands of blind people in the halls of a colossal Orlando convention center, a forest of canes tapping and colliding, and for the first time I felt the power of being in a space where the blind outnumbered the sighted. I met blind activists from across the political spectrum who made annual visits to their representatives in Congress, and others who marched in street demonstrations with their white canes in one hand and placards in the other. In California and New York, I met blind geniuses working at the cutting edge of digital accessibility who spend their days soldering circuit boards, designing 3D-printed objects, and editing TV soundtracks. I found myself drawn to these media-obsessed tinkerers, who seemed to approach their blindness as a feature that spurred creativity and invention.

I met people who said that their blindness meant nothing to them—that it was a mere attribute, like hair color—and others whose blindness utterly defined and upended their lives. Some recoiled from any mention of the medical cause of their blindness, let alone the prospect of a cure, while others cultivated personal relationships with research ophthalmologists, demonstrating an impressive fluency in the argot of cellular and molecular therapeutics. I sympathized with all of these positions, even as I wondered which attitudes I would adopt for my own life. I tried to understand how blindness was changing my identity as a reader and a writer, as a husband and a father, as a citizen and an otherwise privileged white guy.

In the middle of the COVID-19 pandemic, I took a trip to Colorado, where I spent two weeks at a radical blindness training center. I wore vision-occluding sleep shades for eight hours a day, five days a week, relearning how to use a gas range and chef's knives, and how to cross busy Denver intersections, all from a team of blind instructors. It was only a simulation of blindness, but one that helped me understand how I might respond, and who I might become, when the ice cubes of my residual vision finally melt away.

Figuring out what sort of blind person I should be has become in some ways indistinguishable from the ongoing process of figuring out what kind of person I am, or want to be, regardless of my disability. As I breeze past forty, it seems obvious that one never fully escapes the painful, exhilarating process of self-exploration and reinvention that begins in adolescence.

The more I explore the world of blindness, the more I come to think of it as a domain that extends well beyond the realm of disability. The late critic Greg Tate wrote:

> Race, generally equated with politics, is really in the American context a branch of metaphysics, aesthetics, and anthropology representing a far broader body of concerns where you can readily leapfrog between sex, death, religion, criminality, linguistics, music, genetics, athletics, fashion, medicine, you name it, in the name of African liberation and self-determination.

Is blindness, then, another branch of American metaphysics, with its own concerns one can leapfrog between? Sex, death, and religion, to be sure, alongside medicine, technology, assimilation, cinema, art, literature, mythology, politics, and on and on. Following Tate's formulation, these concerns also point toward liberation and self-determination: all of blindness's intersections and interventions into the wider world come with an awareness of the marginalization that blind people experience in their contact with sighted society, whether in the form of overt oppression (blind people denied employment or educational opportunities solely on the basis of their disability) or more insidious and subtle diminishment (the everyday experiences of blind people made to feel incompetent or miraculous as they go about accomplishing the basic tasks of living).

I feel an immense sense of connection to this world, alongside a persistent feeling of discomfort and alienation. This is part of the experience of becoming disabled—entering a club that millions unwillingly join every year. But it's also a basic feature of contemporary life: you may not like your family, but that's another club you can't leave. Even more voluntary identities, like one's religion, hobbies, career, or tastes, can have this character of clubs one both values and disdains. Susan Orlean, describing the bitterly competitive, insular world of orchid collecting in her 1998 book *The Orchid Thief*, wrote that it, too, was like a family: "It was some kind of way to scratch out a balance between being an individual and being a part of something bigger than yourself, even though each side of the equation put the other in jeopardy." Blindness is becoming all of these things to me: a bickering, annoying family and a loving, supportive one; an interesting hobby, whose fellow hobbyists can inspire and delight as well as irritate and depress me; an identity that I embrace and revile, that defines me and has nothing to do with who I really am. Orlean identifies this contradiction as fundamentally American: "the illogical but optimistic notion that you can create a union of individuals in which every man is king." In this way, I have a uniquely American experience of going blind.

The progression of retinitis pigmentosa—gradual, narrowing tunnel vision that usually ends in blindness, at an unknown date—is a powerful engine of ambiguity. I have become intimately familiar with the pain of living in between: not quite blind and not quite sighted. I called a guy with RP who'd lost his usable vision decades ago for computer advice, and after telling me I was a "lucky bastard" to still have the central vision I did at my age, and that he'd "kill" to be able to see the screen of his TV or laptop, he added sincerely that he thought his life was easier now than it was when he was in the thick of losing his vision. "I don't have to wake up and worry about what's going to happen with my eyes today," he said. "I know they won't work, and I can get on with my life." The RP Facebook page refreshes itself every day with accounts of people afraid to unfurl their collapsible canes in public for fear of being called out as frauds, the challenges of their own partial blindness (spilling drinks, asking for rides) overshadowed by the looming threat of "real" blindness, qualified by their constant assurances that they "still drive" or "still work" or "still get around OK" with the shrinking central vision they're so lucky to have, but God help them if it ever gets to the point at which they can no longer rely on their eyes.

Visiting that page is among my guiltiest pleasures. Reading the endless scroll of self-pitying posts, buffered by the cheerleading replies they generate ("you got this"; "RP strong"), I feel another kind of alienation: it feels less like a blindness community and more like a community of disease-sufferers, praying for cures and living in fear of the inevitable blindness to come. But as easy as it is to judge these fellow travelers, I engage—in my own way, and usually not on Facebook—in the exact same cycle of self-pity, fear, and football-coach-style encouragement (*cloudy eyes*, *full heart*, *can't lose*).

We all live with this sort of ambiguity: beginning in 2021, many people I know celebrated the end of the COVID-19 pandemic again and again, each time thwarted by a new variant, a new spike in deaths, until we finally had to accept that the virus was never going away, and that a more complicated, confusing, and infinitely less comforting endemic reality would persist. So much of life, and loss, exists in this space between binaries: a divorce that doesn't end a relationship; a move that brings too much baggage to the new destination; a dying relative who's no longer alive in the way we remember him, even as he breathes the same air we do for years. As painful as the extreme might be in these situations—severing the relationship, forgetting your homeland, mourning your dead—finality also offers relief that ambiguity denies us. Living in this weird shadowy landscape between blindness and sight has forced me to reckon with this, and to try to let go of my desperate desire for resolution.

My inclination is to just put my head down and barrel into blindness, becoming proficient in all of the skills it requires and then moving on with my life. But the reality of RP makes it hard to turn entirely away from sight. I feel as stymied by the vision I still have as I do by the vision I've lost.

When I was in Colorado, wearing sleep shades and learning how to navigate with a white cane, I had to enter unfamiliar environments and orient myself within them. I'd listen to the echoes the metal tip of my cane made as it hit different surfaces—that's carpet, that's tile, this sounds like it must be the metal fire door. Any engagement with the unfamiliar is like this—by degrees, we feel our way through a situation that can at first seem strange and unwelcoming. But with enough persistence, and a spirit of discovery, solid and defined contours gradually emerge. The space becomes familiar, and eventually it feels like a room you've lived in for months or years. This is what writing about blindness has done for me. It's no longer a legendary, proverbial sci-fi country, and has instead become a real place, populated by real people. My hope is that this book will encourage the sighted reader to likewise discover the largely invisible terrain of blindness, as well as other ways of living and thinking they might not have previously considered.

There are a few common souvenirs that sighted tourists tend to take away from day trips to the country of the blind. The primary one is pity masquerading as empathy: "How difficult their lives are," one might conclude, while more quietly affirming, *Thank god for my eyesight.* There's also the satisfaction of a voyeuristic curiosity: How do they eat, or find their way home from the store, or really know how attractive their partner is? But a longer stay raises more philosophical questions. How does anyone know the world? Does vision deserve the privileged place it holds at the top of the hierarchy of the senses? How much of perception happens in the eyes, and how much takes place in the mind, regardless of which senses supply its stimulus?

The questions I'm still hounded by arise from the conflict I see between the value of disability—the beauty and power I've found in blindness—and its almost definitional sense of loss and exclusion. How can a thing that causes so much alienation also be a source of growth and joy? How can something that estranges us from so much of the world also bring us closer to it? Activists sometimes frame their disability in terms that echo those used by other marginalized groups—locating pride in their oppressed identity. But does blind pride require a wholesale rejection of sight? Could I, for example, find a way to truly embrace my blindness, even if I'd accept a miracle cure if one ever came along?

• • •

Oscar recently asked me what my favorite TV show was. (We'd let him watch a few episodes of *Seinfeld*, and he'd loved it.) Before I could answer, he quickly added, "It's probably a show about blindness, right?" I assured him that my favorite show was definitely not about blindness (most TV shows with blind main characters happen to be, as far as I've seen, not great), but I liked that he had identified this tendency in me, the way that in the last few years I've become a sort of blindness collector. After we opened the floodgates on weekday movie nights during the pandemic, we watched the 1940 Technicolor epic *The Thief of Bagdad* together. Early in the film, we meet the main character, a blind beggar (he's an ex-sultan, cursed into poverty by an evil sorcerer). Oscar turned to me and said, simply, "*Blind!*"—as though he were pointing out an eagle that had just landed in our yard. I reached out to give him a fist bump. He was hesitant at first to return it: Why are we celebrating this again? But then he went with it; we're becoming a blind-positive family.

At one point in the movie, the sultan told a princess that she was the most beautiful woman he'd ever seen. Oscar asked, "Wait, how can he know that, if he's blind?" The film had been jumping back and forth in time, to before and after the sultan's blindness, and we'd been following him in his sighted state for at least half an hour by that point. He'd engaged in all manner of activities—breaking out of an underground dungeon, exploring the bazaars of Basra—without any indication that he was visually impaired in any way. So how had Oscar missed that he was sighted?

I decided to take this not as a sign of Oscar's inattention, but rather as another feature of his positive attitude toward blindness. He hadn't yet absorbed the stereotypes of blindness that popular entertainments perpetuate, of the blind as exiled beggars, cursed, stumbling, and miserable. For him, maybe the sultan was simply blind like I am: clinging to a few degrees of residual vision that he used as best he could. It was perfectly natural to accept a blind character who ran around unfamiliar cities engaging in swashbuckling escapades. As I lose my vision, I want to cultivate this picture of blindness—in Oscar and Lily, in myself, and in the world—of a blind person who's an active protagonist in his own life. I haven't seen this vision in many representations of blindness in films, books, art, or TV, which tend to either mock and diminish blindness, or hold it up as a source of occult superpowers, or treat it with condescending pity—deploying it as a metaphor, rather than an everyday style of living. I found the image I wanted elsewhere: in the people I met out in the actual country of the blind, in the teeming variety of their stories of struggle, adaptation, and adventure.

Part I

Phantom Limp

1.

Seeing Stars

There are as many ways of being blind as there are of being tall, or sick, or hot. But the popular view has always conceived of blindness as a totality. The blind bards wandering the countrysides of ancient Japan, China, or Europe, the blind housed in asylums in the Middle Ages, all the pupils in all the schools for the blind from the Enlightenment onward, blind beggars and lawyers, war veterans and toddlers—in the eyes of history, as well as those of most of their contemporaries, they all saw nothing. Modern dictionaries still subscribe to this sense: blindness is the antonym of vision, and connotes a destitution of sight. What else could it mean?

Despite the poetic impulse to equate blindness with darkness, it's rarely experienced as a black veil draped over the world. Only around 15 percent of blind people have no light perception whatsoever. Most see something, even if it isn't very useful, by sighted standards: a blurry view of their periphery, with nothing in the middle, or the inverse—the world seen through a buttonhole. For some, scenes come through in a dim haze;

for others, light produces a shower of excruciatingly bright needles. Even those with no light perception at all have little use for the popular image of blindness as darkness: the brain cut off from visual stimulus can still produce washes of brilliant color and shape. One blind man, whose optic nerve—the connection between the eyes and the brain—had been severed, described seeing a continuously swirling (and distracting) "visual tinnitus." The Argentine writer Jorge Luis Borges, decades into his blindness, still saw color, which sometimes disturbed him: "I, who was accustomed to sleeping in total darkness," he said,

> was bothered for a long time at having to sleep in this world of mist, in the greenish or bluish mist, vaguely luminous, which is the world of the blind. I wanted to lie down in darkness.

The arrival or encroachment of blindness gives rise to a similarly dazzling range of experiences, an efflorescence of blind varietals. There are those born blind, with no visual memories, whose brains—including the visual cortices—develop using four (or fewer) senses to construct their view of the world. Those who become blind in early childhood often retain visual memories that can contribute to an intuitive understanding of visual concepts. The late-blinded may have the most cognitive work to do, forced to relearn basic skills like orientation and information-gathering through new senses, long after their brains' developmental plasticity has hardened. Some late-blinded adults consciously struggle to preserve their storehouses of mental images, like art conservators touching up old and fading masterpieces.

People are blinded by their spouses or strangers, by acts of war or sports injuries, by industrial accidents and bad decisions, malnutrition and infection, genetic inheritances and spontaneous mutations. It's disingenuous to argue that blindness doesn't have a transformative impact on a person's life, but in every case, blindness is only part of the story. The life of a blind person is never fully (or even predominantly) defined by their blindness.

Some (like Borges, and me) lose their sight gradually. I first noticed something wrong with my eyes in New Mexico. My mom and her boyfriend, Jim, had developed a romantic idea about the American Southwest, where they saw themselves riding horses and motorcycles in the high desert, a more genre-appropriate backdrop to their relationship than the strip malls of suburban New York. The summer before I entered fifth grade, we moved to a house about twenty minutes from downtown Santa Fe. I entered my new elementary school awkwardly, sitting on a utility box at recess, reading *The Hobbit* in the Hawaiian shirt and shorts I wore year-round. I made friends, eventually, and by middle school I had found my place in a crew of early-nineties southwestern prep-school bohemians, most of them a few years older than I was. I'd follow them into the hills, which were sandy and dotted with piñon trees and juniper bushes, and we'd smoke pot out of wooden pipes we'd bought from long-haired guys at the farmers' market. If I was too young to be smoking pot, I was definitely too young to be taking psychedelics, but I did that, too, keeping up with this group of brilliant and occasionally troubled weirdos in backward English driving caps and Stüssy jeans. We all hung out at Hank's house, because Hank's mom was maximally permissive, getting stoned with us and letting Hank decorate his room like the set for a post-punk staging of *Alice in Wonderland*.

It was on the hill behind Hank's house that my journey toward blindness really began. I soon noticed that my friends were better at navigating those darkened hillsides than I was. At night, if I wasn't following directly behind someone, or paying painstaking attention, I would walk directly into a piñon tree. My friends laughed and marveled at how high I must have been, and I started to pursue that role: the bloodshot slo-mo wiseacre. The night sky was already perforated, splintered, and fractured, the constellations animated by hallucinogens; how could I be sure that there was anything wrong with my eyes while I was rattling the doors of perception so hard? At other times, the night blindness was more difficult to brush off. At the movies, I was increasingly unwilling to get out of my seat until the lights came up—the prospect of picking my way through a dark, undulating forest of knees and legs in search of the exit was embarrassing, a feeling that was compounded by the confusion I felt about why I seemed to be the only person experiencing it. When I mentioned this new impediment to my mom, she dismissed it: everyone has "night blindness," she said—it's dark at night!

Eventually, I used some pre-Google search engines to diagnose myself. (My dad, who had moved to the Bay Area when we'd moved to New Mexico, had bought me a modem.) Searching for "night blindness" on the early web, I found information about eye diseases on a website whose name I've forgotten—the lean, lost grandfather of WebMD. Your eyes, this ancient website told me, have two types of cells: rods and cones. These make up the retina. The cones allow you to see color and account for central vision. The rods give you peripheral vision and are more light-sensitive; they allow you to see in the dark. Retinitis pigmentosa encompasses a family of inherited eye diseases that gradually kill off the rods. As a result, RP usually appears early in life as mild night blindness, before manifesting as slowly narrowing tunnel vision during the day. (One medical source I found later summarized my story with eerie precision: "Mild night blindness is often ignored by the patients and becomes apparent in the teen age, at evening parties.") RP concludes, usually in middle age, with a flourish: complete functional blindness.

By this time, I was attending a boarding school in Ojai with the children of Montana ranch families and California Central Coast citrus barons. (My mom had begun getting more work as a screenwriter, so we had moved to Santa Barbara.) Night blindness had gone from an ambiguous inconvenience to a fact of life. I assumed I had RP, or something like it, but didn't discuss it with anyone aside from occasionally complaining about it to my mom. When other students snuck into the woods at night to smoke pot, I stayed in the dorm, reading or hanging out with the art-damaged pocket of anti-rancher resistance. I frequently worried that I'd permanently destroyed my intellectual capacity by eating so many psychedelics back in New Mexico; my peripheral vision was filled with flashers and floaters and spinning phantom ceiling fans, visual reminders of the fact that I had ruined a perfectly good brain.

It wasn't until I'd returned home after my freshman year in college that my mom decided I'd been complaining about my eyes long enough that I should get them checked out by a specialist. She got me an appointment at an eye clinic at UCLA, where I submitted to a long regimen of tests, including an ERG, which involves numbing your eyes and then attaching electrodes to your eyeballs to measure the amount of electricity your retinas are putting out in response to light. (It's like testing the charge on a battery, but the battery is part of your face.)

When I finally met with the doctor, a soft mustachioed man named Dr. Heckenlively, he confirmed what I'd gleaned from Wikipedia's great-uncle years earlier: I had "classic RP." I could probably expect to maintain good vision during the day through my twenties and thirties. The night blindness would gradually become more severe, and my peripheral vision would erode. As I approached middle age, the degeneration would sharply accelerate. There is no treatment, he told me, but science is making great progress, so by the time I was *really* blind, in twenty or thirty years, there would hopefully be a cure. In the meantime, there were some vitamins I could take to try to prolong my useful vision. Did I smoke? Yes, of course I smoked. I also had a radio show on the college station called *A Thousand Frowzy Steams*. Well, the doctor told me, I'd need to quit immediately—cigarettes are terrible for ocular health. Can you see stars? he asked. This was something I'd already noticed: starlight had become too dim for me to register. It was also the detail that brought it all home for my mom. She sat up straight: "You can't see stars!"

I don't remember sharing my mom's dismay. Part of this must have had to do with the fact that I'd already successfully diagnosed myself, and I felt validated by the doctor's confirmation of what I'd pieced together from the web. My main memory of the day is of Dr. Heckenlively himself, whom my current retinal specialist refers to with awe as a "giant in the field." His manner was so serious that it almost seemed inappropriate to have a vulnerable response to what he was saying—it felt like I was being enlisted into his army, or accepted into an elite internship program. The focus was on our newly shared endeavor, and I now had a grave responsibility. This was no time for blubbering.

As my mom and I left the eye hospital, I wore a flimsy sheet of dark plastic under my glasses, protecting my dilated pupils from the glare of L.A. at noon. I remember fumbling in the bright restaurant we went to for lunch, my eyes struggling to adjust, knocking over a saltshaker as I reached for my iced tea.

Afterward, we visited a museum downtown, where we saw a show of Richard Serra's *Torqued Ellipses*—huge steel sheets rolled into standing curves set within one another, creating open tunnels. Wandering through these brief mazes, each with only two or three turns to make inside, made it feel like the shape of the whole world had changed; the world itself became a torqued ellipse, with only a strip of the outside splashing in. I felt at once claustrophobic and expansive. The sculptures somehow made the world feel larger.

• • •

Ancient Greek had one word for totally blind people, *tuphlos*, and a different one, *ambluôpia*, for "dull-sightedness." Ancient writers shared our modern predilection for using blindness as a metaphor for heedlessness and various other moral, intellectual, or spiritual failings. The Greeks and Romans spoke of blind ignorance, blind leadership, and the blindness of wealth and love; the Old Testament described bribery blinding its recipient, and the blindness of those who don't heed the voice of the Lord—those who "have eyes but are blind" (Isaiah 43:8).

Bruegel's 1568 painting *The Blind Leading the Blind* makes literal (and adds several participants to) the biblical proverb "If a blind man leads a blind man, both will fall into a pit." The painting shows six blind men in a line across the canvas, each holding the shoulder or stick of the man in front of him. The blind guy at the back of the line looks like he's doing all right. As the eye travels across the composition, though, the aspect of disaster gradually increases: the faces contort with growing confusion and distress as the men grimace and stumble, until we see the final blind man, arms and legs thrown wide, falling backward into the proverbial pit. The rest of the men are about to fall in on top of him.

Most disability histories describe the plight of blind people in these terms—as though they spent their lives in this muddy, cold pit. "Want and suffering were the rule rather than the exception and the blind were an economic liability," Richard S. French observed in his representative study, *From Homer to Helen Keller.* "Toleration alone makes such abysmal beggary possible, and rarely does the blind man rise above it." A tour through the Western canon offers a highlight reel of blind abjection: the pathetic stumbling of the cyclops Polyphemus, his eye pierced by Odysseus with timber that had been sharpened and then heated to a glowing red point; Oedipus taking long pins from his mother's garment and plunging them into his eyes ("The bloody pupils / Bedewed his beard. The gore oozed not in drops, / But poured in a black shower, a hail of blood"); the third-century BCE biblical story of Tobit, who goes blind after a swallow shits in his eyes, believes his wife has become a criminal to support him, and prays for death.

Several sources describe the practice in Athens and Sparta of killing congenitally blind babies, as well as those with deformities—"club feet, webbed hands, fused fingers"—and more severe conditions the Greeks classified as *terata*. The infants would be carried outside the settlement and placed on the side of the road, or in a hole, sometimes in clay vessels, to be killed by being "exposed to the elements," a weird euphemism we use to refer to the actual causes: hunger, cold, heat, animal attack, a flood of water.

Beyond these grim portrayals, until the advent of disability studies in the 1990s, scholarly books dedicated to reconstructing the lives of disabled people were scant. Most histories of blindness were promotional tools: blindness organizations commissioned official histories (like Frances Koestler's *The Unseen Minority*, funded by the American Foundation for the Blind), and heads of blind schools wrote their accounts with a view toward assembling compendia of blind suffering to spur donations. Richard S. French, the sighted superintendent of the California School for the Blind, wrote in his own 1932 study that "not only the monstrous and crippled were destroyed but many infant blind must also have suffered a like fate." (French goes on to assert that "among the more primitive peoples . . . old, sick, and crippled persons were a drag upon free movement and a burden to society. They were disposed of in various ways, even buried alive and on occasion eaten.")

In *A History of Disability*, the first major study of the subject in Western culture, though, Henri-Jacques Stiker saw little evidence that the blind and Deaf were included in the *terata*. There is no question that some children were in fact "exposed." Plato and Aristotle both apparently approved of the practice. But Stiker points out that the ancient Greeks drew a distinction between *defect* (which "jeopardized conformity," and suggested a curse from the gods) and *illness* (which was seen merely as a weakness, and thus worthy of compassion). Sensory disabilities were, he argued, categorized as illnesses, not defects. Stiker also cites Cicero, who wrote that blindness and deafness can be rewarding, offering "'pleasures of the dark and of silence' that cannot be enjoyed by those who see and hear."

A reader of these lines in the ancient world would have likely thought of Homer. Later scholars have questioned Homer's identity as a historical figure, a single blind man who authored the *Iliad*, the *Odyssey*, and an impossibly vast range of other poems. But the story of the blind bard or rhapsodist, traveling from city to city to sing his epic poems of gods and war, was widely known and esteemed.

Perhaps the Homeric legend opened other doors. The historian Martha L. Rose finds several primary sources that suggest that blind people contributed to ancient societies (and their economies) in ways that extended beyond the stereotypes of blind bards like Homer or the blind beggar stumbling into a pit. Rose acknowledges the likely presence of blind fortune tellers, itinerant bards, and beggars in ancient Greece (there are similar traditions of blind bards and mystics in China and Japan), but she also offers historical evidence for blind scholars; those with the means would likely have dictated their writing to slaves (who surely experienced far greater oppression than the average blind person in antiquity). There were probably blind shepherds and dairy farmers, miners and rowers. Rose even suggests that blind people might have fought in wars, pointing to a line from Plutarch that describes the Greek general Timoleon: "In his camp at Mylae, his vision was obscured by a cataract in the eye, and it was plain to all that he was getting blind; he did not, however, desist from the siege on this account, but persisted in the war and captured the tyrants."

The blind person in the developed world of today must contend with roads filled with deadly traffic and appointments that might be dozens of miles away, and a tremendous social and civic premium placed on the ability to read print and interact with visual information. Life in an ancient Greek village, by comparison, had no cars to mow one down, and generally offered little reason to travel beyond one's ambulatory orbit. Any information one might need could be conveyed aurally. The world, even to a newly blind person, might seem eminently manageable. When I proposed this idea to my friend Sheri Wells-Jensen, she agreed. "Being blind in a little village in Ecuador, where I lived in the Peace Corps," she said, "was a little easier than trying it in the US."

• • •

Dr. Heckenlively's prediction turned out to be accurate: during my twenties, years passed without my really noticing a change in vision. I came close to getting beaten up once, when I stepped on a rockabilly's boot at a dimly lit dive bar. I stayed in my seat until the credits had rolled at the end of every movie. Games like tennis got harder—I couldn't track the ball as it whizzed in from my absent peripheral vision. I left people hanging for high fives and handshakes. But real blindness was still mostly abstract, a distant eventuality, in the same category as fatherhood, or death: this will probably happen someday, but not today. My life held the lightest flavor of blindness, like a single lemon wedge floating in a pitcher of ice water.

During these years, I enjoyed a series of spectacularly doomed romantic relationships. Then one of my Jewish insurrectionist friends from high school set me up with a friend of his, Lily. She was a fifth-year comparative literature PhD finishing her dissertation at Berkeley; I was living in San Francisco by then, working at a literary magazine. It was a blind date. Our eyes met. She had long brown hair, large, watchful eyes, and a hyphenated last name. The second part of her surname, Wachter, means "watcher" in German—it was originally Wachnachter, a likely permutation of *Nachtwächter*, or "night watchman." Her dissertation dealt with attention, the ways that a nation during wartime must be on alert, and how that experience of watchfulness gets reproduced in its poetry. This seemed cool. I fell in love with her. We moved in together, the night-blind and the night watcher, and adopted a dog. Soon she got her first job offer, at a university somewhere in Missouri. I drove her through the rain to the Marin Headlands, where we walked our dog up to a dramatic promontory overlooking the Pacific Ocean, a few yards from a crumbling antiaircraft mount. As she walked ahead of us, I knelt down and said to our dog, "Oh, no, what have you eaten?" Lily turned around and said, "What did he eat?" I presented her with a small jewel box. "Oh, what did you do?" she said, and I asked her to marry me.

On our walk back down the trail to the car, the leaves on the trees still dripping with rainwater, I felt the need to say, "You remember I'm going blind, right?" At the time, it felt like a joke. It *was* a joke, because of course she remembered. We'd talked about it many times. It was also a joke because it seemed so distant, like reminding her I was mortal. But blindness was present in our relationship from the beginning. When we went out dancing, as we did that night after we got engaged, I made my way through the club with a hand on her shoulder, to avoid treading on any more rockabilly feet. I was still driving during the day then, and more than once I'd had to race the sun to get us home before my driving became (even more) dangerous. Part of me, though, really wanted to know: Did she realize what she was getting herself into? Did she know what it meant to be blind? (Did I?) Mirroring my joke, she replied, "Oh, really? You are? Maybe I shouldn't marry you, then." But then she added, "I know, and yes, I still want to marry you."

Later that year, I retired from driving altogether. I was making a left turn, having checked and seen a clear path, and suddenly a furious pedestrian was banging on my hood, shouting "Open your fucking eyes." A few weeks later, at a four-way stop, I hit the gas and Lily yelped as a cyclist zoomed past, inches from the car's grille. I was in my early thirties, and my retinal degeneration was just starting to rev up. We moved to Columbia, a university town in the middle of Missouri, where Lily had gotten the job. She drove us the whole way.

Our house turned out to be a forty-minute walk from downtown. The days got short, snow covered the ground, and we knew almost no one. Working from home, I started to feel isolated, like a dog waiting to be walked, springing to life at the jingle of car keys, tail wagging, wondering, Where are you going? To a park? Can I come? I casually researched blindness support groups online. A retinal specialist in San Francisco had written the name of one on the back of a brochure years ago, but I hadn't felt like I needed such a resource then—my night blindness was a conversation piece, a humorous liability at parties. But now, more blind, I was becoming more curious, and probably, though I couldn't quite admit it, more in need of support. I found a meeting of the local chapter of the National Federation of the Blind (NFB) and reached out to two of the organizers, who invited me to their fall picnic at a park ten miles from our house. I invited Lily along—in part because otherwise I would've needed to take a taxi, but also because I didn't want to show up alone.

At the park we wandered among giant gazebo-like shelters, cicadas screaming. Eventually we found the group, about fifteen people gathered around a few picnic tables covered in an intensely midwestern potluck spread. The meeting was already in progress. The handful of sighted people there looked at us silently, and it seemed safe to assume that none of the blind people knew we were there. We stood uncomfortably at the side of the shelter as the group argued about the best ways to promote an upcoming trivia night fundraiser. Was buying an ad in the local paper worth it? I felt Lily's discomfort burning next to me like a radiator. "Are you OK?" I whispered. "Do you want to leave?"

"I can stay if you want to," she said, desperate to leave. When we got back to the car, she said, "That was really weird." I agreed, but I also recoiled from her characterization. I had noticed the blind woman in a wheelchair, using a strange device that looked like it somehow converted the text on a laptop screen into metallic braille. I'd noticed the other people with multiple disabilities, and the modest scale at which the group was operating—arguing over how to spend their tiny publicity budget. If I had gone to the meeting to find other blind people whom I might commiserate with or learn from, or befriend, the first impression was more off-putting than I'd expected. Part of it was surely just geographical culture shock, but a greater part was a different kind of culture shock—our discomfort with disability. I know now that the people there had experience and knowledge that could have helped me. But I didn't go back to another meeting.

Being newlyweds in central Missouri with no friends or family for hundreds of miles made having a baby seem like an obvious next move. Though RP is an inherited condition, I can't find it in my family history, and Lily and I didn't spend much time worrying over the possibility that we'd be passing it on to our child. Our understanding of the genetics was fuzzy: the doctors didn't know which mutation had caused my condition. In the examination room at the ob-gyn's office, before our discussion of what disabilities we wanted to test for and under what conditions we would terminate the pregnancy, I found an activity book on creationist biology called *Understanding God's World* tucked into the magazine rack, which added a note of ancient superstition to our visit. A technician scrawled the word *boy* on a scrap of paper and folded it in half. We walked to a lakeside park next to a beach slick with goose shit to read it.

That October, a few days before Lily's due date, we watched Paul Ryan and Joe Biden bicker and snipe at each other in the vice presidential debate and fell asleep. A few minutes after I'd drifted off, Lily woke me to say that her water had broken. Her mom, who was visiting in hopes that she'd be in town for the birth, drove us to the hospital. The roads were wet and empty, and I exerted a useless vigilance from the back seat. In the delivery room, I tried to stay out of the way. I tend to miss signals that someone needs to use the space I'm occupying, so I found a patch of wall that was empty of medical equipment and parked myself there, moving forward to rub Lily's back and then receding when the nurses took over. Early the next morning, when Oscar was finally born, tiny and beautiful and screaming, the nurse asked if "Dad" wanted to cut the umbilical cord. This seemed like a terrible idea, handing surgical scissors to a part-blind guy and asking him to use them on the most tender creature on earth. I awkwardly declined. The nurse pushed back—this was in the printed-out birthing plan we'd brought along. "Nope, that's your job, Dad!" They showed me the stretch of umbilical cord they'd marked between two clamps. I was to take the gleaming scissors and cut right there. I belabored these instructions; the possibility that I would accidentally slice his belly or otherwise puncture him seemed real. Then I inhaled and cut the cord.

When I held him for the first time, his tiny red face filled my central vision. I could see nothing else.

I couldn't drive to the store in the middle of the night for diapers, but once the diapers were in the house, I became proficient at changing them. Walking with Oscar, I had to double my care; I occasionally slammed my head against cabinets, and I was haunted by the prospect of accidentally crushing his face into a doorframe. There were some close calls, though no more than a fully sighted parent might've had, including one mild concussion at a playground that was, in my defense, pretty unsafe for any child. We managed not to kill him.

As he learned to speak and soon wondered aloud why I couldn't see the fork I'd just dropped, I tried to explain my vision to him. For some reason, in these conversations, I always used the word *peepers*. Like, "I couldn't find the fork because I have bad peepers." I was trying to find soft, fun language for blindness. I didn't want him to see it as a sad thing. When he was four, I overheard him say to a friend, "We need to clean up these toys now, otherwise my dad will trip over them. He has bad peepers."

The world looked more or less as it always had, but my blind spots were growing ever larger. If before I was surprised that I couldn't find a pencil or a mug, now entire cars and small buildings went unnoticed until I swiveled my head into just the right position. I was teaching part-time at the university and one day the two women who ran the English Department office greeted me on their way to lunch.

"How's your leg doing, Andrew?" Sharon asked.

"My leg?"

"Yeah—we saw you limping yesterday," Paula added. "Did you hurt yourself? Are you feeling better?"

I chewed on the question until I finally realized what they were talking about. My vision had degenerated to the point where even during the day I was worried about running into people, or fire hydrants, or anything that might fall into the growing chasm of my dead peripheral vision. So I'd developed a mincing gait that I unconsciously employed in order to brace myself against any unexpected impact—call it a phantom limp. No false moves: I was treading lightly, gingerly, through the throngs of frat guys walking in unpredictable vectors across campus. I had already purchased a collapsible white cane that I carried in my bag but rarely used—I was deeply self-conscious about it, and only unfolded it when I was alone in a dark, crowded, unfamiliar place, or while traveling, where the alternative would be knocking everyone's beer into their laps (as I did once, back in San Francisco—two full beers directly into the laps of a pair of women, one of whom, my friends later told me, was a winning contestant on *Top Chef*).

Lily got a grant that released her from teaching for the year to finish her book, and we temporarily moved into the garden apartment below her dad and stepmom's place in New York. My vision was deteriorating at a faster rate—I noticed changes with each passing season, rather than every year or two. One night, after watching a concert in Harlem with my friend Jason, we finished a joint and decided to walk the length of Manhattan back downtown. I decided that tonight was the night I'd break in the cane for real. Pantomiming blindness, I swung it awkwardly in front of me, as we walked south, passing through darkened parks and into and out of many bars. We tried to use the cane to get into a fashion party we wandered past near Chelsea Piers, Jason appealing to the bouncer's potential sense of pity—*Here, sir, is a totally blind man, who merely wishes to attend your event! Won't you let us in?*—as I stood drunkenly by, holding the cane in my fingers like a giant fountain pen, doodling on the pavement. The bouncer didn't let us in. When I fell into bed that night, I felt like I'd broken the seal on cane-walking. Picking up Oscar from day care the next week, I unfurled my cane as we descended into the subway station. Waiting for the train, Oscar secured to my torso in his carrier, we absorbed all the stares we got, the blind guy surely about to fall onto the tracks with an innocent baby strapped to his chest.

The first night I used my cane in front of Lily, we'd left Oscar with her dad and stepmom to go out to dinner with some friends in Greenpoint. The restaurant was fashionable, which means it was lit by a single Edison bulb running at half power. Finding a bathroom in a dark restaurant was up there with leaving a movie before it ended, in terms of normal social activities that inspired deep anxiety in me. But then I remembered I had my cane, still faintly glowing with the new power it'd absorbed on my night out with Jason. I excused myself from the table and unfurled it with a sheepish, self-conscious flourish. As I stood up, Lily surprised me by saying that she didn't think I needed the cane here. The moment was so fraught with shame even before she spoke that I immediately accepted her suggestion. A waitress walked by, and I asked her where the bathroom was, folding the cane back up as I followed her. Lily and I had barely discussed the cane before that night, and she didn't fully understand why I needed it. She'd never seen me with it in public before. She had no sense of my anxiety about finding the bathroom, for example; the appearance of the cane had caught her totally off guard.

The problem with the cane is that, like the word *blind*, people read it as a signifier for a total absence of sight. I was faced with a dilemma: use the cane and feel fraudulent, like I'm trying to pass as a blind guy, or pass as a sighted person and risk increasingly serious injury and mayhem to myself and others. I have wondered if that moment in the restaurant set me back a year or two, cane-wise. I know I would've benefited from using it more—not so much to tap around, using the cane as an extension of the body, as more fully blind people do, but as a signal to others to give me space. For Lily, though, the cane made me look vulnerable—helpless as soon as I unfolded it. That dinner forced us into an uncomfortable confrontation. Even now, almost a decade later, I still feel pangs of cane-related embarrassment or fraudulence nearly every day.

Lily got a new job, teaching at a liberal arts college in New England. I resolved that when we arrived, I would start fresh as a full-time, out-of-the-closet, cane-wielding blind person. When I met her new colleagues, I held the cane in plain sight. These days, though I still have enough vision to read large print and recognize faces and see when the DON'T WALK sign starts flashing, I use the cane everywhere I go. It's cured me of the limp. When my cane connects with something—a curb, a hydrant—that I genuinely had no idea was there, it's gratifying. In these moments, my pantomime of blindness, the feeling that I'm faking it, fades. I feel, for a moment, like a real blind person. I can now track the decline in my vision month by month, rather than year by year. This can be so scary that it sometimes makes me feel like I can't breathe. And yet alongside the panic, there are the beginnings of a weird solace.

Walking to Penn Station to catch the Amtrak home from New York on a recent spring afternoon, I spotted a guy leaning with his back against a deli, watching me. As I passed, we made brief eye contact, and I saw something sour in his expression. I looked away, and he said the thing that I've read on so many strangers' faces since I started using the cane: "You can *see*." He spoke in the sneering voice you'd use to say *gimme a fucking break*. I felt a painful, vindicating satisfaction, a long-deferred confirmation of the thing I'd always suspected everyone was thinking about me anyway. With some shrillness, I replied, "Actually, I can!"

Standing in the crowd at Penn Station afterward, I thought about my periodic desire for the eye disease to just get it over with, and take the rest of my sight. I wanted to be relieved of seeing the way people look at blindness: the scorn, the condescension, the entitled, almost sexual leer. Skepticism, pity, revulsion, curiosity. I know I've looked at blind people this way too—like when Lily and I stood at an uncomfortable remove at the National Federation of the Blind's mid-Missouri-chapter picnic in that sweltering park years ago. But I was a different person then: I didn't really think of myself as blind.

Lately I'd begun to feel a stronger desire for solidarity, for community—to meet other people who'd had this experience of the many ways that the sighted world expresses fear, discomfort, or condescension around blindness. I felt ready to take a more purposeful step across the border, into the country of the blind.

2.

National Blindness

As soon as I passed through the sliding doors of the convention center, everyone was blind. A blind child was nestled in his sighted mother's arms, asleep or just taking refuge in her neck, his short white cane dangling from his hand. A nuclear family in brightly colored vacationwear walked past, blind parents guided by their two sighted children. A pair of hotel employees stood guard over the place where a guide dog had had an accident, protecting the crowd from flowing into it.

The National Federation of the Blind's national convention draws more than three thousand attendees a year, nearly all of them blind. I kept repeating this number to myself and in messages to friends: *I'm hanging out with* three thousand *blind people in Florida!* It was such a novelty—blindness was a group activity. The sound of dozens of canes tapping on the tiled floors echoed through the lobby.

The fact that more people were blind than sighted created a different sense of space. The social order—of movement, of distance between individuals—had shifted. Pairs of blind people walked together down a wide hallway. They looked like they knew where they were going, so I followed them. A moment later, I found myself overcome with emotion. I pulled off to the side, leaned against a closed shop's window, and tried to figure out what had happened. It was physically stressful to be there—if I stayed still, chances were good that someone was going to gently plow into me. But as I stood pressed against the beachwear boutique, I absorbed how alone I'd felt in blindness—even my provisional, junior-level version. Entering a space where it was the norm, where *we* outnumbered *them*, was overwhelming. Even before I'd spoken to anyone, I could conceive of myself, in a small but sincere way, as a member of a blind community. I had brought an audio recorder with me; listening back to the recording, the sound of tapping canes envelops my sniffling. "It's super intense," I mumbled into the recorder. I made my way farther down the hall, but I kept having to retreat into various little alcoves to cry and murmur some more.

The Rosen Shingle Creek is colossal—the NFB occupied an entire concourse, but it was just one piece of a much larger honeycomb. Reading the list of meetings scheduled at the center that day, blindness seemed like just another American industry, a trade union, with its own periodicals and subcommittees, banquet dinners and corporate sponsors. I pressed my way through the swarm of canes, trying to find the main hall.

• • •

The most salient factor determining the quality of a blind person's life may not be what culture or historical period they live in, but the economic and familial situation they're born into. Today, as in the Middle Ages, there are blind people who live at the margins of society, shunned by their families, living lives of unremitting poverty, while blind contemporaries live lives of relative ease. John of Luxembourg, the fourteenth-century king of Bohemia, ruled for the last decade of his life without vision; Nicholas Saunderson, blind from infancy, held the Lucasian Chair in Mathematics at the University of Cambridge ten years after Isaac Newton.

But the reality is that such people represent a tiny minority of the blind experience. The disability historians Catherine Kudlick and Zina Weygand write that "despite the complete absence of statistics, we can be certain that in nineteenth-century France, as in earlier times, most blind people came from the lower classes and faced extremely difficult lives." The lower classes made up the majority of the population, and the causes of blindness—"illnesses, poor hygiene, malnutrition, and accidents on the job"—were all "far more likely to accompany poverty."

As I've hung around blind communities, I've encountered a few joking references to "the blind 1 percent": the kids who show up to their blind summer programs with the latest assistive technology, which can quickly add up to tens of thousands of dollars' worth of braille gizmos and smart goggles. I've likewise been struck by the message board posts of blind people who casually mention the reams of tech they buy every year, complaining of the difficulties they have syncing their Apple Watches to their iPad Pros ever since they upgraded to the latest iPhone. It seems likely that I will join this privileged blind class. My grandfather Marvin Neil Simon, the grandson of Russian immigrants, grew up in a crowded apartment in Washington Heights but dropped the

"Marvin" from his name and found success as a comedy writer, turning the stories of his working-class childhood into blockbuster Broadway plays and films like *Brighton Beach Memoirs* and *Lost in Yonkers*. As a result, I have a financial cushion to soften my fall into blindness; when I recently became convinced that PCs were more accessible than Macs, for instance, I impulsively bought myself a second laptop with Windows and a license for the JAWS screen reader (which works far better with Microsoft Word) without having to agonize over the cost or petition my state's blindness commission for assistance.

I've made a career for myself as an editor, an audio producer, and a writer, all work that I can theoretically continue even without the central vision I still have. I feel confident that I'll be able to keep finding jobs, but I'm just now entering a space where blindness is really intruding, and where anyone googling me will instantly know I'm blind. I have the naive sense that my accumulated professional experience will insulate me, that I'm not about to be shunted into the "blind trades"—industrial labor like caning chairs or tying straw onto brooms. But the doubts that keep blind people out of other jobs will soon affect me too: magazine fact-checkers have tactfully begun asking how I know what I've reported in ways that I'm sure they don't ask sighted writers. These doubts find their way into my own thinking: How will I work as a journalist once I can't gather visual details independently?

Walking around the NFB convention in Orlando, I felt the simultaneous sense of belonging and alienation that has come to mark my experience of blindness. My own provisional blindness played a big part in this ambivalence—didn't I have too much vision to really be a part of this club? Another part of it was what some activists call "internalized ableism": I was looking at blind people with the prurient, condescending curiosity that felt so hurtful when turned on me. But there was also a sense of class consciousness burbling beneath the surface. Only 16 percent of blind Americans have a college degree (less than half the national average), and more than a fifth don't finish high school (more than double the rate of their sighted peers). Blind people are twice as likely to live in poverty. But the really astonishing statistic concerns blind labor. The US unemployment rate usually averages around 5 percent, peaking at the height of the pandemic in 2020, when nearly 15 percent of Americans were out of work. For blind people, the unemployment rate is *fourteen times* that of the general population, hovering at around 70 percent. It's hard for me to accept this: that holding a full-time job, any job, is a minority position among the blind, even in the US, even in 2023. As I try to understand blindness, a depressing reality emerges: one of the fundamental experiences that most blind people share is joblessness.

Encountering these statistics changed the stakes of what it meant for me to become a member of a blind community. I'd initially approached it as a sort of cultural or philosophical question: What is the phenomenology of blindness? What's its flavor, its folklore, its vibe? But as I considered the lives of most blind people, the question of what blindness is became inescapably political. Every state in the US has its own commission for the blind, staffed by vocational rehabilitation counselors trained to help blind people find employment, with government dollars earmarked for essential tools and services—canes, screen-reading software, magnifiers, training. But clearly this system—overwhelmingly run by sighted administrators and teachers—was failing blind people. State support, supplemented by relief from private charitable institutions, has proven itself insufficient in the face of that astonishingly durable 70 percent unemployment figure. What was the source of this problem? Was it purely based on the low expectations that sighted people had for the blind, or did blind people themselves play a role?

The NFB's official history reports that one of the "greatest disappointments" of its founder, Jacobus tenBroek, "was the reluctance of many successful blind persons of the professional middle class to be identified with a movement of rank-and-file blind people who not only were often unemployed but were categorized as unemployable." What could blind people do to pull themselves out of this economic marginalization?

• • •

I found my way into the main hall. It was massive, and about two-thirds full. I saw a handful of people using the braille labels hanging from poles marking each state affiliate's location to find their destination, but the approach most people used was a technique I came to think of as Addressing the Void. A blind person would stand, stopped midstream, holding their cane vertically, in a resting position. They looked off into oblivion with the semi-arbitrary gaze that blind people often have. (Sight gives a target for the gaze to follow: with sight removed, the gaze remains—and by *gaze* I just mean an intelligent face pointed in the direction of the thing it's regarding. You don't need working eyes to have a gaze. Statues have gazes. But with sight removed, the gaze tilts and strays.) The expression on the face of a blind gazer paused in the world takes on an inwardly whirring, computational, deep-listening aspect. After a few moments posed in frozen, careful attention, this person would announce, firmly and loudly (to whisper was futile; whoever responded would need to both hear them and realize they were being spoken to), "IS THIS NORTH DAKOTA?" Because the hall was so dense with people, this approach usually worked. "NEBRASKA!" someone cheerfully replied, her own gaze aimed past the questioner. "Keep going!"

I arranged to meet the journalist Will Butler outside the Independence Market (so called because it sold tools, from talking thermometers to digital braille notetakers, that allowed blind people to function independently, without sighted assistance). I'd first come across Will's writing online a few years before—he published semi-gonzo dispatches for *VICE* from music festivals and other events with taglines like "Horse Racing Is Totally Depressing When You're Blind." He was working as the communications director for LightHouse for the Blind and Visually Impaired, a blindness rehabilitation agency in San Francisco. Introducing myself, I mentioned where I was with my RP: legally blind, using a cane, but still reading print. Normally, people respond to this information with an expression of sympathy, borderline condolences. Will replied, "At the risk of sounding like an insane person, whenever someone tells me their son has RP or they're going blind, I have to stop myself from saying, 'That's awesome!' Because aside from a few obvious obstacles, blindness has really opened up a lot of intellectual doors for me."

At the Independence Market we caned our way past dozens of booths, slick corporate displays and homemade setups from local delegations. It was an aural assault—on top of the roar of chattering convention-goers, there was an army of "talking signs," volunteers who called out "Candy bars from the NFB of Wisconsin!" or "NFB T-shirts here!"

Will had to leave for a meeting he'd scheduled with a blindness-tech-startup CEO, and when I met him for lunch the next day, I was surprised that he didn't recognize me, even as I got close. He obviously had some vision—during the general session, I watched him use his phone visually, though he did hold it pressed almost to his nose—but I might have assumed that he could see more than he does. I tried to figure out a natural way to tell him that I was next to him. "Will!" I bellowed, about twice as loud as necessary. "What's happening!" He flinched, and I hated myself, making a note to find a better technique than violent cheerfulness to indicate my arrival to a blind person.

We made our way over to the restaurant. As we read our large-print menus, Will said we might have to move tables. Why? I asked. "It's stressing me out," he said, "watching these blind people get off course and crash into us." We were sitting at the first table in the hallway from the convention center to the hotel, and it had become a sort of shoreline that washed up person after person making their way down the hall. We both watched as a woman walked directly into our table. She apologized and asked us where the lobby was. I gave her bad directions: "If you move to your left . . . go straight five feet . . . and turn right?" She veered off course into a little cul-de-sac the hotel had festooned with low tables and upholstered wing chairs. "Should I go help her?" I asked.

"She'll figure it out," Will said. "This is the one place where I don't feel bad giving bad directions. There are so many people who can help them."

• • •

The blind have always lived in tension with the sighted people who make it their business to help them. The world's first state-run hospice for the blind, called the Quinze-Vingts (French for "fifteen twenties," a reference to the three hundred blind people who originally lived there), was founded in Paris around 1260. Its residents wore special yellow fleur-de-lis badges to signify the king's protection and, in exchange for their labors, could count on room and board. Some had steady jobs—"the bell ringer and the crier were blind," the historian Zina Weygand writes, "as well as the managers of taverns situated within its walls"—but for the most part, they were employed as full-time beggars, going out into the city accompanied by a sighted guide for a set number of hours each day. At first, the blind residents exerted some autonomy, meeting with sighted administrators to advocate for changes. But by 1522 a porter was installed to monitor the residents' activities, and they were required to maintain "good behavior" and perform various religious obligations.

The Quinze-Vingts solidified the public image of the blind person as a professional beggar, and created a sense of resentment toward them, a perception that they were, as Weygand writes, "the quintessential aristocrats of mendicancy" (a fancier-sounding and less racially loaded version, perhaps, of the contemporary image of the "welfare queen").

Parisians expressed this resentment in a brutal "entertainment" that they organized a few blocks from the hospice in 1425. They dressed four blind men in battle armor, instructed them to carry a banner emblazoned with the image of a pig, and then marched them—along with an actual "strong pig"—down to a nearby park. The blind men were given batons and told that whoever killed the pig could keep it. A violent, inverted game of blindman's buff ensued—"a very strange battle," as one chronicler observed; "when the stronger ones believed that they hit the pig, they hit each other, and if they had really been armed, they would have killed each other." Evidence from French literature suggests that "entertainments" like these were a regular occurrence.

It wasn't until the late eighteenth century that the first schools for the blind in Europe were established. For the first time, a poor blind person could enter an institution that was designed to educate rather than merely house them as "impotent" mendicants. But as revolutionary as this development was—leading most notably to the development of braille, and literacy for the blind—it didn't solve the problem of acceptance in mainstream society. When Samuel Gridley Howe established the Perkins School, the first American school for the blind, he found that the success he had in socializing and educating blind children didn't result in opportunities for higher education or job placements in an industrializing nation. Students returned to Perkins frustrated by their search for work, and in 1840 Howe built a workshop to train Perkins students in semiskilled labor—"blind trades." Over the first half of the twentieth century, schools for the blind and then independent contractors established hundreds of these "sheltered workshops," paying thousands of blind people subsistence wages to produce goods like brooms and mops, some with exclusive government contracts for their sale. "In this department," Howe wrote, "the blind feel perfectly independent, being assured of the bread they eat; and if any surplus remains to them, it is far more prized than would be ten times the amount of alms."

• • •

I asked Will if he'd gotten blindness skills training at one of the NFB's centers—he seemed so adept, so comfortable. He told me he's never had any training, but he thinks he gets around OK. He'd just returned from Japan, where he went on a few day trips alone. But he's quick to underplay his own abilities. "Honestly, the cane is not that complicated of a thing," he said. "It's the epitome of low tech."

When he was a freshman at Berkeley, Will was totally blind in his left eye, but he was otherwise "normal"—he drove a car and had a serious girlfriend, with plans to take a summer trip to Paris with her. Then his good eye started to fail. He underwent three retinal detachment surgeries, and to recover, the doctors made him lie flat on his stomach for three months straight. At the end of that meditative but agonizing period, he was legally blind. He and his girlfriend never went to Paris, and soon broke up.

Then he gradually began to reenter the world. Like me, Will spent those first few years ashamed of his cane, which he owned but never used, until it finally became clear that something had to change. One night, Will couldn't find a place to use the bathroom, so he peed in a quiet parking lot—which turned out to be that of a police station. He was nearly arrested. Run-ins like this started to add up. His friends knew he had vision problems, but no one apart from his mother encouraged him to get help.

"No sighted person says, 'Get a cane, dude,'" Will says now. "No one would ever think that, because sighted people view the cane as a sad thing, as tragedy."

The turning point was a trip he took with friends to Montreal. On the last night, Will and his friends stayed up all night partying, then took a five a.m. bus back to New York. At the border, customs officials gruffly roused them after everyone else had already exited the bus to go through customs. Will was deeply hungover, and holding on to his much shorter friend for guidance. "We probably looked like we were tripping," he said. He got an extra-long grilling at passport control, and the whole bus had to wait as he tried to convince the border agents that he wasn't on drugs. As soon as he got back to New York, he resolved to use the cane from then on.

That evening, he brought the cane out for the night for the first time. "I just happened to be with some good friends who were like, 'Dude, just bring it. Don't worry about it,'" Will said. They showed up at the bar where they were meeting a larger group, including a woman he'd never met before, a friend of a friend. As they all sat down, occupying a cluster of tables, Will could hear her, two tables away, turn to his friend and say, "Who's that?" She was talking about him. "Oh my god," she said, "my roommate would love him. He's totally her type." Will spoke about this moment with reverence. "I mean, I walked in there with a cane, thinking, Is anyone even going to talk to me? Like, am I going to be totally ostracized? I felt the lowest I'd ever felt. And this girl somehow just had the capacity to look beyond it. It was almost like she didn't see it. It was like a gift from a higher power. To be like, It's going to be OK. People are going to treat you fine."

I told Will about my own anxieties—how I felt like an impostor, constantly vacillating between feeling too sighted to be blind, and too blind to be sighted. "You might be going blind for a long time," Will said. He chewed a little, then added, "And at a certain point, you have to ditch the 'going blind' narrative. That sounds kind of harsh, but . . . you'll just be blind. And then you might be less blind or more blind, but you're still just blind." This did sound harsh—like he was suggesting that I was playing up my experience of going blind for effect, even holding it over someone like him, who's already had his "going blind" moment in a dramatic and concentrated way. Even the phrase *going blind* is problematic for him now, Will said: "*Going blind* has baked into it all the loneliness and isolation that we associate with blindness. A much more accurate way to describe it is *becoming blind*; blindness is much more an arrival than a departure."

It felt good to sit there and talk to Will. The few blind people I'd met up until then had all been at least thirty years older than I was, which made the kind of easy, honest conversation we were having now feel out of reach. Will said he wished he'd found someone to talk to like this when he first became blind. Now he gets to come to the NFB, where he's less blind than a lot of people: "So I get to hold that over them." We laughed at this joke, even as we both recognized that it wasn't entirely a joke. The hierarchy of sight turned out to be more than a vague sensation I thought only I might feel; it was a common dynamic among blind people. It was a relief to hear him acknowledge it. "Imagine," he said, "there's probably eight hundred people here at the NFB who get treated as incompetents every day of their lives. And they get to come here and help people. That must feel so good."

• • •

Early schools for the blind didn't prepare students for college or lift the prejudices of mainstream employers. But they did form the nucleus of a new, politicized brand of blind group consciousness, and the seeds of the organized blind movement. The cradle of this movement, and of so much disability activism in the US, was in the Bay Area. In the 1880s, at the California School for the Blind (CSB) in the soon-to-be-incorporated city of Berkeley, Newel Perry was in tenth grade. He'd begun thinking seriously about his postgraduation prospects and would sit up at night with his friends trying to imagine what their future might hold. "We'd never heard of a blind person going to college," he recalled, so they decided to write letters to the superintendents of all the state secondary schools for the blind they could find, explaining their talents and asking what they thought of their plans for higher ed. "I think half of them answered, and none of them told us they thought the idea of college was good," Perry recalled later.

> Several said, "Don't try it." One of them said, "You would be educating yourself only for a life of discontent," meaning, of course, if we did get through the university and we couldn't do anything, we'd be in an awful fix. Maybe we'd be better off if we stayed ignorant.

Nevertheless, Perry's teacher encouraged his ambitions, and in 1890 Perry became the first blind student to attend Berkeley High. He went on to become one of the first blind students to graduate from UC Berkeley, and by all accounts had a distinguished academic career: after receiving a fellowship to teach math at Berkeley, he eventually earned a PhD in mathematics from the University of Munich. But as he entered the job market, the low expectations of those blind-school superintendents were echoed by university math departments. His return to Berkeley in 1912 to work as a teacher at the CSB can be seen, from one angle, as a failure—rejected by the sighted world, he returned to the field of blindness. But Perry's passion for raising the prospects of blind people also made his decision a powerful one. This is still a common trajectory for many blind people: they achieve mainstream success, graduating from college, working in the real world, but then return to the blindness field, to work as teachers or assistive-technology trainers or accessibility consultants. It's a move animated in part by frustration with sighted prejudice, but also by a sense of solidarity with their blind compatriots.

Perry—the kids knew him as "Doc"—became a celebrated mentor at CSB, urging generations of blind students to follow his example and attend mainstream high schools and universities. He traveled up and down California by train, eventually forming the California Council of the Blind, a statewide organization led by and for the blind to advocate for their rights. He was a savvy political player, often writing bills himself that he would encourage legislators to adopt. During his time as the first president of the California Council, he got the state to pay for readers for any blind student attending college, hire job-placement workers at schools for the blind, and reform several "legal aid to the blind" laws.

As with any great teacher, one can find the strongest evidence of Perry's legacy in the success of his students: they became legislators, scholars, and businessmen. (CSB was coed, but Perry focused his efforts almost entirely on his male students; while he was ahead of his time in his thinking on disability, his views on gender were, unfortunately, far more representative of his era. Schools for the blind were also subject to the same segregation laws that mainstream schools were, and CSB was a white institution.)

His most celebrated student, Jacobus tenBroek, had much in common with Perry. Both men grew up in rural poverty and both lost their vision in traumatic early childhood accidents: at eight years old, Perry contracted a terrible case of poison oak that would burst his eyeballs and temporarily put him in a coma; at seven, tenBroek peered through a hole in an archery target, unaware that at that moment, his friend was letting his arrow fly, and would fatefully hit his mark. The arrow instantly blinded tenBroek in his left eye, and a case of "sympathetic ophthalmia" soon blinded his right. TenBroek—nicknamed "Chick"—followed Perry's footsteps: a mainstream school, Oakland's University High, and, in the 1930s, UC Berkeley, with a few blind classmates alongside him. Like Perry, tenBroek found academic success, completing a law fellowship at Harvard and a PhD in political science from Cal. But despite this robust CV, he experienced the same prejudices in the job market that Perry had: a department head at a large midwestern university that had expressed interest in hiring him to teach public law dropped his pursuit when he learned tenBroek was blind. TenBroek briefly contemplated following

Perry to CSB to become a teacher of the blind himself before finally finding a job as a professor in the newly formed Department of Public Speaking at Berkeley—not the law professorship he'd coveted, but a foothold, and one he turned into a distinguished career.

During this time, the landscape of government assistance to the blind was shifting. In the 1910s and 1920s, Perry had focused his efforts on state legislatures. But the Great Depression spurred the federal government to get into the business of welfare. For the first time, the US established federal agencies tasked with distributing "aid to the needy blind."

Perry and tenBroek now realized that they needed to think bigger. In November 1940, tenBroek, representing the California Council of the Blind, traveled to Wilkes-Barre, Pennsylvania, to meet with fifteen other leaders of similar organizations. TenBroek wore a trim Vandyke beard and the tweedy suits that befitted his background as a prewar Ivy League legal wonk. The attendees voted to make him the first president of their new organization, which they called the National Federation of the Blind. "The problems of the blind are now national in character," tenBroek said in a banquet speech in 1944, "and the organization of the blind must also be national in character."

• • •

The NFB philosophy straddles two seemingly opposing ideas: On the one hand, the organization argues that blindness is an incidental attribute that doesn't affect one's ability to accomplish nearly anything a sighted person can. On the other hand, the NFB demands accommodations and special benefits for blind people. These two ideas are difficult to hold at the same time: Are the blind equal to everyone else, or do they have special needs? But in practice, they needn't be mutually exclusive; in fact, they're the central tensions of the American way of life. Our laws are in constant tension between personal liberty (the decision to lift mask mandates in the midst of a pandemic, for example) and public welfare (protecting the immunocompromised from a deadly virus). The paradox of the American republic is that it at once enshrines our benefits while at the same time insisting on our liberties. This is also the paradox a blind person must confront. In a job environment where the vast majority of employers have no conception of how a blind person might be able to independently catch a bus or fry an egg, let alone manage a restaurant, benefits such as pensions or tax breaks are necessary. But these benefits must be administered thoughtfully, the NFB argues, leaving the blind person their privacy, dignity, and freedom to choose their own path and profession.

At the first NFB convention in 1940, tenBroek recalled that the delegates focused primarily on "the havoc wrought by the Social Security Board, the desirability of a national pension, and the unmitigated dastardliness of social workers." The Social Security Board, he argued, operated under a view of blindness that dated back to the Elizabethan Poor Laws, where relief was offered in exchange for a lifetime of menial sweatshop toil, with no levers in place for pulling a person out of poverty. Under the US system, benefits were conditional on income—if a blind person was lucky enough to find employment, their benefits would be cut off as soon as they saved more than a set dollar amount. TenBroek argued for a middle path, where the blind could keep more of their earnings, incentivizing them to work. Thanks to the NFB's lobbying efforts, blind people can earn nearly 70 percent above what other disabled groups do before they lose their benefits. But while blind people sometimes require more training than other disabilities, it hardly seems fair that they receive more generous benefits than other groups. And regardless of these disparities, the laws governing the distribution of Supplemental Security income (SSI)—one of the primary sources of disability benefits in the US—are long out of date, and all but ensure that their recipients remain in poverty. As Maggie Astor reported in *The New York Times* in 2021, SSI provides a maximum benefit of $9,528 per year, "three-quarters of the federal poverty level"; recipients are penalized if they earn more than $85 in outside income, if they have more than $2,000 in savings, or even if they accept gifts of "groceries or even shelter from loved ones"; and the benefits haven't been adjusted for inflation since 1972.

TenBroek told the first NFBers in 1940 that their goals "can only be accomplished by a militant, aggressive, group-conscious national organization of the blind." Over the years, the NFB made good on this promise of militancy. They fought legislative battles with the Social Security Administration and won Senator John F. Kennedy's support for a blind "right to organize" bill (which ultimately failed) to protect them against the pressure they faced from state blindness commissions—a kind of disability union-busting. They also brought attention to individuals who were denied rooms for rent, rejected as blood donors, denied jobs as civil servants, rejected for jury duty, and so on. Today, the NFB advocates for blind prisoners denied access to basic programs, blind people unable to cast private ballots in elections, and blind parents separated from their children solely on the basis of their blindness.

TenBroek modeled the federation on labor unions, and saw a direct analogy between the blind person and the industrial worker. Both, tenBroek said, "are forced to extend to each other a good deal of mutual aid and to ask society for protection and to some extent for assistance." Newel Perry, tenBroek's mentor, remarked that people knew him as a Republican in most aspects, but that "for the blind, I'm a Socialist." The NFB's membership largely reflects the US political spectrum, including a large base of conservative rural whites. But when it comes to issues affecting their blindness, a sense of collectivist solidarity tends to win out over conservative sentiment. In Orlando, I met Barbara Loos, a blind Nebraskan working a table at the Braille Book Fair. When I asked her how she got involved in the NFB, she told me she was a "Republican who believes in civil rights." She said she was put off by the NFB at first because of its reputation as a radical organization. "But I looked up *radical*," she told me, "and it just means 'at the root of things.'"

The NFB's radicalism has earned it a reputation for stridency, dogmatism, and autocracy. Its organizational structure, based on the organized labor model, does give its president a tremendous amount of power once the votes of its rank-and-file members are counted; the NFB's first forty years were dominated by two charismatic leaders whose voices became synonymous with the movement. There are still those in the federation who speak of one of tenBroek's successors, Kenneth Jernigan, with a kind of nostalgic activist fervor, as though he were the Malcolm X of blindness.

But by the end of the 1950s, a group of Federationists had become increasingly frustrated with tenBroek's single-handed control over the organization. They accused his administration of financial mismanagement and an undemocratic consolidation of presidential power. This led to a period known as the "civil war," concluding with the purging of the "dissident" factions within the organization and a dramatic scene at the NFB's 1961 national convention in Kansas City. Dozens of the defecting members staged a walkout from the convention floor, crossing the street to a separate hotel, where they officially incorporated a new national organization: the American Council of the Blind.

The ACB resembles the NFB in many ways—it has bylaws ensuring that a majority of its members are blind (making it another organization *of* and not just *for* the blind), a national convention, state affiliates, local chapters, lobbyists in Washington, and so on. But the ACB is smaller, and tends to strike a more conciliatory tone toward the agencies that the NFB gleefully excoriates. (It also has a reputation, at least among some blind people, for leaning more politically progressive than the NFB.)

As the NFB rebuilt itself after the schism, and grew in membership, it continued its aggressive interventions into policies that affected—and, they said, oppressed—blind people. These actions sometimes put them at odds with other blindness organizations, including the ACB. In the 1970s, audible pedestrian signals were introduced in the US—those electronic bird chirps that sound when it's safe to cross an intersection. The NFB came down swiftly against their use, arguing that they reinforced the image of the blind as helpless people who can't figure out from the sound of traffic when the light has changed. For decades, this was a controversial split between the ACB and the NFB, sowing confusion among local municipalities baffled by the warring groups of blind people arguing for and against the signals. There are still members of each organization that snipe at the other: several NFBers I spoke with condescendingly described ACB conventions as rife with older blind people who over-rely on assistance from their sighted companions, and there are ACBers who cannot speak of the NFB without heatedly describing its dogmatism and stridency. But these grievances are largely limited to the older generations, who still harbor resentments from the civil war era. There's movement among younger members of each organization to move past the old conflicts between these two groups that should, at bottom, share the same goal: removing the barriers that prevent blind people from living full lives.

• • •

Two days after my lunch with Will, in the wake of a long, monotonous afternoon session, everyone returned to their rooms to change for the final banquet. I sat in the lobby, half dozing, and woke to see them emerge from the elevators, resplendent in formal evening wear. And once more, I caught myself questioning the basic dignity of blind people. Shouldn't a blindness convention be like working from home—can't we all just wear pajamas? Why place all this emphasis on formality and pomp? Nearing the end of my fourth day there, I was exhausted by the emotional effort it had taken to confront blindness—in myself and in others—over and over again. The worst thoughts that people have about blind people kept arising. *What's the point of looking nice if you can't see?* But people did look fantastic coming out of the elevators. And I recognized the foolishness of the thought even as I rolled it around my mind like a bolus I was afraid to swallow or spit out. The banquet's dress code was about self-respect, the human dignity that everyone has, or has a right to. The ability, no matter your circumstance, to feel presentable and elegant. It was why, I'd heard, the NFB headquarters in Baltimore have the cleanest bathrooms you'll ever use. (I've also heard that the federation's college scholarship committee has enlisted a sighted person to describe the wardrobe of their blind applicants, in order to evaluate their personal appearance as part of their decision-making process.)

When I found my table, an older woman and a guy with an intellectual disability in a wheelchair who looked to be about my age were already there. I introduced myself, and the woman, Susan, immediately began telling me their story. Within the first minute, she'd explained that her son's name was Jared, and that he was a shaken baby. "I was at work and my husband was with him," she said. "He lost his optic nerve and developed the equivalent of cerebral palsy. When Jared was sent home from the hospital, they said, 'Oh, by the way, he's blind'—so I was trying to find anybody who could tell me how to raise a blind baby." This is how she found the NFB, which has a division for parents of blind children. As she spoke, I had another thought that made me feel like an ableist jerk even as I had it. What does it matter, I thought, that he's blind, if his other disabilities are so severe? Why focus on blindness, when he has all these other problems too? Shouldn't they be at a shaken baby convention? Which is a deeply ill-conceived question. Jared and Susan have just as much right to a blindness community as I do. So why did he make me feel so uncomfortable?

I'd been cultivating a sense of blindness not as a disability, but instead as some rare and wonderful literary attribute: something that's touched great poets like Homer or Borges. I had begun to collect clippings of blind brilliance, like a passage from an essay John Milton wrote in response to a critic who used Milton's blindness as a metaphor for what he saw as the gaps in his reasoning. Milton's response draws a sharp division between visual and mental impairment:

> I would, sir, prefer my blindness to yours; yours is a cloud spread over the mind, which darkens both the light of reason and of conscience; mine keeps from my view only the coloured surfaces of things, while it leaves me at liberty to contemplate the beauty and stability of virtue and of truth. How many things are there besides which I would not willingly see; how many which I must see against my will; and how few which I feel any anxiety to see!

Intellectual disability didn't fit into this elevated idea of blindness. I've been leaning too hard into Will Butler's story of blindness as an opening of intellectual doors. There's pathos in vision loss, but it's the grand, refined pathos of King Lear, who says to the blind Duke of Gloucester, "No eyes in your head . . . yet you see how this world goes." (Gloucester's reply is awesome: *"I see it feelingly."*)

Jared's story challenged the patness of that fantasy. My reaction, in turn, was a shamefully basic case of discomfort and fear around disability. I can see that intellectual disability is another impairment with its own diversity of experience, one that's also cloaked by stigma, estrangement, and fear. But in the moment, I wasn't anywhere close to finding my way into that understanding, and instead I ignored Jared as I spoke to his mother.

The Johnsons, a family of four from Louisiana, sat down at our table: a blind boy, who looked to be about Oscar's age, and his older sister and parents, all sighted. Just like Susan, this boy's mother began narrating her son's medical history to me almost instantly, nearly unbidden, and as though he wasn't there. "This is Isaac," she said. "He has hypo-optic dysplasia. When he was six months old, I thought, Why isn't he focusing on toys like normal babies?"

Isaac sat down next to me. He was small and funny.

"How old are you?" I asked.

"Ten."

"When's your birthday?"

"I don't remember. I remembered—but I forget."

We ate for a while in silence, listening to the scholarship announcements blasting from the stage. Isaac said, "That salad was good. I haven't had a tomato for five months."

"Do you like tomatoes?" I asked.

"I found a tomato once at my school," he continued. "I took it to the office. It had fallen out of a basket." In retrospect, this is my favorite moment of the entire convention: the image of a blind, tomato-loving ten-year-old in Louisiana, playing in his school's yard. He notices something on the ground. Does he kick it? Move it with his cane? Perhaps his foot brushes against it. He kneels down to investigate. It's warm, soft, firm. He brings it to his face and inhales. Definitely a tomato. Would Isaac have eaten it, if he'd known no one was looking? When you're blind, do you ever really know that no one is looking? As a kid, I remember the feeling of being unobserved, relishing my solitude. But Isaac doesn't furtively eat the tomato. He reports it to the authorities, who confirm that there is in fact a missing tomato, fallen from a basket a teacher has carried across the yard.

I loved this story because of the matter-of-fact wonder with which Isaac communicated it. In the moment, it reminded me of Oscar, who I missed, badly. But I also loved it because after a week of blind politics, blind tech, blind culture, blind struggle, it restored to me a sense of blind life with regular contours. This nonstory—*I found a tomato*—might have done more to illuminate the NFB's ethos—*blindness is not what defines you*—than anything else I'd heard or seen that week. Isaac and his tomato gave me hope. Hope that I will still love the things I love, that I'll still find them in the world. That I won't crush them, or miss them every time—that sometimes I'll accidentally touch one with my cane or foot, and it will be a blessing.

Our conversation ended when the NFB's president, Mark Riccobono, approached the podium to deliver his banquet speech. I felt a small splash of horror as he announced that the theme of his speech would be "synergy." But it turned out that this wasn't corporate-speak—or, rather, it was corporate-speak of a special kind, channeled through Ray Kurzweil, the famous futurist and Google engineering director, who has attended the NFB national convention nearly every year since 1975, and who nodded approvingly from his place at the table behind the podium. Riccobono used *synergy* to capture an idea that academics and millennials (and, a few years later, the culture at large) would probably call "intersectionality": the synergy of identity. The NFB, he said, is women, it's LGBT people, it's blind people. Riccobono spent much of his speech focusing on the underappreciated role of women in the organization's history. But this feminist emphasis only went so far: as an identity marker, he said, blindness must supersede all other attributes. "That they were women," he explained, "was not nearly as important as the fact that they were *blind people* who believed in equality, had a hope for the future, and were willing to participate actively in the efforts of the National Federation of the Blind." This was a strange sort of intersectionality—celebrating one identity without diluting the hard-line privileging of another. It's a liability of the prioritization of group consciousness that the NFB's leaders established at its origin—blind solidarity above all. After the banquet, I learned that this is all awkward new territory for the federation. The NFB's LGBT meetup struggled for recognition for years—its first official meeting was only in 2017, the year before I attended. Isaac said loudly, "I wish this speaker was done."

The speech turned toward its conclusion and the audience began to lose its shit in earnest. "Vision is not a requirement for success in the world!" Riccobono shouted, and I saw that he'd gotten the attention of Isaac, who was now clapping along with the crowd. People were screaming, crying, hugging. My ears hurt. Jared was full of life in his wheelchair, shaking his fists and hollering. As the speech ended, I heard wailing behind me; a group of three people had stood up from their table, embracing one another in a tight circle. One of them was just falling apart, weeping uncontrollably, held up by the other two. The emotion in the room rippled through the assembled body in immense waves. These were people who'd been discriminated against, who'd felt shunned and isolated and subordinated and disdained, and here was a moment of overwhelming defiance, solidarity, and inspiration. This was what they'd been waiting for all year.

After the speech, there were more presentations, but the Johnsons got up to leave—the kids were tired. "Bye, Mr. Andrew," Isaac said, and I warmly told him goodbye as he stood next to me. After an awkward pause, Isaac said, simply, *"Hand"*—and I realized I'd left his extended hand dangling, unseen in the dead zone of my peripheral vision. I found and squeezed it, and the Johnsons walked him off to bed.

3.

Blinded by Definition

My first visit to Mass Eye and Ear (MEE) started like any garden-variety optometrist's appointment: with the eye chart. Using my good central vision, I could still see the big *E* at the top, and with glasses and proper lighting, I could read several of the smaller lines beneath it. I put some feeling into it. "*Bee-aye cee*," I said to myself, to the nurse, to the audience listening at home. (In keeping with a vague idea I'd developed of producing a podcast about going blind, I'd brought along my tape recorder.) "*Oh, dee? El kay, queue em bee-tee. Oh, pea . . .*" As I made my way farther down the rows, the letters began folding themselves into vibrating, illegible, starlike clusters of silver pixels. I start to sound a little more desperate on the recording. "*Kay-tee?? Ell-zee kay??? Oh dee, oh zee, are . . . KAY?!?!?*"

I wished the nurse could just scan my eyes with a *Star Trek* tricorder and learn everything she needed to know. But vision is a powerfully subjective substance, one that is still most accurately measured by the patient's own report. Doctors appraise all the senses this way, with odd quizzes designed to standardize an elusive, highly interpretable impression. Patients indicate pain level as a point along an affective spectrum, from a happy face to one with a grimace, eyes squeezed shut and skin red with agony. Audiologists pipe a sonic version of the eye chart into our ears, benign nouns like *dog* and *child* that the auditor must repeat back. Raised in a culture that worships the authority of doctors, I find it difficult to trust entirely in my own report. Reading the chart and answering their questions, I felt like an unreliable narrator of what should be indisputable: my own direct observations.

The tools that doctors use to measure vision are recent inventions. In 1836, Heinrich Küchler, a German ophthalmologist frustrated by the lack of consistency in eye examinations, cut out a selection of pictures from calendars, books, and newspapers, collaging and arranging those images—farm equipment, military weapons, and animals (he chose camels, frogs, and birds)—in descending order of size, just like the alphabetic eye chart I was reading. Pulled together from such disparate sources, Küchler's frogs and cannons all appeared in different styles, print qualities, and line weights. (They also depended on the patient's ability to identify an eclectic range of industrial and zoological specimens.) The collaged eye chart failed to catch on.

A few years later, Küchler tried again, this time making a chart with letters. He chose a black-letter typeface (like the *New York Times*'s logotype, but even busier, denser, and narrower), and printed full words on the chart. Patients were able to guess the lines based on the context of the most legible letters, and the black-letter typefaces used by different printers led to wide variations in size and inconsistencies in the measurements of patients' visual acuity. All of these problems were solved twenty years later by the Dutch ophthalmologist Herman Snellen, who created the eye chart more or less as we know it today: lines of descending, random letters, printed in Optotype, the font Snellen designed to regularize the weight, size, and shape of the letters, no matter what press they were printed on. Eventually, producers of the Snellen chart had to print variations on the letter arrangements, since the chart had become so ubiquitous—including on coffee mugs, shower curtains, and throw rugs—that some patients had memorized the first few lines, like the lyrics to a popular song.

• • •

Mass Eye and Ear is a hundred miles from my house, so I'd spent the night before my appointment in a hotel at the edge of the hospital complex in the Beacon Hill neighborhood. I wandered across the frozen medical campus, blearily scanning each facade for signs of the eye infirmary. I decided to stop at a Starbucks, and as I stood in line, I suddenly felt firm hands on my shoulders, steering me aside. A stranger, thinking himself helpful, had just moved me out of the way of a woman I hadn't seen—who I never really did see, beyond a patchy peripheral feminine blur—who was apparently trying to get past. Strangers, I'm learning, frequently touch and guide blind people like this in public, without warning or consent, feeling the need to manage us like furniture, or animals, or toddlers. This was my first such encounter, and I was too surprised to say anything.

I found Inherited Retinal Disorders on the third floor of Mass Eye and Ear. As the doors of the talking elevator shut behind me, I walked past a vitrine displaying relics from the institution's history—MEE is the second-oldest eye hospital in the country, a fortress of philanthropic medicine, originally designed to treat the "deserving poor," which meant mostly Irish laborers blinded by cataracts or industrial accidents. I stopped in front of a series of six oil portraits of eminent Massachusetts ophthalmologists, and snapped a few photos on my phone: Instagram fodder in the form of this weird visual celebration of the mild-mannered men who had devoted their lives to the preservation and extension of vision.

In the waiting room, I held my pile of recording equipment sheepishly in my lap, too shy to ask anyone if it was all right to use it. I listened, wishing I was recording, as the husband of a woman off somewhere having her eyes dilated talked about how she had kept driving long after her deteriorating vision should have stopped her. One day she rear-ended a dump truck, which was so much higher than her car that she managed to actually wedge her car beneath it. Midway through this harrowing story, his wife returned from the examination room, and cheerfully delivered the kicker: "I was almost decapitated! If anyone had been in the passenger seat, they would have been." Her husband confessed that for years he'd encouraged her to limit herself to driving to and from work. "It was such a short drive," he said. What could be the harm? She was diagnosed with RP at seventy years old. Bryan Bashin, who runs the LightHouse for the Blind in San Francisco, told me that "RP is the most potent denial machine." Because people with RP hang on to the ability to see something throughout our degeneration, "down to the last photon," there's a powerful incentive to think, *Well, I can still see—I can't actually be blind just yet.*

After the eye chart, the next step was the visual field test. I dreaded this one even more than the way they pried my eyelids open, *Clockwork Orange* style, for the electroretinogram that was coming later. I sat in a rolling office chair, and the nurse asked me to press right up into what amounted to an awkward embrace of the squat metal machine, which hummed with electrical current. Then I peered through a scope on the side, which offered a view into a tiny amphitheater with a dull yellow light shining in its center. The nurse handed me a game-show-style buzzer, which she told me to press whenever I saw a pinprick of wobbly light moving from the periphery of the amphitheater toward the light at its center. For most people, this test is as routine as the eye chart, a little medical carnival game. But as I waited to see the wobbly lights emerge from my dead periphery, impotently clutching the buzzer through the long silence, certain that the light would have been visible to someone with a normal visual field many minutes ago, my anxiety grew. Finally, a light appeared directly in front of me, and I gave the buzzer a squeeze, the worst contestant in the history of *Jeopardy!*

As soon as we'd finished the visual field exam, the nurse informed me in her terminal deadpan that she'd now give me the double eyepatch. It took me a moment to understand her meaning. Wasn't a double eyepatch just . . . a blindfold? I think of eyepatches in the same category as monocles—they are only ever singular. It's like calling a bicycle a "double unicycle." But *blindfold*, with its daredevil associations, would be out of place in the eye hospital. It would introduce that word, which must only be whispered—(*blind*)—carrying like an infectious disease vector the same unpleasantness my cane brought into the waiting room.

In my chart, I have scotomas, not blind spots. An eyepatch is medical, something a child might have to wear for a few months (Lily wore one for a year when she was five, tripling the cuteness of her childhood photos), but a blindfold is for parlor games, something a ringmaster puts on before he shoots an apple off someone's head, or what they have you wear before you face the firing squad yourself. Before I'd had a chance to fully think through the semiotics, the nurse asked me to remove my glasses. She placed a piece of gauze over one eye and secured it in place with tape. There was a brief pause, as at the peak of a roller coaster's ascent. Then she performed the same operation on the other eye, and just like that, I really was blind—and there's no other word for it.

The nurse guided me back to a seat in the waiting room. It was a different seat than the one I had before, and I bristled at this minor indignity, that I couldn't find my way independently to choose a seat for myself. I rode out an overwhelming desire to look at my phone. My tape recorder was still running, and I held it in my lap, as it (and I) blindly listened to everything that transpired in the room.

Vision is a vector: the eyes point in one direction. But we listen in a field, isolating what we hear with our attention, rather than a directed gaze. Philosophers of sound (and stoned people at rock concerts) are fond of pointing out that while we have eyelids, we cannot close our ears. It's more difficult to direct one's listening; sound just washes up on us, whether we want to hear something or not. In the waiting room, I hear someone sit down next to me, and I greet the void, addressing myself to the creak of an ass connecting with a chair.

"Hey there," a voice said. I wondered if it belonged to the same guy I'd spoken to earlier, who I'd chatted with about commuting from the western half of the state for hospital visits. We were interrupted by the trembling sound of a paper cup being filled with water, accompanied by the rumbling percussive bass of the plastic bubbler. I was sitting next to the watercooler! The surprise of its proximity transformed a banal sound into an explosive interruption.

I found chatting with this man easier with the double eyepatch. There was no pressure to maintain eye contact, and the silences felt like they'd been made material, sublimated into a soothing mist that suddenly filled the room. He told me about his wife's eye problems; he was waiting for her to return from testing, and I nodded, reflecting on the strangeness of nodding without sight. Is he registering my nods? Is there even any point in nodding anymore?

After half an hour of this, the nurse returned to guide me into the ERG room. I'd been double-eyepatched because I needed to be utterly dark-adapted in order for the electroretinogram test to work. Only major eye hospitals have the equipment; I hadn't taken one since I was first diagnosed. The room was black as the nurse peeled off the patches and inserted specialized contact lenses into my eyes. The lenses have small wires coming out of them, and blinking became awful: it felt impossible even as I did it, like swallowing with a thick plastic tube running down your throat. I tried to blink around the wires.

When I finally met my doctor, our conversation was a reproduction of the same one I'd had with all the other retinal specialists: you have classical RP, there's still no treatment, vitamin supplements might be effective, come back to see us in two years. It made me wonder what the point of these visits is—many people with RP simply stop going after a while, deciding that it's too upsetting to keep making scientific measurements of a process whose progress they don't need medical equipment to observe.

The doctor showed me the results of my failed appearance on optical *Jeopardy!*—the visual field test. This was that schematic that had once reminded me of ice cubes, the one that described how much vision I'd lost: the roughly symmetrical pair of diagrams, one for each of my eyes, with small, wobbly ovals at their centers (the twin portholes of my residual central vision), flanked by two slender, curved shapes (representing my periphery). The doctor said that those slender shapes were the bits of vision I was using to get around. There's a clinical term for this: *ambulatory vision*, or the patient's ability to see objects at close range. If a patient can't visually navigate a room, whether or not she's able to read large print or see what someone looks like, then a doctor will determine that she's lost her ambulatory vision.

My doctor's deceptively innocuous phrase—"the vision you're using to get around"—rang in my ears for the rest of the day—and for the next two years, until my next visit. The idea of ambulatory vision made it sound like the loss of my sight was effectively the loss of my legs. As soon as I lose these strips of peripheral vision, I imagined, Lily will nod, rise, and walk silently to the basement to retrieve a rocking chair she's kept hidden there for this purpose. She'll guide me gently into the chair and hand me a blanket, which I'll smooth in my lap. I'll pat searchingly around the coffee table for the remote control, which, once I find it, I'll clutch for the next fifty years, listening to the television until I die peacefully, still seated in the chair. My official cause of death: prolonged blindness. (I thought I'd invented this fictional malady—*terminal blindness*—until I read Samuel Beckett's *Endgame*. In that play, the half-blind Clov blames the totally blind Hamm for the death of an unseen character, Mother Pegg, because Hamm refused to give her oil for her lamp. "You know what she died of, Mother Pegg?" Clov asks Hamm accusingly. "*Of darkness.*")

Of course, all the doctor meant to say was that without ambulatory vision, I won't be able to use my sight to get around the way I do now—she wasn't denying that it's possible for blind people to do things like climb Mount Everest (as Erik Weihenmayer did, in 2001) or travel independently around the globe more than anyone, sighted or blind, had up to that point in history (James Holman, 1786–1857). Had she invoked such inspirational blind achievements, or described the potential for blind people to find independence, it would have been obnoxious, maudlin, and probably not very useful to me in that moment. But that's not her style. Her default mode is dry, compassionate frankness, probably an effective posture for someone who has to inform or remind people that they're going slowly, incurably blind, every weekday. I appreciated her honesty, but it also instantly formed this hopeless image—immobile imprisonment within my skull—that she didn't do anything to alter.

At the end of our conversation, she said she thought I qualified as legally blind in Massachusetts, but that the visual field test they'd given me that morning hadn't followed the proper parameters for the state to approve it. If I wanted the official designation, I'd have to take the test again. The US has only had a legal definition of blindness since the 1930s, when it emerged as a way to decide who was eligible for the New Deal's slate of federal services and entitlements for the blind. "More people are blinded by definition," the director of the Blinded Veterans Association later observed, "than by any other cause."

Today, there are two main ways you can achieve legal blindness. The first is poor visual acuity: if you're unable to read the giant *E* at the top of the Snellen chart—even with corrective lenses, through your better eye—you're legally blind. My bid for legal blindness hung on the other metric, the visual field. This measures the narrowness of one's tunnel vision. Normal vision is roughly 140 degrees; 20 degrees or less puts you into the domain of legal blindness. My doctor suddenly seemed awkward around this question, in a way that she wasn't when she was telling me that my traditional mobility would soon be obliterated. She delicately offered me the second visual field test as a choice, emphatically and entirely up to me, only if I wanted it, and she'd understand if I didn't. But why wouldn't I want to be legally blind? Some patients resist it, she said. They don't feel blind, don't want to be blind, and don't want the word pinned to them. Many of them still drive (though they shouldn't), or still have careers in fields that require vision. They don't want to be blinded by someone else's definition. I glanced at my cane, leaning faithfully in the corner. Becoming legally blind was just the sort of justification I'd been waiting for. With legal blindness, I'd own my blindness better.

Soon I was peering again into the tiny amphitheater, clutching my buzzer and playing a final round of doomed optical *Jeopardy!*, with a new prize at stake.

When the doctor returned after the test, she said that I had indeed qualified, and that she'd give me a form I could send to the state commission for the blind to register for services. She told me this somberly, in case I'd suddenly become one of those patients she mentioned, devastated by the introduction of the word *blind* into their legal identity. But I felt a rush of excitement at the news; congratulations were in order. For the first time that day, I felt as though I'd passed a test.

• • •

A few years later, my family went to an outdoor Rosh Hashanah service at the synagogue near our house. We never did things like this, but Oscar was starting Hebrew school soon, and we thought we should make an effort to participate in some way before we started dumping him there twice a week. My mom happened to be in town, the weather was fine, and we all sat together under a huge white tent.

No one spoke to us as we arrived—kibitzing was forbidden by COVID protocol—and I felt my cane draw its customary stares, particularly from the children; kids are always less subtle in their ogling. The service was sweet, boring, fine—there was a lot of music, and kids from the school kept coming to the front to read prayers or lead songs. I wasn't overjoyed with the idea of Oscar going there, but I didn't feel any deep opposition either.

Then the rabbi asked one of the leaders of the children's program to share a poem. It was by Billy Collins, they said, written in the voice of a boy whose mother responds to his every complaint with the injunction to *"Fall to your knees and thank God for your eyesight."* I stiffened the way I do now whenever a movie or TV show makes a negative or pitying reference to blindness. "'My bicycle only has three gears,'" they read. *"'Fall to your knees and thank God for your eyesight.'"* The poem went on and on like this, repeating this refrain, as the poet's childhood peevishness evolved into grown-up gratitude to his mother—and, it seemed clear, to God—"'for giving me the eyes to see the world, to regard these words.'"

As we walked home after the service, Lily, my mom, and Oscar each earnestly agreed that the poem had made them uncomfortable. Oscar seemed delighted to join our increasingly critical conversation about the synagogue and Billy Collins. My family's solidarity was delicious. We briefly considered how we might interpret the poem differently—had we missed something? Was it as bad as we remembered? But then I found the text on my phone—it had been published in *Tikkun*, the progressive Jewish magazine—and yes, it was as bad as we remembered. What was there to misunderstand? *Fall to your knees and thank God for your eyesight.*

A week later, Lily cc'd me on an email to the rabbi. "My husband, Andrew, is legally blind," she wrote, "and we all felt uncomfortable joining a new community only to hear a poem instructing us to be thankful for our eyesight. I hope you will be more sensitive to this issue in the future, and to the kind of ableism texts like that reinforce. There are certainly plenty of more interesting and less problematic poems about gratitude out there."

It felt, oddly enough, like a milestone in our marriage. Not so much Lily's defense of me—if I was sufficiently outraged, and not just deeply annoyed, I would have written to the rabbi myself. But her message suggested that she had begun to internalize my experience of blindness. The irritation she felt at the poem wasn't simply on my behalf; it was her own. That touched me.

The rabbi responded with an apology that placed the brunt of the problem on our own reaction ("I am sorry that it made you feel uncomfortable"). I chalked it up to garden-variety ableism, but I also harbored a creeping suspicion that it reflected some kind of particularly religious attitude toward blindness. Was the rabbi thinking of the passage in the

Torah that prohibits disabled or disfigured people from offering sacrifices or serving as priests?

> No one at all who has a defect shall be qualified: no man who is blind, or lame, or has a limb too short or too long; no man who has a broken leg or a broken arm; or who is a hunchback, or a dwarf, or who has a growth in his eye, or who has a boil-scar, or scurvy, or crushed testes.

A passage in the Talmud places the blind among four "types" (the list also includes the poor, lepers, and "those who have no children") who are "considered like the dead."

Oscar dreaded the start of Hebrew school. But once he found out that it was mostly games and singing and not anything like that long holiday service, he loved it, and so I accepted it too. I had also already begun to find other reasons to connect my blindness and my Jewishness, starting at another appointment at the eye hospital in Boston, two years after my last visit.

• • •

I'm going blind not just once, but over and over. Even when I lose a clinically tiny amount of vision—say, an eighth of a degree of my visual field—the decline feels catastrophic. *Another chunk of sight—gone!* I think. *The whole edifice will surely collapse now*. . . . But then it stabilizes. Months tick by with no new changes. What once felt like a gaping hole in a crumbling ruin begins to feel normal, invisible, an everyday feature of the landscape.

I've mentally cured myself, and then re-diagnosed myself, several times over. Once I adapt to a change, and it's felt stable for a while, I nurture the illusion that, actually, my RP isn't as bad as it seems. I can live with this amount of blindness. I return to the feeling I had in the decade after my diagnosis, treating information about RP—and the entire world of blindness—the way an indifferent student might regard the facts of the English Reformation: this must be important to someone, but that sad, lonely person is very far from here. Then my vision erodes a bit more, and the drama of a fresh diagnosis is reactivated. It's really happening! I've got a degenerative retinal disease!

In this heightened state, everyday moments feel violently altered. One morning, I set a knife and a radish on the cutting board. When I return from the fridge, the knife has disappeared. I stare in blended wonder and horror at the radish, which I know is still sitting next to the knife. But the knife isn't there. How blind I've become! I diligently scan up and down the cutting board, and at last the knife gulps back into view, resting innocently just where I'd left it. Distraught, I slice the radish.

The week I'd chosen for my follow-up visit to Mass Eye and Ear, I was in one of these catastrophic moods, where it seemed like the world was disappearing. When I was first diagnosed, the doctor had told me that the decline would be gradual through my twenties and thirties, and then accelerate as I approached middle age. Now here I was, approaching middle age, swiping my cane past the familiar portraits of eminent Massachusetts ophthalmologists. After the usual tests, I sat fiddling with my tape recorder in an empty exam room. I was surprised to see a young doctor walk in—a fellow, he said, doing his residency under my usual doctor. He asked how my vision was—a trick question, since he had the results of that morning's exams in front of him. Speaking from my catastrophic mood, I said with mellow urgency that it was all finally happening, that the prognosis I'd received as a teenager—the accelerated decline, the plunge off the cliff—was now at hand. I shared the ominous tale of the disappearing knife on the cutting board. He let me finish, and then said, matter-of-factly, "RP doesn't really work that way. The decline is more linear than logarithmic." These mathematical expressions were barely legible on the tiny, wet chalkboard of my mind. "RP doesn't suddenly accelerate," he explained. "The decline tends to remain at a stable, unchanging rate." I cautiously digested this. It was entirely counter to the understanding I'd been carrying around for the past twenty years. "That's surprising," I said. "It's good news! But . . . surprising news."

He asked if I was receiving support services from the state commission for the blind. Eye doctors tend to have a low sense of the lived experience of the visual impairments they diagnose and measure; meeting and listening to actual blind people is not a part of most medical schools' training. A 2021 study found that more than 80 percent of US doctors believed that people with significant disabilities "have worse quality of life than nondisabled people"—a figure grossly out of step with the attitudes of many disabled people. The fact that my retinal specialists were even aware of the blindness rehabilitation services I was eligible for (that could help me figure out how to continue living a full, productive life without sight) put them a step ahead of most physicians.

After qualifying for legal blindness—it even came with a special laminated ID card!—I'd had a first round of trainings with a few of their specialists. They taught me how to use my cane properly, instead of what I was doing before, which was to carry it around ceremonially, as though I were relaying it to a blind CEO waiting nearby. My instructor advised me to imagine kicking the cane with each step, so that as my left foot extended, the cane swung over to my right side, and then vice versa, clearing the path for each foot as I strode forward. The commission had also introduced me to an array of assistive technologies I had too much vision to find useful, like the gadget you hang on the edge of your mug as you pour coffee in, emitting a piercing digital shriek when the cup is full. A few of the vocational counselors I met with even betrayed a sense that I wasn't quite blind enough to be receiving their services. "I thought your vision would be . . . different than it is," one of them had said. I told the medical fellow that I'd planned to schedule a second round of training once I'd passed the milestones I felt were imminent: the loss of my ambulatory vision and my ability to read print.

"You're not going to lose print so quickly," he said with an irritating breeziness. A feeling of deep fraudulence burbled within me. This news should have come as a joyous surprise, but my happiness was tinged with an odd disappointment. The night before, a popular podcast had accepted a pitch I'd sent them about reading technology for the blind. I'd imagined a story built around my own feelings about my imminent loss of print. What perspective was I supposed to offer now? Could I still write a book about blindness? I was in the thick of telling myself, and others, the story of going blind, which Will Butler had suggested I might be ready to move past. But now I felt even more confused about where I stood in my journey.

At the end of the day, after a few more tests, it was time for my tête-à-tête with my real doctor. While the fellow explained once again that there wasn't any evidence that I was losing my sight as quickly as I said I was, my doctor played good cop, softening his accusation by adding that there was probably a good reason why I felt like I was losing my vision so quickly, and that tests only measure so much. This seemed like empty reassurance; it was clear that they both put their stock in medical testing, paying lip service to the patient's subjective but ultimately flawed perception out of some sense of obligation.

Then, another surprise: at the end of my last visit, I'd had blood drawn so that I could get in line for genetic testing. Because I'd declined to pay the several thousand dollars that it'd cost to have my test processed quickly, my sample had waited in a years-long queue to be evaluated for medical research. The results had just come back, and for the first time, the doctor could share with me the particular genetic mutation that had caused my RP. It was called the MAK-1 mutation—most common, she told me, among Ashkenazi Jews. *That's me!* I said, flashing a vaudevillian grin at the two unamused MDs.

This piece of information had a few major implications: it meant that if clinical trials for gene therapy for that mutation came up, I'd be eligible. Previously, I'd only been eligible for general treatments, but the most promising approaches for RP involved targeted gene therapy. The MAK-1 mutation, one of more than a hundred that can cause RP (researchers discover more each year), was only identified in 2010, and there have been only a handful of small studies on patients who carry it. One of these studies, my doctor told me, observed twenty-four people with the mutation, and five of them maintained a small amount of central vision into their seventies. Their *seventies*! The feeling of fraudulence that had come with the fellow's skepticism about my experience of vision loss now gave way to a rush of excitement at the prospect of decades of sight. A high-speed montage flashed through my head: Oscar's high school graduation, Lily's affectionate gaze, the faces of unfamiliar toddlers—my grandchildren, all part of a strobing barrage: sunsets, sandwiches, cinema, C-SPAN, all the images the world will produce for my pleasure and enlightenment by 2060. A moment later, I thought of the assistive-tech instructor who'd come to my house earlier that year. "RP is slow," he'd told me. "A few of my older clients with RP, some of them can still see the screen!" I asked how much they could see—could they read the text? "Oh, no," he said. "I just meant they can register that an event has happened, that an alert has popped up." Was this the sort of negligible central vision these septuagenarians from the study still had? (I imagined a lab filled with old blind Jews, grousing at the quality of the snacks the researchers had provided.) Or was it something more, the sort of vision that lets someone see words, faces, landscapes?

Then there was the question of whether I'd passed the disease on to Oscar. This had been impossible to determine before we knew what mutation I had, but now we could find out easily, and with a fairly high degree of certainty. The genetic counselor patiently explained the basics of genetic inheritance that I should have remembered from eighth grade. The form of RP I had was an autosomal recessive disease. This meant that if Lily had a copy of the MAK mutation, there was a one-in-four chance that Oscar had RP. Lily, being an Ashkenazi Jew herself, had an elevated chance of being a carrier. If she wasn't, then it was very unlikely Oscar had the disease. I assured the counselor that Lily would get tested.

Suddenly my blindness felt like it had become a cultural inheritance as well as a biological one. Biology is of course inseparable from culture; who your parents are is the fundamental biological fact of your existence, as well as the source of most people's cultural DNA. For most of my life, I've felt Jewish in a vaguely biological, mostly secular, and deeply cultural way. My grandfather never went to synagogue as an adult, but he spent his career writing plays and movies that expressed a secular, assimilated Jewishness. His work helped nudge Jewishness through its midcentury transformation toward an American cultural flavor that was palatable to a mass audience, an ancestor to *Seinfeld*. Blindness, on the other hand, had arrived to me without a culture, or with a culture that felt utterly foreign to any sense of myself I'd had before. Disability, in my uninformed view, was built around pity and charity, and was inseparable from a sense of intellectual diminishment—like the special ed kids we never talked to or played with in the years I went to public school. But blindness was now a part of my inheritance—something I hadn't associated with Jewishness, except insofar as Jews and disease did seem to have a special relationship. The MAK mutation had developed because of the closed population that Jews maintained, intermarrying in small diasporic communities, narrowing the gene pool generation after generation, my bright goyish genetic counselor told me, so that certain diseases—breast cancer, cystic fibrosis—became far more prevalent among us.

One of my favorite parts of my grandfather's autobiographical play *Brighton Beach Memoirs* is about illness: Kate, the mother in the play, has a superstitious fear of saying the names of serious diseases aloud; she never utters the words *cancer* or *tuberculosis* above a whisper. Her son Eugene, the play's narrator and stand-in for my grandfather, gets a big laugh mocking her, insisting on whispering lesser maladies, like asthma.

I'd later learn (reading Susan Sontag's *Illness as Metaphor*) that my grandfather had echoed an idea—consciously or not, I don't know—that Stendhal had first put forth in his 1827 novel *Armance*. "The hero's mother refuses to say 'tuberculosis,'" Sontag notes, "for fear that pronouncing the word will hasten the course of her son's malady." Despite mocking this medical superstition, my grandfather was a world-class hypochondriac. When I told my mom how much resistance I felt in myself around understanding RP—the basic details of how the disease worked, which stem cell treatments were most promising, and so on—she said, "Poppa was the same way. 'Just tell me which pills to take,'" he'd say to his doctors, wanting to be done with it.

My grandfather's brand of comedy—complaining, mocking, obsessed with disease and death and suffering but ultimately compassionate and heartfelt—felt deeply Jewish. And now, in my engagements with the world of blindness, I'd begun to wonder if there was something that could be called the blind sense of humor. At the NFB convention in Orlando, flashes of a dark, absurdist sensibility could sometimes be heard from the blind leaders at the podium. The NFB's president, Mark Riccobono, during a raffle: "OK, if you're a winner, raise your hand high, make a sound, or just swing your guide dog up over your head."

I'd heard a version of this joke before. Dan Goldstein, a recently retired sighted lawyer for the NFB, told me a story that laid out the organization's attitude toward humor (and provided the source for the swinging-guide-dog joke). Dan was helping the NFB bring the first digital accessibility lawsuit against a corporation, suing America Online in 2000. The NFB president at the time, Marc Maurer, had given Dan a compliment on some aspect of this work. Being from Texas, Dan said, he has a "po mouth," so without thinking, he deflected Maurer's compliment with a folksy rejoinder: "Well, even a blind hog in a cornfield at midnight in a thunderstorm finds an acorn sometimes." Everyone happened to stop speaking at that moment—they were in the cafeteria at the NFB's Baltimore headquarters, surrounded by blind professionals on their lunch break—and Dan more or less died of embarrassment. Later that night, Dan's phone rang. "Is your stomach in knots?" Dr. Maurer asked. "Well, good," he said. "Let me explain the two kinds of blind humor to you." The first kind, Maurer told him, is unacceptable blind humor, which trades on stereotypes. Mr. Magoo, the bumbling, senile cartoon character unaware of his own imminent physical peril, is unacceptable, because he amplifies the stereotype of the incompetent blind person who endangers himself and everything in his path. Maurer could've pointed to any such example from a long list of mockeries of blindness, including the public spectacle of the armored blind men trying to kill the pig in that park in medieval Paris. Acceptable blind humor, by contrast, tends to be absurdist. Maurer's example: "A blind man goes into a department store and starts swinging his guide dog by the tail over his head. 'Can I help you?' the clerk asks. 'No, thanks,' the man replies. 'I'm just looking around.'"

• • •

At the Quinze-Vingts hospice in Paris, the blind residents wore yellow fleur-de-lis badges on their uniforms, demonstrating the hospice's royal affiliation. And as Edward Wheatley points out in his book on blindness in medieval European literature, Louis IX, the founder of the Quinze-Vingts, forced French Jews to wear yellow badges, which one of his successors would later require the blind residents of the Quinze-Vingts to wear as well. Both Jews and blind people, Wheatley writes, were accused of being greedy and lazy. Each group was seen as socially deviant, associated with acts of dishonesty and criminality. And "both groups were at least partly blamed for having chosen their marginalization, Jews by eschewing conversion and blind people through sinfulness or lack of faith."

By the twentieth century, Jewishness and blindness had come to be understood as biological facts that one could hardly choose to escape. The Nazis made Jews wear yellow badges, too, and in the first half of the 1930s, Nazi civil servants sterilized at least three hundred thousand people, focusing in particular on children and anyone with hereditary diseases, including inherited causes of blindness. During World War II, the Nazis moved on from sterilization to so-called "euthanasia." Before they used gas chambers on Jews, Nazi scientists used them to murder thousands of people with disabilities, including many who were blind. Under this program, code-named Aktion T4, the Nazis ultimately murdered more than two hundred thousand people with disabilities over the course of the war.

Today, disability can be considered as a biological fact (your eyes don't work) or a social construct (blindness is problematic only insofar as the world is built for the sighted). But the lived reality of blindness, as with an identity like Jewishness, exists somewhere in between these two extremes. Disability scholars are now pushing past the medical-social binary and toward—as the critic Jonathan Sterne helpfully puts it—"a conception of biology as having historical dimensions, and history as having biological dimensions."

I'm a Jew because of who my parents are, but also because of something more ineffable, that feels far more cultural than it does biological. I'm drawn to other blind people through a similar sense of shared experience, even as, frequently, I realize that this affinity is superficial, and misguided. At times I'm sure that I have—or want—nothing to do with those groups, even though I am, inescapably, a member of both. The self-hating Jew is a well-worn trope. How about the self-hating blind person?

• • •

After my appointment at the eye infirmary, back in my hotel room, I ate a brutally expensive bag of peanut M&M's from the minibar and tried to read my email through the wash of dilated pupils. My doctor unexpectedly called—she wanted to let me know the results of my blood work. (The vitamin A regimen I was on put me at an elevated risk for liver damage, so I had to take a blood test once a year to keep an eye on things.) She said it all looked fine. As she started to sign off, I stopped her. "I know you just explained all of this earlier today," I said, "but I'm having trouble processing it." Though they'd said it several times, several different ways, I still wasn't sure I'd heard correctly. "When I was diagnosed," I said, "my doctor told me that the degeneration would be gradual until middle age, when it would accelerate. But today you guys said that was wrong, and instead it's going to be a consistent, slow decline. What's changed?"

I was diagnosed more than twenty years ago, she reminded me, and the metrics that doctors used to predict vision loss had evolved. The stability of central visual acuity is notoriously difficult to predict, but the genetic profile they'd just discovered, and the rate of change they'd seen between my first visit and this one, suggested that my vision was declining at a slower rate than what I'd initially been told.

"I'm learning braille over here," I said, hearing my voice turn plaintive. "I've been operating under the assumption that I have only a few years of useful vision left."

"I wouldn't be in a rush to learn braille," she said. "First, because I've heard it's really hard to learn as an adult, but also because I think your vision could be stable for a while. I don't want you to be alarmed that you're rushing down a hill in a roller coaster and picking up steam. Yeah, there's potential for your central vision to change," she concluded, "but hopefully not any time in the next twenty years."

Calling my parents, and hearing their excitement, made it feel even more real. Twenty years! I called Lily. "There goes your book!" she joked. I waited for her to sound excited, too, but instead she was critical—trying in her analytical way to understand it. "What about all those dark pomegranates?" she asked. I'd decided that whenever I felt my vision decline, it was easier to use an arbitrary code name, rather than saying "I feel blind today," to insulate Oscar. *Dark pomegranate* had emerged as my epithet for blindness. "You weren't making those up, were you?" It was a fair question—one that I was asking myself too. Was I making those dark pomegranates up, all the times I'd told her "I feel extra-blind today" and extracted a hug of sympathy?

That night I got hammered at the hotel bar with a couple of South Shore businessmen, who insisted on buying me shots after I told them, already quite drunk, the good medical news I'd just received. I woke up the next morning profoundly hungover, and made my way to South Station to catch the bus home.

It was a bright morning—not as bitterly cold as the last few days, but mounds of snow and ice were still piled up along the streets. I hadn't walked to the station before—I usually took the T—and I made two wrong turns, eventually finding myself in a cobblestoned colonial village, the apotheosis of antique, fancy New England charm. I walked down a little alleyway lined with eighteenth-century town houses, everything empty, silent, rinsed of activity.

My vision felt different. I'd been cultivating an irreverent attitude toward vision loss; the working title for the podcast I wanted to make was *Vile Jelly*, a phrase I'd lifted from the scene in *King Lear* when Cornwall, gouging out Gloucester's eyes, says, "Out, vile jelly! Where is thy lustre now?" Vision was a thing that was failing me, and I was trying to let it go, to lean into that failure with hard-core comic gusto. But that morning, walking up Beacon Hill, blindness had receded, like a morning fog that burns off by noon. Maybe I could allow myself to plan on having vision after all. I'd been living with a kind of visual death sentence hanging over me, one that yesterday a young ophthalmological fellow had casually commuted. I regarded the white cane in my hand. Did I even need this? What else had I been mistaken about?

I emerged from the cobblestoned streets onto Boston Common, a wide patchwork of snow, grass, and low stone walls, and suddenly stopped short—I'd almost fallen down a handful of stairs that sharply descended into the park. I'd had no idea the stairs were there until my cane swiped out into empty space. OK, I conceded, my heart pounding, perhaps the cane still has some use. I am still blind, after all, at least in the eyes of the commonwealth.

Walking through the park, I realized that for the last few years, I hadn't really permitted myself to appreciate visual beauty. Doing so felt too poignant, too cheesy, too painful—the imminently blind man gazing with tender appreciation at the mountainside, the bluebird, the child's face. I'd see something that might qualify as a beautiful thing I'd someday miss, and this would trigger instant confusion and recoil. Should I try to memorize this image? Impossible: there is simply too much to see, and I can't control what images I remember or forget—that's part of the pleasure of looking, the surprise of what ends up becoming indelible in the mind's eye. Instead, I'd wonder how I'd experience the scene as a blind person—what sonic or tactile or olfactory elements will be available to me? What could I get out of it then? What might Lily or Oscar say if I asked them to describe it?

It was a protective response, a relentlessly doubled, rejected vision. But walking through the snow-reflected dazzle of the park, winding my way through trees and birds and joggers and pathways, I experienced the first purely visual pleasure I'd allowed myself in years. The world seemed to pour in and out of my eyes simultaneously.

My vision had been clogged, stopped, congealed. Seeing was difficult, embattled, benighted. What I felt that morning was the ease of seeing, where vision flows from the eyes unobstructed, ranging effortlessly for miles. For the first time in a long time I wasn't watching the world disappear. Full of wonder, it merely appeared. If I wasn't falling to my knees and thanking God for my eyesight, I was certainly closer to it than I'd ever been before.

The feeling lingered for about a month, until my vision declined again.

Part II

The Lost World

4.

The Male Gaze

One night, we went to the house of a family we barely knew for dinner. I'd met the dad for coffee shortly after we moved to town, and found we had a few things in common. The meal was planned with an implicit optimism that we'd all become friends: mom and mom, dad and dad, all the kids. At dinner, Oscar and their kids finished eating quickly and ran around their elaborate backyard, while the dad decided to steer the adults' conversation toward an interrogation of my vision.

This wasn't the usual curiosity about what, exactly, I could see, but a more aggressive and invasive inquiry into how I felt about it all. I've encountered people like this before: arbitrarily tough questioners who approach casual dinner conversation as a chance to hone their journalistic interview skills. I was put out, but not egregiously so, until he'd finished with me and turned to Lily. "It must be difficult to have a *husband* who's going blind," he said to her, chewing the meat he'd grilled. "What's *that* like?" I felt pinned to my chair by a soft harpoon. Lily and

I hadn't really discussed what's difficult about being married to someone who's going blind; I was furious that it had come up as a subject of general conversation. Why should she get into it here and now, in front of this handsome, noxious dad? She looked flustered, and evaded the question.

A year or two later, Lily saw the handsome, noxious dad's name in the local paper. Teasing me—she knew I'd soured on him after that encounter—she said, "Ooh, look who's in the paper!" "I hate that guy," I replied, and then caught myself—I didn't hate him, and I didn't want to hear Oscar start saying he hated people. Oscar had already picked up our exaggeratedly pessimistic style of speaking, our habit of jokingly calling totally benign, mildly inconvenient things (running out of milk, a bad hand in Uno) "horrible"—so I tried to watch how I spoke. Of course, Oscar seized on my comment immediately. "Why do you hate him?" he asked. I fumbled. "I don't," I said. "It's just . . ." Why did I hate him again? "When we were over at his house," I explained, "he said to Mom, 'Wow, it must be hard to be married to someone who's going blind.'" Hearing myself, this was hardly a satisfying or logical answer. But Oscar didn't miss a beat. "Why would being married to a blind person be *hard*?" he asked. I couldn't quite tell if he was dismissing the idea, or genuinely curious. But I chose to interpret his question as incredulity at the noxious dad's presumptuousness.

"Exactly!" I said, flooded with affection for him. He's on my side! What could be hard about marrying into blindness anyway? We had teamed up against the tactless dad, but in the next moment I wondered if we'd also aligned ourselves against *anyone* who dared to suggest that someone else's blindness is a burden—perhaps against Lily. I glanced over at her. She listened to us in silence.

• • •

The world Lily and I build and maintain together is an increasingly blind one. I come to terms with my blindness slowly, a few steps behind my actual rate of vision loss, and she's generally a few steps behind me. When we first met, my visual impairment was hardly discernible. She liked the feeling of guiding me to the table when we went to a dark bar; she thought it was cute that I needed to put my hand on her shoulder. But this minor intimacy in the dark spaces of our courtship didn't point, for her, toward a larger reality of blindness. She'd never known anyone who was blind.

Before I used a cane, Lily's friends would sometimes get confused by my vision. I'd miss their hands, extended for a shake or a hug, and later, they'd ask her what was going on. She didn't tell me about these conversations until recently. Some of them reacted with intense concern, asking for details of my condition, shocked that someday I could be totally blind. Others just didn't get it, and received her explanations with skepticism.

It was confusing for her too. It took a lot of me bumping into things and not seeing people's hands before she understood what my vision looked like. Then, when my vision changed, and changed again, she had to catch up. As it got worse, and I stopped driving and biking, the degenerative part became clearer.

I have a tendency, as many partners do, to assume that Lily has such intimate daily access to what I'm thinking and feeling that what I'm going through should be obvious to her. But our closest intimates still aren't mind readers. Whenever I did bring up blindness, I spoke about it the way I did about everything that made me uncomfortable—in an ambiguously ironic, jokey register. When I brought out the cane for the first time, on what for her was just a random night in Brooklyn, she didn't really think of me as blind, at all; it read as this sudden eruption of blindness into our lives. When we talked about it later, she said that I looked so vulnerable that she felt scared that someone was going to mug me. For her, blindness and vulnerability were synonymous.

I hated that Lily saw me as vulnerable—and not the good kind, the way therapists and lovers want you to be vulnerable. Blindness for her signified the sort of vulnerability your enemies want from you, the kind that signified weakness, an easy target. At one point in planning on making the blindness podcast, I'd invited a friend to our house with their radio kit so Lily and I could record a conversation about all this. We would have the conversation that the tactless dad wanted to hear us have. The microphone, and the presence of my friend, who acted like an editorially minded couples therapist, gave me permission to ask Lily questions I might otherwise have avoided. We sat in tiny chairs in Oscar's playroom—the quietest room in the house, at least while he was at preschool.

"I think going blind as a man comes with particular challenges," Lily said. "So much of this is emasculating. There's this received idea that men are supposed to be in control and protect people." She was trying to be honest—sympathetic, acknowledging how it must feel for me—but I heard it as a confession. The disease was siphoning away my viability as a partner, a diminishment that would continue as I lost more vision. I'd certainly felt this damage to my manhood already: she might have found it cute for me to put my hand on her shoulder in the bar, but I felt, on some reptilian level, that it should have been me leading her through those tables.

Maybe this is what I should have said to Oscar, when he asked me why I hated that other dad: Because he suggested, with an intrusive, unearned intimacy, that blindness would complicate my relationship with your mother. Even if it's true, it wasn't his place, and it made us uncomfortable. His questions suggested that being blind made me less of a man, a compromised husband, and even though I can conceive of a life where your mom can still love and respect me as a blind person—a blind man—there's an unavoidable, painful morass of feelings there that we have yet to fully explore. Also, it didn't help that he looked like an L.L.Bean model and engaged in ostentatious displays of fatherly potency the entire time we were there, as I sat neutered in my patio chair, gorging myself on chips and salsa. Does that answer your question, kiddo?

• • •

When Lily and I moved to New York City for a year, we found that I suddenly had trouble keeping up with her on the street. She got annoyed, and it turned into a fight. My position was: *What the fuck is your problem? Why can't you wait for me?* Her position was: *I've spent my whole life as a New Yorker, walking quickly around the tourists who clog these sidewalks. I don't understand why you can't keep up.* I couldn't believe I had to remind her: *Degenerative retinal disease? It's hurtful to be left behind?* She considered. She understood. She apologized. She slowed down for me on the sidewalk, or I'd grab her arm and zoom along with her around the clumps of tourists. Later, the cane solved this problem all on its own, blasting apart clusters of pedestrians with its powerful semiotic force. But then the process began anew, with some fresh adjustment: the piles of dirt I'd miss while sweeping the kitchen, or a countertop I'd wipe down three-quarters of, thinking I'd taken care of it all. Lily's first reaction would be annoyance—why are you suddenly so bad at cleaning?—until she realized what was going on. Those brief periods, though, when she seemed angry at me for losing vision, were hard to bear.

There have been times when I've tried to prepare Lily for what it will be like when I reach the next two major milestones of blindness: the inability to read visually, and the loss of ambulatory vision—the sight I use to see doors, exit signs, and street addresses. I've tried to explain the adjustments that we'd need to make, without really understanding what they were. After learning to use a braille labeler—not that I needed it yet, but it was an early unit in the braille course I was taking—I cheerfully told her, "We will label all the cans of beans we buy with one of these!" I said this with a confidence that masked the fact that I had no idea what I was talking about. I was surprised, later, during our podcast-therapy session, to hear the impact this injunction had had on her. She said she'd tried imagining herself labeling every can of food, and that it seemed like an unfathomably daunting prospect. I think I'd inadvertently given her the idea that she'd have to become my full-time personal care attendant, spending hours each week labeling all our groceries, and (I heard as the subtext) who knows what else: cutting up my food, dressing me. . . . Her career would end, replaced with taking care of me, her new adult baby. We still haven't solved the bean-labeling issue, but it's pure speculation anyway. The problem has been deferred until such a time as I can no longer distinguish the black beans from the chickpeas.

These conversations have gotten better between us as my vision has gotten worse, mostly because we're forcing ourselves to have them. We no longer need a podcast producer to find our way into this territory. I recently asked her to stop lining the rim of the bathtub with her bottles of avant-garde conditioners and mystery exfoliants, because every time I stepped into or out of the shower, I'd knock all of them over in a clattering mess. Before, little requests like this felt fraught, and she received them in an atmosphere of tense negotiation—another burden my vision had placed on the way she wanted to live. She hated the tone I used to ask, too—a toxic combination of condescension and simpering, backpedaling fear of her response. But now, when I bring up things like the tub clutter, a little more forthrightly, she replies, simply, "That makes sense. I can do that," and we're good. The household has adjusted to my present level of blindness.

• • •

When Oscar was an infant, up screaming every few hours during the night, I would hold him to my chest and bounce semi-violently on a Pilates ball. His face pointed behind me, and I faced forward, watching the first season of *The Walking Dead*. It was a dissonant experience, graphic images of zombies exploding like humanoid water balloons filled with beef stew while I held a precious, tender newborn, whose cries mingled with the screams of zombie victims. But I hadn't had a full night's sleep in months, and I needed something to occupy me as I bounced endlessly on that ball.

The Walking Dead soon entered our home's lexicon as a shorthand for the apocalypse. "In a *Walking Dead* scenario," I'd say, "I'd eat that." Or, "If this were *The Walking Dead*, I could use that as a weapon." Part of the show's appeal was its absurdly elevated sense of exigency, a bit like our lives felt with a new baby: just when things couldn't get any crazier, another dozen zombies emerge from the woods. How are our embattled protagonists gonna find their way through *this* mess?

Even before Oscar was born, during Lily's pregnancy, I felt a powerful new sense of protectiveness. In the mall, on the way to a restaurant, I scanned our surroundings vigilantly for potential assailants and dangers. After Oscar arrived, this feeling shifted and intensified. Watching *The Walking Dead* at two a.m. every night only heightened it. How could I defend the two of them, I wondered, frantically bouncing on the Pilates ball, if that posse of zombies were to attack our house? I couldn't even drive the getaway car. I could probably do some general damage with a baseball bat, or a shotgun, if we owned either. But what if the zombies waited to attack until after I'd lost my ambulatory vision?

The zombies bided their time. I diligently changed diapers, took Oscar to the library, constructed mail-order furniture. The feeling of emasculation and diminishment remained present, but it was latent, gradual, a slow leak I tried my best to stanch.

During our podcast-therapy session, Lily admitted that she worried about how Oscar and I were perceived when we were alone together in public. He was still in preschool then, and she thought that someone might see it as unsafe for a guy with a white cane to be out alone with a small child. *She* thought it was safe, she said, because she knows I'm careful. But how would someone else look at us? This was her *Walking Dead* scenario. My fantasies were about what I'd do to protect our family if we became climate refugees, or if the Trump administration pulled society into a real-life *Handmaid's Tale*. Lily's fears were less dystopian, focusing the disaster just at the level of our family: What if someone sees me with my cane, and thinks, "It'd be pretty easy to kidnap that blind guy's kid"? (Neither of us were aware at the time of the very real cases of toddlers and infants being separated from blind parents by social workers who think blindness prevents a parent from safely taking care of a child.) But both our fears were based on the old idea of blindness as vulnerability. My vision loss made it harder to perceive me as the kind of male figure I thought I was supposed to be, that I wanted to be: the apocalypse sheriff with his baseball bat and chainsaw.

• • •

Sex is a tactile act, obviously, but for sighted people, sexual desire usually begins with sight. Our eyes meet first, and the rest of us follows. The desired person's image is the emblem for everything else we feel affection for—and then, if we're lucky, love. When Lily and I first started dating, I sat in my office a few blocks from her apartment, looking again and again at the same five photos she'd posted of herself (we'd both just joined Facebook), even though we'd spent all weekend together and I'd see her again that evening. When we ate dinner, her eyes looked back at me with a beguiling mixture of shyness, penetrating intelligence, and some mysterious, volcanic third element I still can't quite identify. I feel so lucky to have fallen in love with her. And I'm not worried that blindness will diminish that feeling. I know I'll miss seeing her, beginning with her eyes, our effortless exchange of glances whenever Oscar says something amazing. I will sorely miss the ritual of watching her change out of her elegantly psychedelic outfits at the end of each day. But none of that feels like a prerequisite for feeling love or even attraction.

The Australian theologian John Hull, soon after losing his sight in middle age, started a cassette diary, recording his observations of how his experience of the world was changing—his relationship to his family and friends, to sound and space, his dreams, everything. Hull had his diary transcribed, and turned it into a book, *Touching the Rock*, which is one of the most exhaustive phenomenological accounts of the experience of becoming blind as an adult ever written. It's also more terrifying than any episode of *The Walking Dead*, easily the scariest book I've read. The same quiet method of observation that Hull applies to his experience becomes harrowing when he aims it at his emotional life. I turned the book's pages at the pace usually reserved for horror novels as Hull patiently measured the degree, composition, and cause of his terror, claustrophobia, isolation, depression, and grief. More than once, I read *Touching the Rock* just before bed, and woke up an hour later in the midst of a full-blown panic attack, unable to breathe or see in the darkness of the bedroom. Tinnitus roared in my ears. I felt like I'd been buried alive.

Hull's entry for January 7, 1984, isn't one of the more terrifying passages, but it does illuminate the ways that blindness transformed his sense of himself. Hull writes that desire and image are primordially unified: seeing an object is what gives rise to our desire for it, he says. He may have physical pangs of hunger, but blindness has disentangled image from desire, and he doesn't experience the same sort of yearning for food that he did when he was able to see the meal arranged on the plate. "Somebody says, 'Your soup has come,' or 'Don't start yet; the waiter is working his way round the table with the vegetables,'" Hull writes.

> "But what is it?" I ask. "It's veal cutlet." Now I know. But what do I know? I have this sentence, and I believe it, but the visual cues which excite the actual desire and turn it outwards towards the object are lacking.

For Hull, sex works the same way. Desire has been uncoupled from image, and the excitement has dimmed. He still feels physical pangs, same as with hunger, but "the trace of a perfume and the nuance of a voice are so insubstantial when compared with the full-bodied impact upon a sighted man of the appearance of an attractive woman." It's worth mentioning that most people who lost their vision early in life, or who have been blind for a long time, will find Hull's observations patently ridiculous—they enjoy food, and sex, as much as the sighted person sitting across from them at dinner. Hull's memoir is thus less an account of the general experience of blindness, and more a document of the process of mourning his sight.

I thought, in a vaguely occult way, that if Lily held Hull's book she would understand my fear, along with my burgeoning sense that real blindness held some of its own intellectual, philosophical, mind-expanding possibilities. She gamely flipped through it, leaning against the kitchen counter one Saturday morning, and landed on a passage, similar to the one above, where Hull explored the social implications of not knowing what anyone looks like. Sometimes, Hull writes, he'd ask sighted friends to give him a "sort of thumb-nail sketch" of someone he's just met. His desire to know how a new acquaintance looks is particularly acute when he's meeting a woman: "What color is her hair? What is she wearing? Is she pretty? Sometimes I long to know. I remain, after all, a man, reared in a certain sighted culture, conditioned to certain male expectations." Hull feels ambivalent about his curiosity, but true to the confessional form of his diary, he faithfully reports his feelings as they are. "Perhaps I should change," he says, "and be less influenced in my judgement of women by my male conditioning, but it is painful to have this change forced upon me by mere blindness." He goes on like this, alternately documenting his desire to know what women look like, then chastising himself for it:

> It makes a difference to the way I feel about a new female acquaintance if a colleague, having caught sight of her, remarks on her beauty or her plainness. There is a double irrationality in this. In the first place, my feelings should not be so dependent upon a woman's appearance. I know that, and I apologize. But I still feel it. The second thing is that it is surely a deplorable lack of indepen-

> dence on my part to be so affected by a criterion which can be of no significance to me.

"Uh-oh," Lily said, closing the book. I saw her point—so, it seemed, did Hull—but I was surprised by how defensive I suddenly became. I had hoped that the book would generate some sympathy, and instead she had—sharp-eyed scholar that she is—zeroed in on its most ideologically symptomatic moment, where Hull had chosen to expose and explore his own anti-feminist blind spot.

And what did my defensiveness say about me? Did I share his retrograde feeling? Was I a bad feminist too? Whenever anyone asks me about the things I might miss seeing—it comes about once a year, this question, like a holiday—I always want to undermine such a depressing and impossible thought by throwing an inappropriate joke into my answer. I'll miss seeing Mount Tom, half obscured by fog, I tell them. Franz Kline's giant, calligraphic paintings at MoMA. And butts, sheathed in that modern denim that somehow stretches like yoga pants.

The joke never works. Enough people have told me so that I stopped using it, no matter how irritated I was at the question. I tried briefly turning it into a philosophical rumination—*what happens to the male gaze without sight?*—though this, friends told me, wasn't an interesting line of inquiry either. But privately, I still felt stuck on it: Was it wrong for Hull to want to know what women looked like? Or for me to include women in the list of visual phenomena that I'll be sorry to lose?

I wonder if my persistent interest in this is a distraction I've manufactured for myself. It's all too sentimental, too horrific and obvious, to think about what I'll really miss: Hallmark stuff like those quick, conspiratorial glances exchanged with Oscar as we play together, or a warm smile from Lily that catches me completely off guard, pleasurably disarming me. Robert Hine, another fastidiously observant college professor who went blind in middle age, wrote that "to the blind, no loss can be as great as the dimming of loved faces. There is no substitute for the interchange of a smile." But Hine, too, acknowledges the inescapable link between sight and sex. After fifteen years of blindness, at sixty-five an experimental surgery partially restored his vision, after which he admits to "an obsession with sex," reporting that his "willing" wife, Shirley, and he read *The Joy of Sex* and its sequel together and generally celebrated the end of his blindness with lots and lots of it.

Perhaps I have tried to soften the pain of the loss of faces by joking about the loss of butts. I understand why the joke is unwise. Women aren't *visual phenomena*—they're complex, richly interior subjects. Yes, I wonder, but aren't they also visual phenomena, just like everyone and everything else that's not microscopic or transparent or otherwise obscured? The solution to this is, I think, to recognize that women aren't neutral targets for the gaze. There's a long and violent history associated with the way men look at women. The male gaze, Lily reminded me one evening, as I muddled my way through these ideas, fixes women in an acquisitive, objectifying light, and it's from this kind of entitled, invasive looking that systemic violence arises. What I'm searching for is a way for blind people to retain their sexuality, their ability to look (even with the aid of description) at attractive people, without participating in the objectification that can go along with it. I know that, like John Hull, I will be intensely curious about what people look like—and, I suspect, it'd be disingenuous for me to pretend that that won't include wondering about women. Can I allow that curiosity to exist without extending misogynist culture? It sounds like a joke, but following this line of reasoning, my eventual, total blindness could be a victory for feminism—one more male gaze extinguished at last!

But the loss of sight doesn't actually put an end to the male gaze. Blind people, being people, still want to know what other people look like, for all the reasons that sighted people do, including sexually objectifying reasons. Living in the society of the spectacle, where appearances are so central to every exchange—professional, romantic, familial, casual—the details of someone's looks carry tremendous weight. A blind guy I know, in his twenties, has some residual vision, but not enough to get a good read on what anyone really looks like when he meets them in person. But on his phone, looking at a dating app, he can control the magnification and the contrast with enough precision that he can just make out the photos women post there. On the other hand, online dating offers many of the same challenges that the job search poses to blind people: as soon as they disclose their disability, the conversation almost invariably grinds to a halt.

So my friend relies on parties, and does his best with women he can't quite see. He told me that he finds it maddening not knowing what these women look like. To make do, he uses a pet theory he's developed, about people's visual attractiveness—I've heard variations of it from a few blind people. It's a theory of the voice. His idea is that if someone is attractive, they'll be positively reinforced from a young age by their peers and family, who will imbue them with the confidence that physical hotness brings. After years of this conditioning, my blind friend argued, the hot person's confidence will eventually become detectable in the very grain of their voice. By listening to someone talk, you can determine if they're hot or not. This theory is, I think, total bullshit—most hearing sighted people have had the experience of seeing a photo of a favorite radio personality, and the shock that comes in recognizing the gulf between the image their voice conjured and the reality of what they look like. My blind friend was deeply invested in his theory because it restored some of the power he'd lost, as a young blind guy on the dating scene, to evaluate his sexual partners based on his own visual preferences. He seemed to only half believe his own theory, but he still held on to it as a kind of consolation.

We can laugh at the superficiality of this—Larry David made it a running joke on *Curb Your Enthusiasm*: the shallow blind guy who was obsessed with dating attractive women (Larry sets him up with a Muslim woman, whose face and body are fully covered by a burka)—but the preoccupation is common among blind men and women, as is the desire to present themselves in a visually attractive way. Schools for the blind frequently offer instruction on how blind people ought to present themselves, a skill that's crucial for their integration into the mainstream workplace and successful social relations more broadly. Molly Burke, a blind YouTuber, has several video tutorials on how she applies makeup as a blind woman. (The most popular of these, in which she does makeup for the beauty YouTuber James Charles, has 23.8 million views. Among the video's 26,778 comments: "It's sad that she is so beautiful and doesn't even know it!")

Even people born blind grow up inundated with images that contribute to their conception of beauty—through music, the dialogue on

TV ads, accessible books and magazines, and the comments of their friends and families. It's the same dynamic that creates sighted people's conceptions of beauty. This is especially true today, when so many blind kids can access the internet (including a growing corpus of audio porn) through a screen reader on a phone or computer. Previous generations, if they grew up in conservative families or attended a repressive school for the blind, often lacked any access to mainstream media or sex education, and had to wait until they were out on their own to find material that gave them anything beyond a grammar-school picture of sexuality.

In spite of this reality, many people still think blind people shouldn't care about appearances. Jimmy Kimmel expressed this dehumanizing attitude in especially stark terms on his late-night show when he had the actor and musician Donald Glover on as a guest. Glover told a story about how he got Stevie Wonder's permission to use one of his songs on an episode of Glover's FX show, *Atlanta*. He sent a rough cut of the episode to Wonder, who told him he loved it. "How'd he do that?" Glover said to Kimmel, as the audience laughed at the mystery of how a blind man could enjoy an episode of television. "It's the same thing with his album covers. I'm like, these are so good! How does he *know* they're so good?" Kimmel enthusiastically picked up the thread, interrupting Glover to add, "You see him with women he's married to, or dating, and you're like, 'Wow! She's beautiful!'" Neither Glover nor Kimmel can fathom a world in which Wonder might be able, as a blind man, to appreciate the beauty of his own wife. It would make more sense, their conversation suggests, if Wonder's album covers and romantic partners were plain. Kimmel's and Glover's banter circles around these questions: What could visual beauty mean to a blind person? What right does a blind person have to even be associated with something visually beautiful?

The eighteenth-century French philosopher Denis Diderot had less trouble than Jimmy Kimmel imagining a blind man's appreciation for his wife's physical charms. "The surface of the skin is no less subtly differentiated to him than the sound of the voice," he wrote in his *Letter on the Blind* (1749), "and there is no reason to fear that he might mistake his wife for another woman, unless he stood to gain by it." Some blind people take this position—they get everything they need to know about their partner's attractiveness through four senses. And for the most part, sure, our sense of a person's beauty extends far beyond their visual appearance, and attraction is composed of an amalgamation of factors: a person's smell, the sound of their voice, the feel of their skin, the way they express themselves, the way they treat us, the narrative we write about them in our heads. But if we're being honest, many other blind people say, we want to know about the visual component too. "At some point," my friend Hai, who's been blind since childhood, told me, "you ask that question. What does this person look like? Because we're curious!"

When I was at the NFB of Massachusetts's state convention, Ron Brown, a national board member, gave a banquet address that began with his story of how he got together with his wife, Jean, who's also blind. Soon after they met, Ron asked her out, and asked his brother to drop him off at her door. "Here's the deal," Ron told him. "If she doesn't look that good, you say, 'It looks like it's about to rain.' But if she's fine, you say, '*Ooooh*, the sun is shining bright *today*! *Man*, it's a beautiful day!' You have the plan?"

Ron and his brother go to Jean's house, and he knocks on the door. Jean, who had a contract with a modeling agency before she lost her sight from retinitis pigmentosa in her early twenties, opens the door. "My brother's standing there looking at her," Ron said, "and I'm waiting for the cue." Finally his brother says, "*Wooooo*, the sun is shining bright *today*!" Jean says, "Yeah, it's a nice day." But Ron's brother says, "No, I mean the sun is *really* shining bright. I mean it's a *beautiful* day!" As he goes on and on, Jean's thinking, "What's wrong with your brother? Is he a weatherman?" The crowd of blind NFBers ate this story up. Ron went on to explain that he told Jean what happened six years after they got married, at which point she called him a dog. "Well, you know what?" Ron concluded proudly. "We've been married now thirty-three years, and the sun is *still* shining bright today."

Of course, blind women want to know what people look like too. In her ethnography of blind women's experience of their gender and sexuality, the anthropologist Gili Hammer interviewed forty blind Israeli women. "I'm really interested in how people look," one of her respondents told her. "When a new lecturer arrives to teach a university class, my friends make sure to ask me, 'Aviva, did someone already tell you what he looks like?'" Hammer also found that some blind women experienced the male gaze differently than sighted women do. "I felt like air," one of her respondents said of her experience as a blind teenager. "I felt like they looked through me. . . . I wasn't treated as a woman or as someone who belonged to a specific sex."

This is hardly the worst of it. When Emily Brothers, a blind transgender woman, was nominated as a candidate for MP by the Labour Party (making her, in 2015, the first blind woman to run for Parliament), a columnist for the British tabloid *The Sun* asked, "Being blind, how did she know she was the wrong sex?" The blind person becomes, in the eyes of the culture, celibate, sexless, without access even to their own gender or sexuality.

• • •

Two of the most high-profile men accused of sexual assault in recent years, comedian Bill Cosby and casino magnate Steve Wynn, were both legally blind as they stood trial. Late in his life, Cosby claimed to have developed keratoconus, a degenerative eye condition that caused his corneas to bulge. As he and his lawyers tried to burnish his public image in the face of his indictment for drugging and sexually assaulting a woman—and similar, credible accusations from fifty-nine others—they seized on his blindness as a key to his reputation's rehabilitation. "No 79-year-old blind man could possibly defend himself against a claim that he sexually assaulted someone he supposedly met once, half a century ago," Cosby's lawyers wrote in a statement. "Without his eyesight, Mr. Cosby cannot even determine whether he has ever even seen some of his accusers, let alone develop defenses and gather exculpatory evidence." The argument is absurd: blindness hardly precludes someone from identifying an accuser or participating in the basic activities of mounting a legal defense. Wynn's lawyers took a different approach, arguing that a blind man was literally incapable of possessing a hostile, sexualizing gaze: "Mr. Wynn was legally blind at all times you allege that he 'leered' at [redacted] on the stage." How can a blind man leer?

The idea, the lawyers contended, was absurd on its face. But while retinitis pigmentosa might have damaged or even obliterated Wynn's vision, the male gaze is far too deep and durable to be thwarted by something as incidental as a lack of eyesight.

During my visit to the NFB national convention, I discovered a few satirical Twitter accounts that posted incendiary stories about NFB leadership sexually harassing its members in a flagrant orgy of abuse and revelry. At the time, the allegations struck me as comically exaggerated, but two years later, in 2020, social media exploded with dozens of credible allegations from NFB members describing sexual abuse and harassment, along with a failure of the NFB's leadership to respond properly. The NFB hired an outside law firm to conduct a full investigation (there were ninety-three complaints in total), which found significant evidence for widespread sexual misconduct throughout the organization. One prominent NFB leader, Fredric K. Schroeder, had a distinguished career in the blindness field, including a stint as the commissioner of the Department of Education's Rehabilitation Services Administration, where he ran a $2.5 billion program administering services to people with disabilities; Marc Maurer, the NFB president for nearly thirty years, seemed to be favoring him as his successor. But the external report found that Schroeder engaged in "predatory grooming behavior with young women he mentored or supervised," along with "groping and aggressive acts committed in connection with alcohol consumption." The investigation revealed that NFB leadership knew about this pattern of behavior as early as 2002, and that despite numerous complaints, "Dr. Maurer had no intention of intervening." "An informal network of women formed to protect younger members from Schroeder's misconduct," the report said, "by devising creative techniques for avoiding him or minimizing interactions."

Schroeder quietly resigned from his leadership positions within the NFB, with no explanation or apology to the wider membership. But he didn't leave the NFB, and in 2016 he received support from NFB leadership to become president of the World Blind Union (an umbrella organization linking all the world's major blindness groups). At the NFB national convention in Las Vegas in 2019, one of its speakers had to cancel at the last minute, and many in the assembly were shocked when Schroeder took the podium. As soon as he was introduced, dozens of members stood and walked out in protest. Eighteen months later, the investigation would begin.

When an assaulted woman is blind, she faces an extra layer of disbelief. A member of a local blind meetup I'm part of told our group a story about her experience with this kind of doubled doubt. She was walking through her neighborhood with her guide dog. As she waited at a street crossing, she heard feet shuffling off to her right. Suddenly, a hand grabbed her breast, and she yelled at her unseen assailant to stop. When she got home, she called the police, and two detectives came to question her. Had she heard the perp's voice? No—he hadn't said a word. Well, they wanted to know: she said the assault happened at 3:35 p.m., but how could she know what time it was? She told them she wore a braille watch. "They were quite skeptical that I was able to tell time," she said. "They questioned my going out alone, or going out then, because it was winter. They said they had more important cases—like drugs—that took their time, but they might be able to send someone to follow me to perhaps catch a similar incident. They suggested I go out at a different time of the day, rather than in the afternoon." Her story is a mix of the sort of doubt and apathy that any sighted woman might face, with an added layer of blame and skepticism generated by her disability—the notion that she shouldn't have been out by herself at all. What did she expect to happen, going out alone with her guide dog in the afternoon?

• • •

The tabloids celebrated Bill Cosby's blindness as a kind of divine punishment for his sins. "His alleged victims may take some solace in the fact that he's in his own personal hell," an anonymous source told the *New York Post*'s Page Six. "He has been suffering from a degenerative eye disease and is completely blind. . . . All his Hollywood friends have turned their backs on him." In medieval England, one thirteenth-century lawyer wrote, rape was punished with blindness, by "tearing out the eyes and loss of testicles, because of the appetite which entered through the eyes and the heat of fornication which came into the reins of the lechers." The idea of blindness as a symbolic, punitive castration goes back to ancient Greek drama and the myth of Sophocles's *Oedipus Rex*: the story of the king who plunges long pins into his eyes after learning that he's unwittingly killed his father and slept with his mother. "When I saw Bill Cosby stumble in and out of the courthouse wearing dark sunglasses," a reader of *The Washington Post* wrote in a letter to the editor, "using a cane and being shouldered and assisted by a surrogate daughter (Antigone?), images of blind Oedipus leaving Thebes flashed." But, the letter writer pointed out, Cosby is not an "ill-fated tragic victim" like

Oedipus. Neither, of course, is Cosby's blindness self-inflicted—but that doesn't stop the public from reading his blindness as a symptom of his guilt, justice served for his misdeeds.

Oedipus doesn't feel all that useful to me, as far as images of blindness and sexuality go. For obvious reasons, I'd like to avoid conceiving of blindness as a symbolic castration, no matter how tightly desire may be lashed to the visual. I'm much more drawn to Tiresias, the blind prophet in Sophocles's play, who foretold Oedipus's demise. In Ovid's version of Tiresias's origin story, he encounters two giant snakes mating. He slaps at the snakes with his staff, an act that spontaneously flips Tiresias's gender from male to female. Tiresias spends seven years as a woman, until another day when she encounters another pair of colossal, mating snakes. She slaps the snakes with her staff again, and instantly regains "the shape the Theban had when he was born."

Years later, Zeus and Hera, drunk on nectar, are arguing over who enjoys sex more, men or women. They think of Tiresias, who has tried it both ways, and call him up to settle the dispute. Tiresias affirms that Zeus is in the right: it's much better as a woman. This infuriates Hera, who blinds Tiresias. Zeus can't undo Hera's curse, but he compensates for Tiresias's sudden blindness by giving him the power to see the future, "pairing pain with prophecy."

I have problems with Tiresias, too: his psychic superpowers perpetuate myths about blind people whose deprivation of one sense creates a heightened sensitivity in others. (It's stories like these that lead people to ask me, *Do you hear more than I can? Is music totally amazing for you?*) But I'm drawn to the metamorphoses he undergoes, including all their weird, sexual overtones (giant mating snakes, struck with long wooden staffs, leading to spontaneous gender transition). Tiresias has experienced life, and sex, as a man and a woman, and as a blind and a sighted person; he's an emblem of transition and transformation between forms. His blindness is explicitly connected to his transgression of sexual norms: Hera blinds him for claiming to know more about bodily pleasure than she does. (In another version of the myth, the goddess Athena blinds Tiresias when he stumbles upon her bathing in the nude.)

My own experience of blindness sometimes feels like the beginning of a metamorphosis. The politics of gender and sexuality, while they are uniquely embodied experiences that are incommensurate with disability, still offer a language and a framework that fit the experience in useful ways. When I walked with my cane folded and hidden in my bag, it felt like a form of being in the closet. The day I finally brought it out, it was a risky self-exposure—a kind of coming out as blind. Disability, like homosexuality, carries a stigma (a word that comes from the Greek for a mark made by a pointed instrument—a prick, a brand, a puncture—of the sort Oedipus applied to his own eyes). When I think of how that stigma can be overcome, the most powerful example I've found is in gay pride and the LGBTQ rights movement. I'm not yet comfortable calling myself a *crip*—the disability rights appropriative analogue to *queer*—but I still draw strength from the example.

If someone takes a new shape, in what way can we still speak of them as the same person they were before? Maggie Nelson's *The Argonauts* reads another Greek myth to understand the fluidity of gender identity. Nelson's title refers to the Greek ship *Argo*, which she weaves together with the ancient thought experiment of the Ship of Theseus, whose planks are replaced, one by one, over many years, until there isn't an original piece of wood remaining. Is it still, at that point, the same ship? "The *Argo*'s parts may get replaced," Nelson writes, "but it's still called the *Argo*." Tiresias, "throbbing between two lives" (as T. S. Eliot described him in *The Waste Land*), man or woman, sighted or blind, is still called Tiresias. As I throb my way further into blindness, I'm faced with a choice: I can cling to the old image I have of myself, or I can let it go and try to make peace with whatever comes next. To cling to my old sense of masculinity strikes me as a path to disaster, like an Argonaut trying to sail on without replacing any of his ship's broken planks. If I don't allow my expectations to change, I'll be consigning myself to a life of perpetual mourning, jealously resenting the experiences all the sighted dads have: effortlessly taking their families on road trips, going with their kids on long solo bike rides, catching their spouse's twinkling eyes from across a crowded room. It feels wrenchingly painful to contemplate abandoning these trappings. But thinking of blind Tiresias, I'm trying to find a new form that fits me, even if the shape it takes is utterly unlike the one that came before.

5.

Camera Obscura

On a Tuesday morning in October 2010, Emilie Gossiaux's boyfriend told her he loved her and strapped her bike helmet onto her head. They were both twenty-one, living together in a Brooklyn loft. Gossiaux was taking a semester off from Cooper Union, the New York City art school, and working as an assistant to an artist in Greenpoint. She turned on her cochlear implant, inserted a hearing aid into her other ear, and jumped on her bike and headed to work. An eighteen-wheeler making a right turn slammed into her as she pedaled down a busy street. She ended up in Bellevue Hospital, where her heart stopped for a full minute. She'd undergone a traumatic brain injury and a stroke, and had fractures in her pelvis, legs, and face. After two days, a nurse told her mother that her daughter was gone, and asked about organ donations.

When Gossiaux woke up in her hospital bed, she couldn't see anything, and her dreams blended with reality. Whenever anyone tried to insert her hearing aid or reattach her cochlear implant, she reacted violently, pinching or slapping their hands away. "I really needed to sleep," she remembered. "I didn't want to be bothered." The hospital had heavily medicated her, which in retrospect she believes exacerbated her dissociative state. "I remember waiting for the light to turn on, for the sun to come in, so I'd know it was time to get up to go to work," Gossiaux told me. "It felt like an endless sleep, an endless night. Like I was in so many places at once. I knew people were touching me, but I didn't know who they were."

Her doctors determined that in addition to her other injuries, she'd been completely blinded in the accident. After they removed her tracheotomy tube, she spoke incoherently, alternately cursing and calling everyone "Ms. Dashwood." (She and her boyfriend had recently watched *Sense and Sensibility*.) The doctors thought there was no way to get through to her, and began making plans to put her in a nursing home. Her mother took the day shift, and her boyfriend sat next to her all night. After they couldn't get through to her for several days, her audiologist suggested they try print on palm, a technique some DeafBlind people use to communicate, by tracing capital letters on Gossiaux's hand. She immediately began responding to her boyfriend's questions verbally—she knew her name, she knew what year it was. Her mother said, "Ask her if we can put in her hearing aids." Gossiaux casually agreed. As soon as they turned on the cochlear implant and her hearing aid, Gossiaux woke from her dream. All at once, she said, "I was back in the world. Back in reality."

After completing physical therapy, she had to learn how to live as a blind person. She ended up connecting with Chancey Fleet, an assistive-technology trainer in New York City who's also a leader in the NFB.

Fleet told her about BLIND, Inc., one of the NFB's residential training centers in Minneapolis. Gossiaux spent eleven months there, learning how to read braille and get around with a cane. She also took an industrial arts class, where she learned to use a lathe to make cups and bowls, and a hammer and mallet to make sculptures out of wood. At night, she rode two buses across town to take a ceramics class in which she was the only blind student. At the end of her training, she decided to reenroll at Cooper Union and finish her BFA. "At first it seemed impossible and scary," Gossiaux said. "I really didn't want to go back to school. I doubted whether I could do it at all. It only became possible after I went to BLIND, Inc., and met other ambitious blind people."

After graduation, she worked as a museum educator at the Met, giving tours and teaching drawing classes. She eventually went to Yale to get her MFA in sculpture. Today she exhibits her work in solo gallery shows and in venues like MoMA PS1, SculptureCenter, and the Museum for Modern Art in Frankfurt, Germany.

Gossiaux makes drawings by placing a sheet of paper on top of a soft rubber mat. Then she draws—pressing down pretty hard—with a ballpoint pen, which embosses the page along the same line as her mark making. She can run her finger along the raised lines she's drawn to orient herself in her composition. She adds color using Crayolas, which leave a waxy residue that she can also feel. Her ceramic sculptures look a bit like her drawings in 3D: playful and cartoonish, with wobbly imperfections that could be attributed to her blindness, or simply to her expressive, impressionistic style.

This connection between visual impairment and innovative, expressive forms has existed in art at least since the birth of Impressionism.

Monet's use of color became increasingly wild as his vision deteriorated late in his life (he eventually had double cataracts, which were untreated). "Reds appeared muddy to me, pinks insipid, and the intermediate or lower tones escaped me," Monet said during this period. "What I painted was more and more dark, more like an 'old picture.'" The Postimpressionist painter Paul Cézanne was myopic, and he rejected eyeglasses as "vulgar." Some critics have argued that his poor eyesight might have influenced his paintings' radical approach to form. Cézanne's contemporary, the art critic J. K. Huysmans, described him as "an artist with a diseased retina who, exasperated by a defective vision, discovered the basis of a new art."

Gossiaux called her 2022 solo show in Tribeca *Significant Otherness*. She borrowed the title from a Donna Haraway essay, "The Companion Species Manifesto," about the complex, intertwined species history of humans and dogs. Gossiaux's title puns on the simultaneous estrangement and connection that is a central part of the disabled experience: her guide dog, a yellow lab named London, who appears frequently in her work, is both her partner—a "significant other"—and a marker of Gossiaux's difference. London is nearly twelve years old, and while Gossiaux still uses her as a guide, she's also intensely concerned for her health. On the day I attended the show and met her, in May 2022, she'd left London at home because she didn't want to make her walk down the stairs to the subway, to protect her hips. Many dog owners talk about their pets like they're people, but guide dog users have especially intimate relationships with their animals. The parental—or spousal—feeling of having a creature who depends on you, and who you come to depend on, at least emotionally, is heightened when one also relies on them for safe navigation through nearly every public space.

Many of the sculptures in the show were of London's ephemera: a collar, a leash, a harness, assorted chew toys. There were also several sculptures and drawings of a creature Gossiaux called "doggirl," who sometimes looked indistinguishable from images she's made of London, but other times took on a hybrid, human-dog form, with three sets of nipples and long human legs. There were a few "alligatorgirls" in the show too. (Gossiaux grew up in a suburb of New Orleans, and often saw alligators in the canal across the street from her house.) In one drawing, called *Alter Ego*, a girl's face peers out from inside an alligator's mouth. She doesn't look especially upset to be part alligator; she looks curious, open. She hasn't been eaten, just altered: a fusing of girl and creature.

The day I met Gossiaux at the gallery, she was waiting for her friend Caroline, who was coming to see the show as well. Caroline and Gossiaux had met at the Metropolitan Museum, where they'd led gallery tours together. (Gossiaux has also taught drawing classes to blind and low-vision visitors through the Met's access and community programs.) Caroline guided Gossiaux around the gallery, though it was really Gossiaux who was guiding us through her exhibition. When I'd first walked in, the gallerist, seeing my cane, told me he could offer descriptions if I wanted—I brushed him off; I could see the images. But as I followed Gossiaux and Caroline around the room, I realized I could use the help—I almost stepped on several sculptures of London's chew toys, and had completely missed numerous small drawings on the walls. Gossiaux invited us to touch the sculptures, rubbing our fingers along the wax she mixes with oil paint so she can feel where she's applied color to the ceramics.

Our tour of the room ended in front of a large ink-and-crayon drawing called *London, Midsummer No. 1.* Gossiaux no longer had tactile access to it, since it was behind glass, though of course she knew it intimately. "It's my guide dog, London," she explained, "only a multitude of Londons, dancing around a maypole. But the pole is my white cane, which is collapsible, like this." She'd been holding Caroline's arm, but now took her cane, which was the size and shape of a baton, and demonstrated how it could telescope out to stand almost to her nose. I looked from her cane back to the one in the image, which stood like a monument in the landscape, surrounded by this trio of guide dogs, standing on two legs and holding red ribbons—which were, in fact, leashes—that stretched to the cane's handle, dancing merrily around it amid the green countryside. I was struck by the drawing's delicacy—the bright purple shading on the leaves that littered the ground, and the beatific expressions on the dogs' faces. "It's such a joyful image," Caroline said.

I regard people who cry at paintings a bit like I regard people who cry at the symphony: I don't doubt their emotion, but it seems wild to me that something so formal could create such feeling. I've always looked at art with a cooler eye, as something that was interesting to talk and think about, but that rarely evoked visceral emotions. But after hearing Caroline's remark, as I stood beside her and Gossiaux, I wept at this image, struck by the joy the artist had discovered among the trappings of blindness. Orientation and mobility, or O&M, is the ultimate blindness skill, the ability to safely find one's way through an environment that can feel hostile or bewildering to the untrained blind person. The white cane and the guide dog are the hammer and sickle, the Stars and Stripes of blindness, representing full independence. But in practice, for me, O&M also conjures a sense of dread—I occasionally sharpen those skills by wearing sleep shades, so I can't rely on my residual vision; the amount of anxiety and energy I expend just trying to walk a few blocks without sight can be dispiriting and exhausting. But in Gossiaux's drawing, the cane and guide dog are no longer just tools; they're liberated from this assistive, instrumentalist framework, free to revel in the landscape. In the sky above them, an orange sun and a blue crescent moon hang together, as though day and night have merged—a blind time of day.

• • •

London, Midsummer reminded me of Matisse's *Dance (I)* (1909), which also depicts a circle of dancing figures. Both Matisse and Gossiaux represent their subjects with an elegant rudimentariness; their sketchiness seems to heighten the feeling of celebration they find in their dancing. Matisse's painting, which is nearly eight and a half feet tall and thirteen feet wide, is also the first painting I remember not being able to see in its entirety because of my narrowing visual field. This was years ago, when I'd first started using a cane, at MoMA, and I kept backing up farther and farther in order to see the whole composition, until finally I had to stand in the adjoining gallery and look at the painting from dozens of feet away, through the entranceway.

I later listened to MoMA's audio tour description of the work. "What matters to Matisse isn't some realistic description of what a ring of dancers would look like," MoMA curator Ann Temkin says on the tour. *Dance*, she goes on, is "painted in such a way that you realize that you're not in some kind of specific place that can be identified, but rather in some kind of ideal place, *in the mind's eye*." It occurred to me that the mind's eye was the realm that Gossiaux was working in as well. But her work also raised a paradox: one of the wonders of art is this ability to represent visually things seen without eyes—but you still need working eyes to see it.

In 1863, a British literary magazine published an unattributed essay called "How a Blind Man Saw the International Exhibition." The essay's anonymous blind reporter wandered through the 1862 London world's fair with his four senses blazing. Exploring near the fair's Austrian court, he hears a rumbling that seems to shake the very ground beneath him. "A few steps brought me to an entirely new region," he writes, noting "the vibration under-foot, and the smell of hot oil which saluted my nostrils as I entered." He's found the fair's machinery annex, where he spends a great deal of time, listening meticulously to decipher the various industrial sounds and chatting jovially with the workers who describe the machines' function and arrangement to him. Throughout the fair, he meets obliging exhibitors like these, who both allow him to touch their exhibits and verbally describe them to him. "Many more curiosities he put before me with evident pleasure," the blind man reports of an exhibitor at the Japanese pavilion, "taking care so to explain each object that they became well impressed upon my mind."

It's only at the picture galleries that his experience sours. "In these quiet though crowded resting-places," he writes, "all was hushed; even the tread of feet was muffled, and the voices of visitors subdued to a low murmur, in which every term generally used in art-criticism could be heard cropping out from time to time." Elsewhere in the exhibition he was a spectator, but in the art galleries, he becomes a spectacle, hearing gallerygoers whisper remarks "such as, 'Lor'! I wonder what he's come here for?' or, 'What good can he be doing here? He can't see the pictures?' to which some one would reply, 'Lor', no! Can't you see he's blind?'"

This experience—few opportunities for useful description of the works, the feeling of being an object of fascination on par with the art itself—remains common among blind people visiting galleries and museums today. Some institutions, however, are working to make their spaces more inclusive. The Met and MoMA offer what have become known in the art world as "touch tours," which invite blind viewers to touch works (usually wearing plastic gloves) that are off-limits to the general public. These include sculptures as well as small replicas of large-scale works, and sometimes even relief representations of paintings or drawings. In her excellent book *More Than Meets the Eye: What Blindness Brings to Art*, the writer Georgina Kleege describes the successes and failures that touch tours can offer blind museumgoers. She is largely disdainful of replicas, which, while they can offer a sense of structure, lack what might be called tactile authenticity. When Kleege touched a model of the Parthenon Marbles at the British Museum, she was disappointed by the way it felt. "Plaster has a slick, artificial feel," she observed, "with little in common with the cool pleasure of natural stone." But at MoMA, Kleege found that her direct experience of a

Matisse bronze gave her access to an illuminating, privileged perspective on the artwork that viewers who could only observe it with their eyes missed. "As I cupped my palms around the massive protrusions of the head's coiffeur," Kleege writes,

> I had the sensation that my hands were resting more or less where the artist's hands had once rested, in the clay versions that preceded the cast bronzes. As I understand it, one of the many pleasures of looking at art is the sensation that in standing before the painting or sculpture one assumes the exact position where the artist must have stood in making the work. One has the illusion of viewing the work, as it were, through the artist's eyes. Here, I had the analogous pleasure of feeling a distant relative of the artist's haptic sensation as he molded the forms.

Kleege's epiphany didn't extend to a visual apprehension of the piece, however. "I didn't have the foggiest idea what this thing might look like," she wrote. "I couldn't say for certain how closely the sculpture might resemble the head of a living woman." The nineteenth-century anonymous blind visitor to the London exposition had a similar revelation. "Were I desirous of presenting a blind person with a correct idea of the human face and figure," he wrote, "I should never think of showing him a statue with that object, for the simple reason that he would not understand it, because he could not realize it."

The DeafBlind poet John Lee Clark argues that tactile aesthetics have their own grammar, entirely divorced from the visual appearance of an object. In an essay on tactile art, Clark dismisses the work of the photojournalist John Olson, whose company, 3DPhotoWorks, makes relief representations of two-dimensional images. "Why would we want a representation of a representation of something?" Clark asks. "Why not a tactile representation of that something, bypassing visual representation altogether?" He imagines an exhibition about a protest that features realistic-looking toy tanks rolling through a crowd of protesters. "In the tactile realm," he writes,

> the toy tank is a joke, because it is made of flimsy plastic parts and is light, being hollow and without ballast. If I wished to install an exhibit about the terrors of totalitarianism, tanks rolling over protestors like so much cardboard, I would need tanks with real heft. The protestors can be made of, well, cardboard, and can even be taller than the tanks. But the power is with the heft, and the tanks have it.

Touch tours can offer revelations like this, and inventive curators have made ingenious tactile translations of visual art, as in an exhibition that Kleege cites at the Tate Modern in London, where "large shards of Plexiglas are used to suggest the fragmentation of Cubism, and a silicone pad, similar to a breast implant, is used to suggest the drapey texture of Salvador Dalí's melting watches."

But touch tours are hit or miss. Only a handful of institutions offer them, and they tend to siphon the spontaneity out of the art-going experience: you make a reservation weeks in advance, and there's a limited set of (often quite old) objects you're allowed to touch. To access the full collection, or new exhibitions, blind visitors must rely on verbal description.

• • •

The primary problem of blindness is access to information. Books, magazines, leaflets, menus, labels, signs, maps, graphs, charts, spreadsheets, slide decks, whiteboards, photos, videos, blueprints, tables, diagrams, illustrations, figures: these mediums are hyper-visual by default. A blind friend told me that as a child, he'd go to the toy store and ask his friends to read him the backs of the boxes—not because he was looking to buy new toys, but because he knew that the text held a world of information that was otherwise out of reach. Chancey Fleet—who taught Emilie Gossiaux how to use computers after her recovery, and is a leader in the world of digital accessibility—calls this state of affairs "image poverty." Fleet, who works as an assistive-tech coordinator at the New York Public Library, is passionate about the various technologies—3D printers, braille maps—that allow blind people to design their own images. "As long as we don't have access to the means of production for tactile graphics, and as long as tactile graphics are something that we're handed and not something that we create, we're not going to move forward," she said. With her rhetoric of "image poverty" and blind people seizing the means of production, Fleet strikes me as a kind of Marxist of visual access—a revolutionary advocating for the blind proletariat who are not only plagued by material poverty but also exiled from the ubiquitous flow of visual capital.

Two podcasts for the blind seek to fill, in their own modest ways, this yawning chasm of inaccessible visual information. *Talk Description to Me* takes images from the news (Ukrainian president Volodymyr Zelenskyy's social media presence; footage from the January 6 riot at the US Capitol) or other iconic images that blind people (especially those blind from a young age) might never hear about in visual detail (cave paintings; Day of the Dead decorations; the moon) and describes them, earnestly and thoroughly. *Say My Meme*, cohosted by Will Butler, applies the same treatment to internet memes, describing the image and its caption and explaining the joke. ("Picture a very tired SpongeBob . . . and he's kind of puffing out his cheeks like balloons, clearly doing this long slow exhale," Will's cohost explains. "You know that exhale you do when you're really milking the moment? And the caption is 'Me after I put the fitted sheet on the bed by myself.'")

When he was in grad school at Johns Hopkins in the late 1990s, the writer James Browning told me, he had a job as an assistant to Kingsley Price, a retired blind philosophy professor at the university. Price was a member of the first generation of the NFB, studying a few years after Jacobus tenBroek at University High, then following him to UC Berkeley to get his BA and PhD in philosophy in the 1940s. Browning would record himself reading books and articles for Price and help with his shopping and correspondence. "He wanted someone good at reading junk mail," Browning told me. "He was really diligent about going through *all* of his junk mail." Browning had to read Price everything: credit card offers, rejections from philosophy journals. "He'd come across some howler or malapropism in his junk mail," Browning said, "and a week later he'd still be talking about this stupid thing. It conjured a whole mythology in his mind: Who are these idiots sending me this stuff?"

When Browning told me this, I felt a hit of recognition. When I consider the loss of the visual world, I feel an obligation to privilege a certain strata of "important" images and information: the faces of my wife and child, endangered animals, Picasso. But I also feel fixated on tiny, throwaway things—an evocative piece of trash left on the street, a split-second glimpse of a sleeping man's face on a subway headed in the opposite direction—what Roland Barthes called the *punctum* of a photograph: the detail I don't think a charitable describer for the blind would ever bother to mention, but that pierces the viewer far more than the big, important, obvious themes of an image. "A photograph's *punctum* is that accident which pricks me," Barthes writes, adding parenthetically, "(but also bruises me, is poignant to me)." I think it's what Price was looking for when he made Browning read to the end of every credit card offer and newspaper advertisement. It's the most personal part of looking; when one must rely on others to do their looking for them, I suspect it's the thing one misses the most.

In a happy coincidence, when Oscar started kindergarten a few years ago, it turned out a father of a kid in his class was also blind. The kid's mom, Youme, approached us at orientation night a few weeks before school started and said, "Our family has a blind dad too!" Oscar and this kid soon became close friends. (Was it because they both have blind dads? I think they would've been friends anyway, but it's impossible to say.) Now our families spend a fair amount of time together, and I sometimes watch Hai and Youme's interactions for clues on how Lily and I will be in the future, when I'm closer to Hai's level of blindness. At

Oscar's eighth birthday party (which we threw, eight months into the pandemic, at a corn maze), we walked together through the little fairground, and I listened as Youme described the scene for Hai: "We're passing a little enclosure with animals," she told him, his hand on her arm, "where you can buy cups of feed pellets; now we're passing a platform you can climb to look down into the maze. . . ." In larger groups, Youme does this craftily, weaving her descriptions into the conversation as naturally as she can, masking the fact that she's narrating for Hai's benefit.

One of the attractions at the fair was a real-life camera obscura, a little pitch-black tent with a periscope popping up that projected an upside-down image of the fair onto one of the tent's interior walls. It worked the same way that a camera or an eye does: an image is only discernible when light comes through a tiny aperture, so that it can be refracted and projected. As soon as we entered the darkened tent, I saw nothing—it was like entering a blind eye in the midst of the fair's bright revelry. But Oscar guided me to a bench inside, and as my eyes adjusted, I could just make out the image on the wall, the upside-down world outside, rippling with the movement of the tent's fabric, hazy but still legible.

• • •

When blind people watch movies or TV with their sighted friends, the same dynamic that transpires between Hai and Youme plays out in the theater or on the couch. With talkier shows, like a sitcom or a game show, barely any description is necessary—most of what you need to follow the action is audible in the dialogue or the narration. But there's inevitably a moment that can confuse the blind viewer, or lead them to wonder what's happening (or, sometimes, they won't even know they're missing anything). They might nudge their friend in the ribs, and whisper, *What's going on?*

It was just this sort of ribs-nudging experience that led a San Francisco entrepreneur, Gregory T. Frazier, to develop one of the first formal programs of audio description for TV and film. One night in the early 1970s, Frazier and a blind friend were hanging out, watching *High Noon* on TV. His friend asked him to explain what was happening; since it's a western, *High Noon* is full of scenes that, to a blind viewer, sound like an indistinguishable soup of music, gunfire, galloping hooves, and shouting. Frazier started describing on the fly, narrating quickly, wedging his economical descriptions between lines of dialogue.

"By the time Gary Cooper had shot Frank Miller dead," Frazier's *New York Times* obituary reported, "he was a changed man." Frazier enrolled in a master's program in broadcasting at San Francisco State, and in 1975 he turned in his thesis on the possibilities of a new descriptive service for the blind. After he graduated, the university hired him, and his department chair, August Coppola, joined Frazier to start one of the first audio description (AD) companies, which they called AudioVision. In 1990, August connected Frazier with his younger brother, Francis Ford Coppola, whose film *Tucker* (about the failed independent automaker) became the first commercial film with an audio-described track included with its home release.

By the late 1990s, the American Council of the Blind—the consumer group founded in 1961 by dissenting members of the NFB—was leading the charge in lobbying the government to require the networks to provide description for some portion of their shows, just as they had to make a percentage of their programming available with closed-captioning. The NFB, true to its ethos in that era of taking contrary stances to the ACB (as when they came out against audible pedestrian signals, or the ACB's push to make US paper currency different sizes), expressed deep skepticism about a federal mandate for audio description. But the ACB's efforts were successful, and in 1999, the FCC issued a rule requiring the four major commercial broadcasters and the top cable and satellite providers to offer audio description.

The new FCC rule led to a flourishing of smaller shops that tackled description for the networks. Rick Boggs, one of the few blind actors to find any success in the industry, founded one such outfit. (He told me with pride about his appearance on an episode of *The Net*, a 1990s cable series spin-off of the Sandra Bullock film, where he played a porn site's blind webmaster. It was, he said, a fantastic role, since blind people tend to be cast—when they're cast at all—as "squeaky-clean" characters that capitalize on the pity people feel for their plight. It felt good to do something more controversial.) When Rick heard about the mandate for audio description, he used the money he'd made from acting to build a state-of-the-art studio in Northridge and hung out a shingle for his new AD shop, which he called We See TV (later rebranded as Audio Eyes). The national mandate amounted to only three and a half hours of programming per week, per network, but he soon had a contract with ABC. "We starved during reruns," he said.

One of Rick's first hires was a young blind engineer he'd mentored, Chris Snyder, who had an incredible ear—Rick bragged that Chris could memorize a phone number just from hearing the tones as you dialed it. As a kid in Scottsdale, Arizona, Chris made his own sound library by recording sound effects off his favorite TV shows, like *Deep Space Nine*. His father was a sales rep for a bike company, and Chris made tapes for him to listen to on his long drives between bike shops across the Southwest, using his four-track mixer and a double tape deck to enhance the talking books he got from the Library of Congress's free audiobook program for the blind, dubbing in music and all the sound effects he'd recorded off his TV, producing a kind of radio-dramatic audiobook. It sounded like a rudimentary version of the work he'd go on to produce at Audio Eyes: TV sound effects, narration, and music, mixed together to create a coherent audio drama. In this way, audio-described TV shows and films turned out to be aesthetic relatives to highly produced narrative podcasts like *Radiolab* or *This American Life*.

After a few years, Audio Eyes was doing well, producing AD for *Malcolm in the Middle* and *That '70s Show*. But the NFB persisted in its opposition to audio description. Even if individual members enjoyed audio-described films and TV shows, the NFB as an organization turned up its nose at the idea that a blindness group would ever expend its resources pushing for something as trivial as entertainment access. "Blind people have much larger concerns than whether they can follow the action on a prime-time television program," an NFB leader wrote in 2003, when the Motion Picture Association of America (MPAA) was challenging the federal mandate for AD in the DC Circuit Court (the NFB filed a supporting brief). "The high unemployment rate among working-age blind people, the falling Braille literacy rate among blind children, and the plight of blind seniors unable to get the independence training that would keep them out of nursing homes come immediately to mind."

In its decision, the DC Circuit Court cited the NFB's position that "the regulations should be rejected as arbitrary and capricious, because the FCC failed to assess whether visually impaired persons actually want or need video description." The NFB makes this argument frequently in its public confrontations: because they weren't included in the decision-making process as an organization, it follows that blind people themselves weren't adequately consulted—a way of dismissing and undermining the claim of the ACB or any other group to represent the interests of the blind.

The court ruled in the MPAA's (and the NFB's) favor, and by 2004, the mandate for description disappeared and the industry collapsed. For the rest of the decade, hardly any audio description was produced in the US. Chris moved back to Arizona, and Rick shrank his team down to a skeleton crew. They found odd jobs to get by: a law school in Irvine had a number of blind students and needed instructional videos described, and the National Park Service wanted description for the videos that play in kiosks in their welcome centers.

After a rough six years, in 2010, Rick called Chris again, and jubilantly told him, "We got the mandate back!" The ACB and the American Foundation for the Blind had continued their lobbying efforts, finding allies in Congress like Ed Markey (then a US representative for Massachusetts, where the ACB has a particularly strong affiliate), as well as other disability consumer groups like the National Association of the Deaf. Rep. Markey introduced a bill in the House, and in 2010, President Obama signed the 21st Century Communications and Video Accessibility Act, which reestablished the federal requirement for broadcasters to produce audio description. Chris moved back to Los Angeles, and work flooded into the Audio Eyes studio.

• • •

I visited Rick and Chris at their shop to see how two blind guys produce an audio description track. Their office is in a very late-seventies-feeling office park in Northridge, a city in the San Fernando Valley where most of the nation's professional pornography is filmed. (In 2016, Pornhub, one of the top porn sites on the internet, launched an initiative through their philanthropic arm, Pornhub Cares, that offered audio description for fifty of the site's most popular videos.)

Chris rolled into the office around noon, complaining that he'd only gotten three hours of sleep, having stayed up all night finalizing the AD on a feature film. Rick introduced us, explaining that I was a cane user but still had a decent amount of usable central vision. "So you're *almost* one of us," Chris said with a friendly smirk.

Rick invited me to sit down, saying he'd take the zebra chair. I had yet another sighted-person thought: *How does he know the chair has zebra stripes?* Why, I wondered immediately, is it so hard for the sighted—even for me—to accept blind people's knowledge of the visual world? I later mustered the courage to ask Rick about this. It turned out he'd been shopping for furniture for his old studio with his first wife when she suddenly blurted out, "Hey, a zebra chair!" He asked her what she meant, and he got some pleasure from hearing her description of it. The chair had been with him ever since. For much of his childhood, he told me, he'd felt sadness, frustration, and anger about being blind, and felt beneath sighted people. But then, in his twenties and thirties, he turned a corner, and realized, "Hey, this blindness thing is actually kinda fun!" Now he finds it more amusing than irritating to rely on sighted people's descriptions for details. He likes the unpredictable variety of interpretation: he'll hold up the same shirt for each of his three children and ask them what it looks like, and get three radically different answers.

Rick is white-haired, slender, and often speaks in numbered lists, which makes it easier to follow his complex, rapid-fire lines of thought. Numbered lists, I'd learned from producing radio myself, are excellent for oral storytelling, and thus, they're useful for blind speakers and listeners too. At a glance, a visual reader can see how ideas are structured on the page, but for a listener, lists offer a framework to hang on to—they're audible signposts. Throughout our conversation, Rick stopped to attend to his phone's notifications, lapsing into a fractured conversation with its screen reader's hyper-speed robotic speech as he fired off messages to the various scriptwriters and engineers on his team, and then—thanks to the handy mnemonic of the numbered list—picked up our conversation precisely where he'd left off.

Rick told me about the theory of audio description he'd developed after years of producing it. "You can grab a blind guy off the street," he said, "and ask him what kind of description he likes. And if you give me his answers, I can tell you: one, when he went blind; two, how much residual vision he has; and three, how much AD he's heard." The congenitally blind, and those without any residual vision, tend to prefer minimalist AD: Just give them what they need, and nothing more.

Describe the stuff that's impossible to follow from the dialogue, and leave out opinions. Don't explain emotions, and don't try to suggest why things are happening. The description should be "absolutely objective," Rick said. "Don't say 'beautiful blonde'—just say what she *looks* like." Rick lost his sight at five years old, and he prefers this minimalist style of description—although, because he does have some visual memory, he sometimes appreciates details like what color things are.

The other consensus group, those with some residual vision, or those who lost sight later in life—generally, those who retain a visual orientation toward the world, or who still have strong visual memories—tend to prefer a more maximalist approach. They want "lots of color, facial expressions," Rick said. "Is he mad? Keep me informed on the story line." This is the category I'm gradually falling into myself. I want to know everything: the Barthesian *punctum* of the local newscast, whether it's the gap between the weatherman's teeth or the way the news anchor's helmet of blond hair shivers slightly as she laughs. Rick has conducted surveys of blind AD consumers and read (and contributed to) the growing literature on AD, and his conclusion is that people who once had sight, on some level, want their vision back—and while they watch a show, they want the audio description to replace it. But ultimately, he's skeptical. "A picture may be worth a thousand words," Rick said, swiveling gently in his zebra chair, "but those words don't match the image."

Because it serves both kinds of blind viewers, Audio Eyes tries to split the difference between the maximalist and minimalist approaches. The critical thing for Rick, and what he thinks other shops miss (nearly all of them are run by sighted people), is the focus he and his team put on the question of what the blind person already knows. The most egregious, infuriating thing that bad AD does, Rick said, is explain what a blind viewer has already figured out from context or the soundtrack. "Don't tell me the phone rings, or that John's sad about his mother," Rick said. "Don't say he gets in the car when we hear the car door slam." So many sighted people, without realizing it, have exceedingly low expectations of blind people. Too often, we adopt a patronizing attitude: *How does he know it's a zebra chair?* No matter that it's his chair, sitting in an office he furnished himself. One day, a delivery guy who brought lunch to the Audio Eyes office asked Rick, as he handed over the bags of food, "How do you eat?" These paternalistic attitudes worm their way into the audio description sighted people write—hence the NFB's anti-custodialist objections to the technology. The writer Hector Chevigny, before and after he went blind in 1943, had a successful career during radio's golden age. In his memoir, he explicitly aligns good radio writing—leaving plenty to the listener's imagination—with his experience as a blind person. Bad radio writing overuses the narrator, who explains things that the listener can easily infer. As a result, he writes,

> we feel a little as if we had been talked down to, as if we had been addressed as children. Perhaps this will convey a little of the feeling the blind get when they have been understanding everything perfectly well yet some well-meaning individual insists on carefully explaining the conversation that has just been heard.

The day I visited, Rick and Chris were cutting a descriptive track into a promotional video for Panasonic cameras. One of Rick's sighted employees had watched the video and written a script, filling in description between the video's preexisting narration and dialogue. A blind employee had edited this script, making sure that nothing was confusing or condescending or presumptuous or otherwise distracting. All that was left to do was for Rick to record the descriptive track, reading off a braille script. Chris and I sat in an adjoining studio, where he directed Rick's performance and cut his narration into the video on the fly. (Nearly every feature of Pro Tools, the industry-standard audio-editing software, is accessible to blind users, who listen to the computer's synthetic speech to tell them what's happening on the screen—a state of affairs that's largely the result of Rick's advocacy.)

After watching him work for a while, I finally asked the question that had been eating at me: What's the point of describing a promotional video about cameras for a blind audience? Rick laughed, acknowledging the apparent absurdity of the job even as he prepared to explain its importance. First of all, he told me, there are blind people who use cameras—he happens to be friends with Bruce Hall, one of the more well-known blind photographers. But beyond that, who's to say a blind person might not want to know about cameras for whatever reason? Rick's first wife was a photographer, and he'd bought her a camera as a gift. "I can't say, 'I can't buy you a camera because I'm blind!'" he said. Rick's team had also described nearly 350 promotional videos for Sherwin-Williams, the paint manufacturer. "Blind people aren't going to appreciate the quality of one hue of paint versus another," Rick said. But they still might want to hear the pitch. When Rick's teenage daughter wanted to paint her room, he'd warned her that the color she'd chosen was too dark, and she'd soon grow tired of it. She didn't heed his advice, and six months later, he turned out to be right.

While I was at Audio Eyes, I felt overwhelmed by the Sisyphean task before them: the rising piles of television in need of description, and every day a new mountain of content added to the heap. For the most part, the commercial work that finds its way to them is arbitrary, selected by the studios and networks to fulfill their mandate. It's tempting to start thinking of a hierarchy of how content should be prioritized: start with the emergency alerts, of course, but then what? Educational content, children's programming, news and documentaries? A blind friend complained to me recently that the Criterion Collection is almost entirely undescribed, and I'd add the same for the entire history of video art. Farther down the list we'd have entertainment, descending from prestige TV to the latest season of *Man vs. Bear* (which a sighted engineer was working on in another room while I was at the studio). Below that, near the bottom, would be the special circle of AD hell reserved for advertisements.

But this attitude, as pragmatic as it might seem, ultimately tells blind people what they should be interested in, as a parent might. I'd rather be able to wander aimlessly through the media landscape, plucking whatever strikes my fancy, art or trash, instead of accepting a charity package of nature documentaries and emergency alerts. It's the same impulse that made Kingsley Price hire a grad student in creative writing to read his junk mail to him. I want the freedom to know the unspoken on-screen URL in the TV ad for the weird fitness product that I feel ashamed of being interested in. I want to watch what everyone else is watching, even if it's a soul-crushing training video, or a bad sitcom, or an ad for paint.

Chris scrubbed back in the Panasonic video—which showed a group of models standing in a CGI cityscape, demonstrating the camera's superior ability to capture color—to listen to the section they'd just recorded. "The blonde in burgundy stands in front of the windows with a strip of hot pink on the horizon behind," Rick's voice said over the studio monitors.

"I don't speak color," Chris said to himself softly, listening to Rick's narration, "but . . . that's an interesting picture."

6.

The Library of Babel

To give his tortured eyes a rest, James Joyce sometimes enlisted friends to take dictation as he wrote and revised *Finnegans Wake*. For decades he'd been through bouts of iritis, glaucoma, and synechia; he'd undergone nearly a dozen eye surgeries with intermittent success. By the time he was composing *Finnegans Wake*, he was nearly blind. His notes for the novel were written in exaggeratedly large handwriting, and he frequently walked with a cane.

One day in the early 1930s, as his friend Samuel Beckett was taking dictation from Joyce, there was a knock at the door. Beckett didn't hear the knock, and when Joyce said, "Come in," Beckett dutifully transcribed the words. Later, as Beckett read the manuscript back to him, Joyce stopped at this phrase.

"What's that 'Come in'?" Joyce said.

"Yes, you said that," Beckett replied.

After considering a moment, Joyce said, "Let it stand."

Finnegans Wake is a supremely aural (and oral) novel, full of multilingual puns and invented onomatopoeia, like the notorious hundred-letter lightning-crack word-sound on the first page—*bababadalgharaghtakamminarronnkonnbronntonnerronntuonnthunntrovarrhounawnskawntoohoohoordenenthurnuk!*—that combines words for *noise*, *thunder*, and *defecation*. Joyce himself seemed happy to promote the novel as an aural experience, recording his performance of one section for Cambridge's Orthological Institute in 1929, and telling his friend Claude Sykes, "It is all so simple. If anyone doesn't understand a passage, all he need do is read it aloud." But his biographer, Richard Ellmann, dismissed the idea that *Wake*'s aurality had anything to do with its author's failing eyesight. "The theory that Joyce wrote his book for the ear because he could not see is not only an insult to the creative imagination," Ellmann wrote, "but an error of fact. Joyce could see; to be for periods half-blind is not at all the same thing as to be permanently blind."

I can attest to the truth of that last claim, but as Ellmann's own biography shows, through its anecdotes of Joyce's generative encounters with dictation, blindness did influence his composition of the novel. Most writers have the experience of watching their manuscript absorb elements of their daily experiences, but this tendency was extreme in a writer like Joyce, who Beckett later described as "a synthesizer." "He wanted to put everything, the whole of human culture, into one or two books," Beckett said. "It is not to be read—or rather it is not only to be read," Beckett wrote elsewhere of Joyce's novel. "It is to be looked at and listened to. His writing is not about something; it is that something itself."

Other blind writers have explicitly acknowledged the impact of their disability on their literary style. In his essayistic documentary *Vision Portraits*, the filmmaker Rodney Evans confronts his own vision loss from RP by profiling three blind artists. One of them is the writer Ryan Knighton, who also has RP. In a scene in Knighton's office at Capilano University, where he teaches creative writing, Knighton shows Evans how quickly he can listen to his computer read back the words he's written—his own private robotic Samuel Beckett. "I can go faster," Knighton tells Evans as his Toshiba's synthetic voice babbles incomprehensibly behind him, "but what I find is I can't think as fast as I can listen to it." Knighton, who can no longer see the words on the screen, tells Evans that blindness has fundamentally changed his style as a writer. "I have this very ongoing, odd, triangular relationship with the computer voice as my mediator," he says.

> But I'm very superstitious about it, so I don't change it. My writing style has emerged as very oratory. It's very oral. That's my reading experience. Sighted people read, they have a voice in their head. I don't have one. I haven't had one for years because I never read to myself.

During the years it took me to write this book, I retired from print. When I started writing, I struggled through regular printed books, unwilling to give up the power of the jotted marginal note, the ability to scan and skim, the well-ordered, physical bookshelf that never crashed or lagged or needed a reboot. But this became exhausting, and unsustainable, so I moved on to ebooks. My ebook reader's font-size meter soon looked like a thermometer on a record-breakingly hot summer day, and the temperature was still rising. I hovered longer than I should have at the second-to-highest setting—at the largest type size, I'd need to advance the screen every five or ten words. So I held out. Whenever I went to enlarge the type one last time, I looked at that final little unfilled space on the thermometer with alarm, and turned back. It seemed unthinkable to lose that voice I hear in my head when I read. Once I'd maxed out the font size, and even that became too small for comfort, where could I go from there?

• • •

Turning on my computer's built-in screen reader made me feel like I was using a computer for the first time, trepidatiously trying out commands and hoping they worked. A screen reader is a piece of software that allows the blind user to control her computer without vision. Turning on the screen reader moves all of the computer's functionality—organizing files, editing text, clicking a link, skimming a PDF—into the keyboard. Any text it encounters, from a menu item to a blog post to a Word doc, is spoken aloud via a text-to-speech synthesizer (think Siri or Alexa). This is true only if that text is coded in a way that the screen reader can handle, and thus the contemporary blind person must constantly navigate around inaccessible web pages, documents, and software that breaks or omits crucial information when they try to use it. But when they work, screen readers allow blind people to read a huge swath of the internet and its growing libraries of digital editions. These include public-domain services like Project Gutenberg and the Internet Archive, digital marketplaces like the Kindle Store and Apple Books, and collections that only serve print-disabled readers, like Bookshare and the National Library Service (NLS).

In the past, if blind people wanted to read (or write) a book, their options were severely limited. Before the development of tactile reading systems like braille, the only recourse for a blind reader was to find someone to read to him, and a writer needed to find a scribe. Starting in the 1650s, John Milton composed batches of verse from *Paradise Lost* in his head, and then got whoever was around to "milk" him, as he put it, taking down the lines he'd produced overnight. His family members, visiting friends, and hired amanuenses would take these variegated scraps and write them out into a clean copy.

Independent reading for the blind began (after some notable but isolated historical instances) in the late eighteenth century, in France, with a happy accident. Valentin Haüy, who started the world's first school for the blind in Paris in 1784, hired his first and most precocious student as an assistant. One day, the assistant, François Le Sueur, handed him a funeral notice from the papers on his desk, remarking that he was able to feel the letters quite distinctly. Haüy, who was at the time developing the world's first curriculum for blind students, was intrigued, and set to work researching and designing a raised-letter reading system.

These first books for the blind were colossal: I saw (and touched) one at the archive of the Perkins School near Boston, and it looked like an exploded, waterlogged spell book. The size of a jumbo briefcase, it weighed nearly ten pounds, and the words rose steeply off the pages, like scar tissue. Raised-letter systems had the advantage of being legible to sighted and blind people alike, which sighted teachers of the blind preferred. Tracing the shape of a raised letter, though, turned out to be less than ideal for a blind reader, particularly because Haüy preserved eighteenth-century printing conventions—the letters were Gothic, florid, dripping with ornamentation. Distinguishing even between simple letterforms is a challenge under the fingers—close your eyes and imagine how a capital *C* might feel, if you encountered it with your index finger moving from left to right. Now imagine distinguishing that shape from a capital *O*, read the same way. It's only once you've arrived at the far edge of the letter that you can identify it, and you'd probably need to run your fingers back and forth a few times to confirm the distinction. This is not a recipe for fluent, efficient reading. Raised-print books' size also made them cumbersome to move and store, and incredibly expensive to produce. While they learned to read raised print at Haüy's school, as soon as they graduated, students no longer had access to these books, and quickly lost their literacy.

But this moment still marked the birth of literacy for the blind, and Haüy's students embraced their massive new books with enthusiasm. At the Perkins Library archive, a researcher showed me a page in one of these early tactile books—a passage from the Gospel of Mark—and pointed to a visible darkening over the word *spit*, in a sentence describing Jesus's miracle cure of the blind man of Bethsaida, which he performed by rubbing his holy saliva into the man's eyes. The word had been darkened, the scholar suggested, from the accumulation of finger oils after repeated touching—the wear of reading and rereading. It reminded me of the maps posted in the New York City subway system, where the point representing the station you're in gets rubbed away by thousands of fingers touching that same spot every day: *We are here*.

In 1808, Charles Barbier, a former officer in Louis XVI's army, began publishing the results of his experiments in developing alternative writing systems of his own. Popular histories of braille paint Barbier as a career officer who created these codes with military applications in mind, in order to allow French soldiers to communicate with one another without lighting their lamps and alerting the enemy to their location. But in the first decade of the nineteenth century, Barbier's military career was behind him; he was engaged as an engineer and inventor, writing on the possibilities of a universal language. His interest in universality led him to think about the challenges of blind reading: in the 1815 publication that described his most successful tactile reading system, he wrote that it would be of use to "those blind since birth [who,] forever deprived of the ability to read our books or writing, also experience great difficulty in correctly drawing the shapes of our letters." His new writing system became known as *écriture nocturne*—"night writing." Unlike Haüy's books, it employed a code of raised dots, embossed on a page using an awl. Barbier soon began a correspondence with Alexandre-René Pignier, the director of Haüy's National Institute for Blind Youth in Paris. Pignier presented night writing to his students, who immediately saw the value of the system over the raised print they'd been using, and set to debating its flaws and making alterations.

Among these tinkerers was a student named Louis Braille. Louis had been blinded when he was three, in an accident with a pruning knife; he'd used one to puncture a piece of leather in imitation of his father, who worked as a saddler in the workshop that stood on the Brailles' property. When he was twelve, Louis began to use a similar tool to tweak and refine Barbier's system, adapting it to the needs of blind readers and writers. He cut the number of dots in a single cell in half—Barbier's twelve-dot cell required a reader to feel up and down as well as left to right in order to discern all of the dots, but a braille cell is composed of a two-by-three grid of just six possible raised dots, numbered from the upper left (1) to the lower right (6). Which of these six dots are raised determines their meaning: dot 1 on its own is the letter *a*; a cell with only dots 1 and 2 raised is *b*; dots 1 and 4 is *c*; and so on. Braille's six-dot cell could be felt in its entirety in a single pass even by a child's small fingers.

Braille also altered the code's relationship with the French language. Barbier wanted his system to be phonetic, transcribing syllables as they're spoken, with cells representing sounds, not letters, and didn't include capitals. But braille did away with Barbier's sonography, transcribing words as they appeared in ink print, punctuation and all, so that blind readers had access to the same degree of literacy as sighted ones did. This also meant that blind readers could hear the silent, internal reading voice that Ryan Knighton says he lost with his vision. As a braille reader's fingers pass over the page, they can listen to their own voice reading just as a visual reader can.

In 1829, with the help of his headmaster, Pignier, Braille published the *Procédé* (its full title in English is *Process for Writing Words, Music and Plain-song Using Dots*). At the Perkins Library, I saw an edition of the *Procédé*, and felt a thrill to see two tactile writing systems on the same page, like the Rosetta Stone, as a half page of raised-letter French explaining his system gives way to the raised dots of the new braille alphabet itself. Raised print, as one blind critic wrote, was an instance of sighted teachers "talking to the fingers in the language of the eye." With the invention of braille, the fingers had found their native language.

Blind students instantly took to the system, but it met with resistance from many of their sighted teachers, who preferred the familiarity of raised letters, which didn't require that they learn a new, "arbitrary" code—never mind that the symbols comprising the Roman alphabet were themselves equally arbitrary. Braille had immense advantages over raised print: it was more compact, quicker to read, cheaper to produce, and, most crucially, it gave blind people the ability to write independently. All they needed was a piece of relatively heavyweight paper, a frame (called a "slate") that locked the page in place, and an awl (called a "stylus") that the writer could use to emboss the page with lines of raised dots. Writing with a slate and stylus was still a little tricky to learn, because the writer needed to write backward, like a typesetter; once the page was removed from the slate and flipped over to reveal the raised dots on the other side, the right-to-left order of the embossed dots was reversed.

Braille spread across Europe to the other schools for the blind that had been established after Haüy's model, and that had adopted their own languages' versions of raised-print systems. Everywhere it was met with a similar dynamic: blind students immediately apprehended its power, while their sighted teachers resisted its alien, arbitrary appearance. If the goal of education for the blind was integration into mainstream society, they argued, wasn't a system like raised print—where sighted and blind people could read the same edition of the same book together—preferable to an obscure-looking code like braille? This attitude was a variation, perhaps, on the universalism that inspired Barbier to invent a "language" he thought everyone could use: the best system would seem to be one that the most people could understand.

Samuel Gridley Howe, the founder of the first school for the blind in the US (and an early, influential proponent of oralism, which made a similar argument against ASL in favor of lip-reading and speech for Deaf students), visited the Paris institute in 1831. At around the same time that Louis Braille was working out his system, Howe was developing and then promoting Boston Line Type, an angular but otherwise mostly standard Roman alphabet. By the 1850s, as braille flourished among blind European students, the US had become a battleground for a cluster of warring tactile reading systems. In the decades that followed, a library at a school for the blind might have books in a half dozen different tactile reading systems: raised-letter systems like Moon Type and Boston and Philadelphia Line Type, alongside braille and its knockoff variants, like American braille and William Wait's New York Point. (Wait described this situation as "a confusion of types for the blind, like that of tongues at Babel.") In one attempt at a partial synthesis, the DeafBlind writer Morrison Heady invented a machine he called a "diplograph" that could, with the flip of a switch, produce three different varieties of embossed type (braille, New York Point, and standard Roman).

Helen Keller and many of her blind contemporaries were compelled to learn all of these systems, since any given library for the blind was likely to contain an assortment, each distributed by their own fierce promoters and defenders. Blind students resented what came to be called the War of the Dots, and the need to stay fresh on multiple codes in order to read the scant books that were available to them. Throughout the nineteenth century, braille remained in some US schools a kind of contraband: at the Missouri School for the Blind, students passed one another notes—and, reportedly, love letters—in braille, since they knew their teachers wouldn't be able to read them if they got caught. Michael Anagnos, who succeeded Howe as the head of the Perkins School in 1876, reportedly said, "If anyone invents a new system of printing for the blind, shoot him on the spot."

I first learned this history from a cheerful sighted curator of blind history named Mike Hudson, who works in Louisville, Kentucky, as the resident historian at the museum of the American Printing House for the Blind, which since 1858 has been the center of federally funded production of textbooks and educational materials for blind students in the US. Mike told me that the War of the Dots effectively concluded in 1909, as rapidly expanding cities like New York realized that, for the first time, they had enough blind children to start building day schools for the blind. "And so," Mike explained in his superb Kentuckian museum-docent drawl, "they have a nice, big, two-day, knock-down, drag-out meeting of the New York Board of Education to decide which code they're going to use in the New York City schools."

Mike and I were on a break during an academic conference on blindness and literacy at Harvard, sitting together in a glass-walled group study room in a library at the edge of Harvard Yard. Describing that debate at the New York Board of Education, Mike said, with genuine excitement in his voice, "It's awesome. They bring in all the heavy hitters. They bring in Mr. Wait; they bring in the heads of the schools; they bring in the head of the American Printing House for the Blind. I mean, everybody who's anybody in blindness testifies before this body. And at the end they take a big vote, and they vote for braille. And not modified American braille, but the French braille code. It's the beginning of the end for the competing codes."

By 1917, a newly standardized braille had become the main way blind children were taught to read in the US. Empowered to read and write independently, blind people were better able to integrate into mainstream society—more blind children were able to enter public schools and later enroll in colleges. Braille shorthand had been developed in the UK in the 1890s, followed a few years later by the first braille typewriters, which now allowed many blind people to secure office jobs as secretaries and stenographers.

But as braille became the standard in Europe and then in the US, there remained readers for whom learning the system felt like an impossibility. With the right instruction, blind children can learn braille as easily as sighted children learn print, but adult learners labored to develop the necessary finger sensitivity, and then struggled to master the code's dozens of arbitrary-seeming contractions. Even if they passed these hurdles, adult braille learners still struggled to push their reading speed anywhere close to the rates attained by those who learned the code as children, or that of sighted print readers.

• • •

This has been my experience too. I knew it'd be difficult, and could take years to master, but as someone who's organized his life around reading and writing, it seemed foolish not to try. I started learning before I'd even given up on regular-sized print. After my retinal specialist declared me legally blind, making me eligible for services from the Massachusetts Commission for the Blind, I reached out to my MCB caseworker and told her I wanted to learn braille. She informed me that in our technological age, screen readers made it unnecessary for most blind people, who can just listen to any text they'd want to read, whether it's an audiobook or an email. She added that it took a long time to get proficient, and that at my age, it'd take even longer. She made me feel a bit like the middle-aged guy who, after reading a few epics in translation and watching some sandals-and-swords movies, declares that he wants to learn ancient Greek.

Since the advent of talking books—the first audiobooks, developed in the 1930s exclusively for the blind—several generations of blind students have been discouraged from learning braille. After talking books came video magnifiers, optical character recognition (OCR) software, and screen readers. Teachers and social workers make an argument similar to the one that the MCB made to me: that a student can just "use technology" to read, getting by with magnification or letting an iPad with a screen reader speak anything that their school might throw at them. Many blind students now enrolled at mainstream schools have limited access to teachers of the visually impaired (of which there is a major national shortage); they might be offered braille instruction once a week, if at all. We take for granted the degree to which sighted children are surrounded by visual language everywhere they go; it takes concerted effort to immerse a blind child in a commensurate amount of braille.

But relying on screen readers, some braille evangelists argue, leads to students who are, in a technical sense, illiterate. They listen only to the language, and they might graduate from college (if they make it that far—about 60 percent of blind students who pursue a college degree end up dropping out) having written papers, read books, and passed their exams without direct contact with a text's spelling, punctuation, orthography—the trappings at the heart of what they see as legitimate literacy. Even those students who rely on magnifiers might lose their sight as they get older, or have to enlarge the type so much that an over-reliance on visual reading becomes a hindrance, leaving them to page through a document one highway-sign-sized word at a time. (I heard a story about a blind person who quipped, "I read print with my nose"—pressing his face almost to the page to discern the letters—"and braille with my fingers.")

But what is literacy? If a blind person can aurally read and understand college-level books, and aurally compose essays whose arguments are commensurately sophisticated, does it matter that they don't recall the difference between *their* and *they're*, or that *pseudoscience* starts with a *p*? For the typo sensitive, screen readers can also be adjusted to read every letter and punctuation mark aloud, though of course this sort of reading happens rarely—it's much easier to turn a text up to five hundred words a minute and let it rip. This hyper-speed synthesized speech sounds unintelligible to the untrained ear, like a coked-up C-3PO trying to record an audiobook, but with practice, listeners can comprehend aural reading speeds of more than six hundred words per minute. Most blind people I've met crank their screen readers up this fast, especially when they need to burn through a series of menu selections—they slow it down for a more dense or literary text, but there's no point in savoring a spam email or a series of computer alerts they've heard a thousand times. Sighted listeners practice aural speed listening, too, as evinced by the appearance of 2x and even 3x settings on mainstream podcast and audiobook apps. And while many blind writers use dictation, most are also touch typists, so to call them functionally illiterate is an exaggeration at best. They merely rely on spellcheckers and autocorrect, like so many of their sighted peers. By this logic, John Milton was illiterate at the time he composed *Paradise Lost*.

Does *close* reading, though, happen only through the eyes or the fingers? Neuroscientists have found that when a blind person reads braille, their visual cortices are activated in much the same way a sighted reader's are. They're activated when we listen to language, too, though one study suggests that this may be to a far lesser extent, even in congenitally blind people. This research bears out my own experience as a reader: when I listen to a book, I can get absorbed in it, but in the end I don't feel like I have quite as strong a handle on the text—the language, the structure—as I do when I read visually. I recently read (or should I say listened to?) Dostoyevsky's *Notes from Underground* at double speed. At first it sounded ridiculous, but the ear adapts, and by the end I felt I could understand everything that was going on at least as well as I would have had I been reading visually. Still, if the novel is a forest, it was as though I'd driven through it at 45 miles per hour, as opposed to walking—or lightly jogging—through the novel's wooded terrain. "If I decide to read a book in braille," one lifelong braille reader told me, "it's a badge of honor. It means I have a lot of respect for the literary merit of that book, and I want to savor it."

Braille has the air of a status symbol among a certain class of blind professionals. I always admire the office setups of these braille-savvy knowledge workers I've visited: they all have forty-cell (or larger) refreshable braille displays sitting in front of their QWERTY keyboards. Refreshable braille displays are about the size of a normal computer keyboard, but boxier. As the name suggests, they can display a line of braille from a digital source, and then instantly refresh to show the next line. At the front of the display, around where the space bar would be on a normal keyboard, runs a strip of empty braille cells—little pieces of metal with holes drilled into them. As the display receives a digital source text, it pushes soft pins up through these holes, presenting the proper braille words and symbols for whatever it's reading. When the user hits a button to advance, the pins plunge back down and then pop up again near-instantaneously to display the next line, like a tactile Kindle that only shows forty characters at a time. If a braille display user needs to proofread an email, or carefully parse a document, or a foreign word or name gets garbled in their computer's synthesized speech, their hands move swiftly down from the keyboard to the braille display, like a sighted person slipping on a pair of reading glasses or leaning into their monitor to examine something more carefully. One friend told me she leaves her left hand on her braille display "half-heartedly" as her screen reader burns through a document; she's listening far faster than she can feel the words, but her fingers still give her useful snapshots of the text as she listens.

I know many successful blind people—including prolific novelists and screenwriters—who never learned braille, but I aspire to be like these professional power-users. Though the majority of visually impaired adults are unemployed, several studies found that blind people who use braille have a higher rate of employment and report greater job satisfaction. "Any time I want to dig into a text, really immerse myself, I read it in braille," Robert Englebretson, a professor of linguistics at Rice University, told me. "I always have a braille display hooked up to my computer. I thrive on braille."

• • •

My first lesson was with an affable sighted vocational rehab teacher who—after more arguments about whether I really needed braille in spite of the easier-to-use text-to-speech technology that was already available to me, and another warning of how difficult braille was to learn as an adult—my state blindness agency finally agreed to send to my home. He was kind and patient, but I quickly became skeptical of his skills. I was using one finger to read, and I found myself constantly tilting my finger onto its edge, where I thought I could feel the dots better. When I asked him if this was OK, he told me, "I've never seen anyone do it like that before, but you should do whatever works for you." He added, "I read braille by sight, but the woman who taught me the code was blind, and she read with multiple fingers on both hands. I don't know what that's about—that's really advanced. When you learn, I think you'd better just stick with one finger." Learning to read braille from a sighted guy, I began to wonder—wasn't this like learning to ride a bike from someone who didn't ride themselves, but had watched a lot of YouTube videos about cycling and knew several bike riders personally?

Around this time, I went to my first NFB convention. While I was there, I wandered into the Braille Book Fair just before it closed for the day. The room was nearly empty of people—instead, I saw rows of folding tables piled high with books that looked, to my eyes, like hulking sheaves of blank paper, spiral-bound at the local copy center.

Near the back of the hall, I found Barbara Loos standing behind a table stacked with braille books. Loos was blind, and had recently retired from her job as a braille and adaptive-technology instructor in Lincoln, Nebraska. She was in her late sixties and wore dark, aerodynamic-looking sunglasses that wouldn't have been out of place on the head of a ski instructor. Barbara asked me about my background and my blindness. Almost immediately, I felt like her student, come to learn from this elder dean of blindness, with her lifetime's experience of blind activism and braille reading. She suggested that I attend one of the NFB's residential training centers, which offered programs ranging from nine months to a year to give a blind person all the skills they'd need for independence, including intensive braille study. When I balked at the length of the program, she prodded me. "Think of it like college," she said. "Immerse yourself in blindness."

Barbara told me about Jerry Whittle, a beloved braille instructor at one of the NFB training centers who had died that year. When someone asked him how an adult braille learner could attain high reading speeds, he famously replied, "Read till you bleed!" I told Barbara that this reminded me of the way the pad of my index finger heated up after a half hour of practice. I could imagine pushing too far, and reading for so long that eventually blood would spurt from my finger, streaking the pages of my practice book. (I'd later hear stories about blind students whose fingers actually did bleed from prolonged reading.) Barbara told me I was probably pressing down too hard on the page. "Braille requires a light touch," she said. Excited by her advice, I told her about my sighted instructor back in Massachusetts, who'd told me to read with one finger. Barbara winced. "You're developing bad habits," she said. "You'll *never* finish a whole book with one finger." This stung. "How many fingers do you use?" I asked. She reached for a book and pulled it onto the table between us. "Always two hands, with about three fingers on each hand," she said, as her hands slid across the braille at the top of the page. "Once you get really fast, about halfway across the first line, your left hand will move down to the beginning of the next line while your right hand keeps reading to the end, and then it slides down to meet your left, ready to go." Reading braille this way, the fingers almost mimic the saccadic movements of the eyes, which don't travel in straight lines from one line of print to the next, but bounce around, constantly reorienting as they move across the page.

When I got back home, I fired my sighted braille teacher and enrolled in a free braille correspondence course instead, figuring that a blind-designed curriculum with a distant blind teacher was better than learning in person with a sighted guide teaching me what Barbara had convinced me were bad habits. I set up a little braille desk in my attic, the centerpiece of which was a Perkins Brailler, a braille typewriter largely unchanged from the version that shipped out to blind writers from the Perkins School beginning in 1951. It's a gorgeous contraption, made of smooth, heavy metal, and it looks and feels something like a classic Olivetti Lettera typewriter might, had it been designed by Chevrolet in its midcentury heyday. When I got it, I had an urge to climb in and drive it around my neighborhood. Next to the Perkins I piled a sheaf of heavy-stock braille paper, along with my slate and stylus and a braille eraser (a poky little tool I could use to press back down on any dots I'd embossed by mistake). I also had a pile of spiral-bound braille workbooks, and an NLS talking book player—basically an oversize, government-issue MP3 player, with big, satisfying, elder-friendly tactile buttons—that I used to listen to my lessons.

I did feel like a hobbyist up there in my attic, like a ham radio tinkerer or amateur student of ancient Greek, working away at this obscure skill I wondered if I'd ever really use—whether because I'd manage to hang on to enough residual vision to keep reading with magnification forever, or because I'd never get fast enough for braille to be worth my while, beyond labeling spice jars. Still, I'd resolutely type up my homework (transcribing the sentences that an anonymous voice read aloud on my talking book player's cartridges) and send it off to my instructor at the Hadley Institute, Pamela Bortz, who lived in Arizona and had worked as a braille transcriber and proofreader for most of her life. When she sent my work back, stapled to a sheet of her corrections (also, of course, in braille), there was a surprising intimacy in the knowledge that her fingers had passed over the same dots that I was now reading. Plenty of mailed correspondence has this sort of aura—the sense that the piece of paper in your hands was once held by your correspondent—but braille intensifies it, as you feel along each line, touching all the words that she's touched, down to every last morsel of punctuation.

Learning braille felt like becoming literate all over again. At first I labored over two- and three-letter words, averting my eyes so I wouldn't be tempted to learn visually, and the dots felt like a raw mash under my fingers. Then, gradually, the sensations in my index finger began to resolve themselves into letters, which slowly aggregated into words. I'd only learned the first seven letters of the alphabet, and each new word I read felt like a revelation. I read a *b*, then an *e*, expecting more letters, but my finger ran on smoothly into space, like Wile E. Coyote running off the cliff—oh. That's it, then—*be*. As soon as I deciphered it, the word lit up on the marquee of my mind's eye.

I spent a while deciphering *edge*. All the letters of the word seemed nestled and pressed together; in the beginning I had difficulty determining where one braille cell ended and the next began. It's much easier for the eyes to make such fine distinctions than it is for the fingers. My fingers' own edges buzzed with the friction of practice. Barbara Loos was right: I was pressing too hard, and I couldn't help but read too deeply into these first words of my life as a braille reader. Even with seven letters, they still sent powerful messages. *Cage!* What cage could the authors of this textbook possibly be describing but a mental one—they'd have written "the prison house of consciousness" if they'd had more letters to work with. Longer words brought the pleasure of achievement. I cheered inwardly as I carefully decoded *decade* and *cabbage*.

After two years of this, in half-hour increments, I was able to read grade-two braille (the more condensed, advanced version), unbelievably slowly. I still had to look up contractions or punctuation that I'd forgotten. I enrolled in a pilot program through the Library of Congress, and received a twenty-cell digital braille display on permanent loan. It was the size of an Amazon Kindle, but as thick as a novel. On its face were the same buttons that were on my braille typewriter, for entering braille text, but there was no screen: instead, a strip of 120 holes, comprising 20 braille cells, ran across the bottom of the device. It functioned much like the beefier 40-cell versions I'd seen in various offices: as the device's internal computer read a braille book file, it sent firm, rubbery pins up through each cell to display the first 20 characters of a sentence in braille. I'd run my fingers across the strip, reading the line, then hit one of the panning buttons. With a little clatter, the pins reassembled themselves to form the next 20 characters of whatever I was reading. (I'd have to advance the display 4 times to read the short sentence you're reading now.)

At first this device mystified me, and I left it in a box next to my braille station in the attic. But once I'd finished my last course, I brought it out again, and fell in love. Reading on the braille display was a palliative against my anxiety about going blind. The more facility I gained with it, the more I could imagine a rich life for myself as a blind reader. I signed up for Bookshare, an online book depository for print-disabled readers that has digital braille (and screen-reader-friendly) editions of more than a million books, including many that have just been published.

"The blind community never, ever had *anything* like it," Deborah Kent Stein, a writer I met at the NFB convention, told me. When she was a child, she could get braille books from the NLS, which mailed them to her one volume at a time (braille takes up a lot of space, and even short books require multiple telephone directory–size volumes), along with the talking books that played on specially designed portable turntables manufactured for the Library of Congress. Their catalog was large but, compared with your average midsize regional public library, still woefully limited. In time, these offerings expanded, but Stein often couldn't find the books that her friends were reading (or that her school had assigned), and had to wait a long time for other titles she wanted. Her mother developed polyps on her throat from reading aloud so much to her and her brother, who is also blind. Today, with her choices exponentially increased, she stockpiles digital books, downloading files by the dozen, "just in case." I told her she sounded like someone who grew up during the Great Depression, hoarding canned food even after it was available in abundance. "Yes, exactly!" she said. "We grew up in the book famine."

• • •

One of my biggest braille motivations is my love of reading aloud. I want to keep reading to Oscar for years, and then to potential grandkids or any other stray children who wander into my orbit. And reading aloud is crucial to my work as a radio producer—I have to be able to glance at a script or notes on the fly during a recording. When I finished my final braille course, Pamela Bortz told me reading aloud was a good way to keep practicing. She said I might start with some easy children's literature.

When I mentioned this to Oscar, he got excited, and suggested a bunch of titles. Even though he was reading *Harry Potter* and *Percy Jackson*, he was still a first grader, and enjoyed a good picture book too. That night, I wasn't sure he'd still be interested. "Should I read you a bedtime story in braille?" I asked. "Yes!" he said quickly, bouncing up and down. I warned him: It's going to be painful. I'm going to read to you like I'm a first grader, and not a first grader like you, who's so fluent at reading out loud. "I like that!" he said. "I love when you read like a first grader!" I think he loved it because it pulled me down to his level, or even below his level—the same pleasure of grown-up reversal that he took whenever I tried to haltingly learn the songs he played with impressive fluency on the piano. We went through some options on Bookshare, downloading *The Lorax*, a few Frog and Toads, and Daniel Pinkwater's *The Big Orange Splot*, which we finally settled on.

By the time I'd gotten the book loaded onto the braille display and hunted around for the first page, it was already past his bedtime, but I let him stay up late for this special occasion. I read so slowly that Oscar spent the whole book trying to guess the end of each sentence. "'When . . . the . . . paint . . . was . . . gone . . . ,'" I read, trying my best to push my speech toward something approximating fluency—buying myself time by stretching out the words dramatically, and infusing each! and! every! one! with feeling. It felt like pushing a truck down a driveway, hoping the engine might miraculously start even though I knew the battery was dead. "'When the paint was gone,'" I read again, buying time as I advanced the display to the next page, "'the . . . roof . . . was . . .'"

"Blue? Orange? White?" Oscar shot back, smiling big.

"'—blue. The roof was blue.'"

"I love this so much," Oscar said, in a voice that made it clear that he meant it. Partway through the book he realized he'd read it before, which only made the game of guessing the ends of sentences more fun.

Every other page had an illustration, and whoever had transcribed the book had inserted a bracketed "[Image]" where the illustrations would be. These were accompanied by useless descriptions. After the text described Mr. Plumbean painting his house in multicolored splotches, for example, we got "[Image: a house]." This identical description recurred several times through the book as the house took on different colors. Perhaps it's redundant to describe the image if it's already been conveyed in the text, but it still felt paltry, like the blind reader didn't matter. Oscar said, "I wish we could see the pictures," so I turned this into another game. "OK," I said, affecting a friendly kindergarten-teacher tone, "who wants to see the picture?" Then I'd add in a gruff deadpan: "Image: a truck." And he'd laugh, adding his own commentary, parroting mine: "Thanks a lot! That's very helpful! 'A truck!'"

"I feel bad for the blind kid reading this, though, who really does want to know more about the pictures," I said, unfairly pivoting into a pious teaching moment. Oscar was quiet. After twenty minutes, we still hadn't finished *The Big Orange Splot*, and it was now long past his bedtime. We left the last few pages for later.

• • •

At that time, the Perkins Library—Massachusetts's primary branch of the Library of Congress's free circulating braille book service—wasn't mailing any books out due to the pandemic. This is one downside of braille's intimacy: in a time when many people were still wiping down their groceries, no one wanted to run their fingers along the same brailled sentences that someone else had just touched. In lieu of the lending library, I took an absurd level of care in browsing Bookshare to find a first grown-up book to download for myself.

I had a number of false starts. I tried the stories of Flannery O'Connor, but even though the collection was an edition from a reputable publisher, the file I downloaded was riddled with strange typos. I later learned that in the early days of Bookshare, the service got all its books from volunteers—blind and dyslexic readers with flatbed scanners who diligently scanned each of the hundreds of pages of a book they wanted to read, then let their computer's optical character recognition software convert these scans to digital text. Then—maybe—they'd proofread them. The quality was accordingly uneven, and the selection was limited to what those blind people wanted to read badly enough that they were willing to scan it. They reminded me of the file hounds who ripped rare vinyl LPs onto their computers, uploading them to torrent streams linked from message boards—a Napster for blind bookworms. I later learned that Bookshare was, in fact, directly inspired by Napster: in the late nineties, Jim Fruchterman, who founded Bookshare, lived one house over from Eileen Richardson, Napster's CEO, and their teenage sons played in a band together. One day, Fruchterman's son showed him the platform (decades before Spotify, Napster first popularized cloud-based music distribution) and Fruchterman instantly thought of the thousands of blind people using his OCR software to scan books. When the first Harry Potter book came out, Fruchterman told me, a hundred thousand blind people scanned the book a hundred thousand times. What if he could create a "Bookster" platform, and have one blind scanner share the file with all the rest? A lawyer friend of his told him that this idea was, in fact, perfectly legal—President Clinton had signed the Chafee Amendment in 1996, freeing all literary works in accessible formats from copyright restrictions in the US. (He also convinced Fruchterman to choose a better name than Bookster for his new service.) Hundreds of publishers now just submit their finished books as digital files directly to Bookshare, as a matter of course, cutting out the scanning step, which results in much cleaner editions and a huge selection of new academic and trade titles.

I decided a potboiler was what I needed: something that would keep me turning the pages. I wanted a book whose sentences would be more likely to finish where I expected them to. I tried William Gibson's *Pattern Recognition*. It seemed appropriate given that the device I was reading it on, my chunky little twenty-cell Orbit Research digital braille display, felt like something out of a Gibson novel: retro-futuristic media tech, a little screenless computer that output a code developed by an unlikely collaboration between a blind nineteenth-century schoolchild and a French military officer turned inventor. As I made my way through the novel in bed one night (*écriture nocturne*, in its natural habitat!), Lily rolled over to ask what I was doing. I lay on my back, the braille display on my lap, my glasses off, and my eyes roaring with the flashes and floaters I always see in the dark. "Reading," I said, and she was momentarily baffled until she remembered that you don't need light to read braille. (It does, however, require warmth. The blind writer Jacques Lusseyran spent the winter of 1941 in occupied Paris, attending university by day, organizing for the French resistance in the evening, and starting in on his reading for the next day's classes at eleven each night. His family's apartment was heated by a single stove, and shut away in his quarters, he could barely feel its heat. "To be able to read braille," he observed, "the sense of touch does not function adequately below ten degrees Centigrade." As a result, Lusseyran wrote, "I had to keep the meager heat of an electric bowl only an inch away from my fingers." This warming bowl—a 1930s-era space heater—in Lusseyran's freezing bedroom struck me as the blind equivalent of reading by candlelight.)

After a few months, I noticed that as my fingers traveled from one end of the line to the other, my head would involuntarily make a similar movement, as though I were watching a slow-motion tennis game being played on the ceiling. I can't really stop myself from doing this, though I find it strange, a little like I'm possessed. After a lifetime of making unconscious head movements while reading, my brain must have made the connection with braille: as I travel across this invisible page, I ought to turn my head. This doesn't happen when I listen to a book, and it's another piece of evidence for the relationship between the visual and the tactile.

Perhaps the title of Gibson's novel was a draw for me too. *Pattern Recognition* was precisely my task at this stage: reading as much as I could until common word combinations like *of the* or *she said* felt as familiar under my fingers as they did when I saw them on the page. But I gave up on the Gibson novel after making it about a third of the way through. It turns out a techno-thriller isn't meant to be read painstakingly, at an underwater pace. It felt like listening to a punk record at half speed.

• • •

The Argentinian writer Jorge Luis Borges lost his vision—what he called his "reader's and writer's sight"—around the same time that he became the director of the National Library of Argentina. This put him in charge of nearly a million books, he observed, at the very moment he could no longer read them. Borges, who went blind after a long decline in vision when he was fifty-five, never learned braille. Instead, like Milton, he memorized long passages of literature (his own, and those of the writers he loved), and had companions who read to him and to whom he dictated his writing. Much of this work—he published nearly forty books after he went blind—was done by his elderly mother, Leonor, with whom he lived until her death at ninety-nine, and who had done the same work for Borges's father, Jorge Guillermo Borges, a writer who also went blind in middle age. (Borges's blindness was hereditary, and his father and grandmother "both died blind," Borges said—"blind, laughing, and brave, as I also hope to die.") Borges kept his job as director of the National Library, and he became a professor of English at the University of Buenos Aires. But literature had become, for him, entirely oral.

Borges decided to use the occasion of his blindness to learn a new language, and his description of the pleasure of learning Old English reminds me of my first forays into learning to read tactilely:

> What always happens, when one studies a language, happened. Each one of the words stood out as though it had been carved, as though it were a talisman. For that reason poems in a foreign language have a prestige they do not enjoy in their own language, for one hears, one sees, each one of the words individually. We think of the beauty, of the power, or simply of the strangeness of them.

In the newness of Old English, Borges found an almost tactile relief in the unfamiliar words, as though they were "carved," like the raised print in those first books for the blind printed in Paris nearly two hundred years before. But because Borges never learned braille, his experience of literature remained fundamentally sonic: "I had replaced the visible world," he said, "with the aural world of the Anglo-Saxon language."

In the same lecture, Borges listed the "advantages" that blindness had brought him, but they all strike me as banal, things he could have easily had as a sighted writer: "the gift of Anglo-Saxon, my limited knowledge of Icelandic, the joy of so many lines of poetry." He is pleased to have a contract from an editor to write another book of poems, provided he can produce thirty new ones in a year, which he notes is challenging considering he'll have to dictate them. This makes it sound like adapting to blindness for Borges meant, very simply, carrying on his work as a writer. "Blindness has not been for me a total misfortune," he said. "It should not be seen in a pathetic way. It should be seen as a way of life: one of the styles of living."

But in his poems and stories, Borges strikes a less sanguine tone about becoming blind. In "Poem of the Gifts," Borges observes the coincidence that one of his predecessors in directing the National Library, Paul Groussac, was also blind. The poem, which begins with the irony of God's granting him "books and blindness at one touch," is written in a slippery voice that may be Borges's, or Groussac's. "What can it matter, then, the name that names me," he says, "given our curse is common and the same?" Borges cannot distinguish between himself and "that other dead one":

> Which of the two is setting down this poem—
> a single sightless self, a plural I?

The transience of the writer's identity was a long-standing theme for Borges, one he developed in the work published after his blindness. "So my life is a point-counterpoint," he wrote in "Borges and I":

> a kind of fugue, and a falling away—and everything winds up being lost to me, and everything falls into oblivion, or into the hands of the other man.
>
> I am not sure which of us it is that's writing this page.

Written in the years following his blindness, Borges must have dictated both this story and "Poem of the Gifts," and both texts express a kind of authorial identity crisis. I wonder how much of this anxiety grew out of the loss of control he felt once he was forced to dictate his work. I've experienced a form of this anxiety myself, as I confront the loss of my visual relationship with language. Once I can't rely on sight to write anymore, will I, like Borges, no longer be quite sure who is writing this page? When I first tried writing with a screen reader, turning off my monitor to see what it was like, I had a flash of this dissolution: I typed too fast for the screen reader to keep up, so I wrote into a void, the words audible in my mind, but without any confirmation that they were actually being recorded on the screen. It was like writing in water, or calling out into the darkness. Even when I stopped, and the computer at last read the text back, my words sounded strange, echoed in an unfamiliar, mechanical voice.

But in between writing the first and second drafts of this book, my eyes have gotten weaker, and I now leave the screen reader on all the time. The anxiety of losing my own voice to the computer's has given way to a relief that I don't have to strain and stretch so much to see. I'm like a guy who could walk haltingly on his own if he had to, but it's so much easier to just use the crutches. I find myself looking away from the screen more and more, resting my eyes as I listen back to a paragraph I've just written. If I suddenly lost all of my residual vision tomorrow, I know I'd be overwhelmed, and the grieving process I've begun would be painfully accelerated. But I also know I'd be able to finish my work.

I'm still getting used to certain quirks—my braille display doesn't always show me paragraph breaks, and when I'm speed-listening to a book, the reader burns through the ends of chapters and on to the next without stopping. I have to rewind, slow down, and artificially re-create the resonant pause that the blank space on the page naturally offers a sighted reader.

But while I'm losing print, I'm not losing literature itself, which exceeds the eyes. The other day, with my phone's screen reader on, I was reading the newspaper at a pretty furious clip. I'd run across the obituary of Ben McFall, the legendary New York City bookseller who worked at the Strand for forty-three years. The piece ended by describing McFall's deep commitment to his work, even after the pandemic and his failing health had forced him into the Strand's corporate office, away from the line of friends and fans who would wait next to his desk amid the stacks to get a personal recommendation, or just to talk books. The obituary ended,

> Mr. McFall, who was so attached to his Strand name tag that he sometimes wore it around his apartment, chose to keep it on even though he no longer spoke to customers.
>
> It read: "Benjamin. Ask me."

I had the speech turned up so fast that these last two paragraphs—which didn't even register as paragraphs, since the babbling screen reader ignored the line break—took only a few seconds to read. And yet I still felt tears burst out of my eyes at that final image, of McFall's commitment: not just to the pleasure of solitary reading, but to the community of readers who sustained him to the very end. My response felt like a sign that however awkward it might feel to read this way, I still felt the power of that community; I'm still a reader.

7.

The Makers

One of the key scenes in disability history plays out like the start of a Hollywood movie (and, sadly, it contains as much invention and inaccuracy as the average screenplay). It goes something like this:

Ed Roberts rolled his motorized wheelchair up to a curb at the corner of Dana and Dwight. It was after midnight in Berkeley, California, sometime in the late 1960s, and it was hard to tell if the fragrance that filled the air was the snakeberry shrubs that lined the block or the pot smoke that wafted over them from a house party nearby. Roberts got a van ride down this street every day to get from his house to his job at the Physically Disabled Students' Program at UC Berkeley, where he'd just gotten his master's degree in political science. He would have preferred to avoid the rigmarole of the van, but the curb was a foot high, with no slope for him to roll up or down. His friend Eric Dibner, who often helped Roberts with daily tasks like getting in and out of the iron lung he slept in, would have had to lift Roberts and his heavy chair over the ledge—a dangerous, teetering proposition for Roberts, who was paralyzed from the neck down, and for Dibner, who didn't look like the sort of person who knew where Berkeley's athletic complex was located.

But they had a plan. Roberts had obtained some nitroglycerine from a friend who worked in one of Berkeley's chemistry labs. They had a vague notion to use it to detonate the curb and build a slope, but they hadn't had a chance to test it out in advance. Luckily, Dibner had also obtained a sledgehammer. With Roberts posted as lookout, Dibner swung mightily at the curb until it was rubble, hoping that the din from the psychedelic band jamming at the party down the block would give them cover. Once the corner was demolished, they mixed some concrete and smoothed out a new ramp. The next morning, once it had dried, Roberts would be able to roll his wheelchair to work on his own.

In their superb book *Building Access*, the disability scholar Aimi Hamraie calls this guerrilla intervention into the city's inaccessible infrastructure one of "the primal scenes of U.S. disability activism, securing the movement's place within the broader memory of civil rights–era direct action." But this scene is also (as Hamraie explains) largely a fiction. The reality of the actions Roberts, Dibner, and others took to make Berkeley's streets accessible to disabled pedestrians was a bit more, well, pedestrian: their actions involved city council meetings and organized protests, rather than contraband explosives and stolen construction equipment. (Dibner did admit to some DIY concrete pours on inaccessible sidewalks, though they took place during the day, without any destruction required.) But considering the impact their actions had on the city, the university, and the entire history of the disability rights movement, it's no surprise that Roberts and his fellow activists have a reputation for wielding sledgehammers.

After a group of wheelchair users (led by Roberts), who called themselves "the Rolling Quads," successfully lobbied the city council, Berkeley agreed to allocate $30,000 of its annual budget to install ramps on the city's existing curbs and on all new construction. These modifications are called "curb cuts"—slopes or ramps that allow a wheelchair to roll smoothly onto or off a sidewalk. Berkeley became the first city in the US to have a "planned, wheelchair-accessible route," and in the decades that followed, the curb cut evolved from activist architectural intervention to mainstream design feature in hundreds of American cities, now required by federal law.

The curb cut has become the prevailing symbol of universal design: the idea that designing for the narrow case of disability benefits everyone. Soon after curb cuts began appearing on sidewalks, it became clear that they were appreciated by many more people than just wheelchair users. Curb cuts helped parents pushing strollers, elders pulling carts, and little kids riding bikes, and today the "curb-cut effect" refers to any universal-design solution that follows this pattern, from the banal to the transformational. Kenneth Jacuzzi, an eight-year-old with rheumatoid arthritis, inspired his father in 1956 to develop a hydrotherapy pump that he retrofitted onto their bathtub, creating a low-impact massage for his son's joints. Ten years later, Jacuzzi sold his whirlpool tub as a mainstream product; it's since been enjoyed by millions of people without a need to relieve chronic pain. Closed-captioning, which allows Deaf and hard-of-hearing viewers to follow the dialogue in TV and film, has become ubiquitous in any setting—bars, airports—where someone might want to watch TV with the sound off. (It's also helpful for language learners.)

Information technology frequently has its roots in blindness. The world's first typewriters, it turns out, were designed for the blind. In 1808, the Italian inventor Pellegrino Turri built the first working typewriter for his blind friend, Countess Carolina Fantoni da Fivizzano. The American inventor Charles Thurber filed one of the first US patents for a typewriter in 1843, noting that his invention

> is specially intended for the use of the blind, who, by touching the keys on which raised letters are made and which they can discriminate by the sense of touch, will be enabled to commit their thoughts to paper.

In 1993, nearly fifteen years before the first Amazon Kindle was released, blind technologists developed a digital reading format that eventually became EPUB, the current industry standard for all eBooks. With this history as a guide, one can reasonably assume that our future will be shaped by the tech that blind and disabled people are pursuing today. Surveying blind listservs, social media channels, and the aisles of assistive-tech conferences, one sees ideas and technologies that will transform life for everyone, including advances in haptics (devices that use touch and vibration to communicate information), GPS mapping (bringing the detail of Google Maps indoors), and machine vision (allowing a phone's camera and AI to interpret a visual environment). Elon Musk may be excited about self-driving cars, but he's not half as pumped as most blind people I've met.

• • •

The adoption of accommodations like the curb cut, Hamraie demonstrates, is rarely as simple as its popular origin story suggests. As curb cuts spread across Berkeley in the 1970s, the Center for Independent Living (CIL), the successor to Berkeley's Physically Disabled Students' Program, which had grown to support a wide coalition of disabilities, found that the curbs they'd advocated for as wheelchair users weren't as universal as they'd imagined. Blind people complained that if the curb cut was installed too smoothly and gradually, they'd walk right into the street—they relied on the drop-off to signal that the sidewalk had ended. The CIL, in its spirit of "cross-disability consciousness," took these complaints seriously and decided to offset the curb cuts from the corners, out of the path of a blind pedestrian who's lined herself up with the street crossing. But this was sometimes impossible, when a fire hydrant or parking meter blocked the place where the offset curb cut might go. In these cases, the cuts might appear far from the corner, forcing the wheelchair user to roll on and off the curb in the middle of the block, navigating dangerously alongside traffic.

The founders of the independent living movement were adept tinkerers—the CIL offered a wheelchair and van repair shop modeled on the hippie bike kitchens that were popping up at the time. The last generation of children who contracted polio before the vaccine was introduced in 1955—many of whom, like Ed Roberts, grew up with limited use of their limbs—had circulated newsletters with instructions for DIY adaptive tools and wheelchair modifications since the 1930s.

The CIL group kept iterating. One nondisabled member recalled a particularly steep wheelchair ramp at the entrance to a Berkeley apartment building, which he'd sprinkled with paint and cat litter to give wheelchairs more traction. What if this sort of tactile surface on a curb cut could indicate the transition to the street to a blind pedestrian? The hack worked, and became an ancestor to the patches of bright-yellow bumps that appear on many curb cuts in US cities today.

This is, Hamraie suggests, the real curb cut effect: design that emerges from disabled communities that prioritize interdependence, ingenuity, and collaboration—and that is then co-opted by mainstream culture, eliding the role that disabled people play in making it. Access becomes something made for, rather than with or by, disabled people. It's a common story in blind history.

When blind people in the early twentieth century tried to devise a way of reading more quickly, for instance, the process transformed audio technology for everyone. In the 1920s, even as recording technology made huge leaps forward, brittle, heavy shellac 78 rpm records still played only three to five minutes per side. The Library of Congress program to produce braille books was only a few years old when Robert Irwin, the blind executive director of the American Foundation for the Blind, began exploring this new technology, researching how to extend the playing time on records in an attempt to open the possibility of a "talking book" that could bring literature to a greater number of blind people. Irwin worked with a veteran electrical engineer in the industry, and by the mid-1930s, they'd designed a record that played at a slower 33⅓ rpm, was pressed on a tougher acetate material, and fit fifteen minutes of audio on a single side. (In his history of the audiobook, Matthew Rubery notes that in these early experimental pressings, it took about twenty records to hold the average novel.) This was the birth of the LP, and the Library of Congress was soon distributing these talking books, along with the heavy-duty turntables that played them, which were produced (often by blind workers) as part of the New Deal. LPs weren't available to the general public for another fifteen years or so; in addition to producing the world's first audiobooks, blind people were also the first to listen to long-playing records.

Blind readers responded with joy to the new audible literature available to them, and the talking books program expanded over the next several decades. But some readers—particularly students, with looming term papers to write—complained that the single-speed playback was too slow. They wanted to skim or speed-read the way a visual reader would: there are few people, sighted or blind, who would choose to read *Hamlet* at the same speed that they will P. G. Wodehouse's *Very Good, Jeeves!* (both titles among the first talking books produced by the National Library Service). Some blind readers would actually crack open their talking book players in an effort to speed them up. In an article (cowritten with Jonathan Sterne) on "aural speed-reading," the disability-media scholar Mara Mills tells the story of Harvey Lauer, a student at a school for the blind in Wisconsin who was assigned *Ivanhoe* for class and couldn't bear the molasses intonations of the book's narrator. He and some classmates hacked their school's talking book player, "wrapp[ing] tape around the motor shaft to increase its circumference and thus drive the turntable faster." The result was *Ivanhoe* as read by a chipmunk, but at least they could get through their homework without banging their heads against the wall in frustration.

By the 1960s, breakthroughs in recording technology allowed blind listeners to accelerate sound playback without affecting its pitch—speeding up *Ivanhoe*, in other words, without turning the narrator into a chipmunk. Later on, it would be adapted to digital audio, and is now a standard feature on mainstream audiobook and podcast apps. Decades later, Mills writes, engineers and producers adapted this technology again, creating audio effects like beat-matching and Auto-Tune, which uses pitch-shifting to make synthetic melodies in vocal music. Songs like Cher's "Believe" and Kanye West's "Blood on the Leaves" can thus trace the origins of their singing-cyborg sound back to a piece of technology blind people helped perfect decades after devising their own hack.

The technologies underlying the internet also have their origins in the problems blind people encounter trying to access information. Engineers began developing tools that could convert print into electronic signals (what we casually refer to as "scanning" today) as early as 1913, with the Optophone, also known as a "musical print machine," which used selenium's light-sensitive properties to convert the shape of each letter in a book into a musical tone, in real time. Mara Mills sent me digitized recordings a blind reader made (in fact, it was Harvey Lauer, decades after his high school experiments with *Ivanhoe*), demonstrating how he used the Visotoner, a descendant of the Optophone. You can hear the fall and rise of a capital *V* as he reads, which under the eye of the Visotoner sounds like commensurately descending and rising musical notes. Some people managed to read entire novels using this system. As Mills writes, optophonic technology was later repurposed, and led to inventions as varied as the pulse oximeter (those little scanners doctors clip to your finger in order to measure your blood oxygen level and pulse) and the video-game light guns that, in elementary school, I used to hunt ducks on the original Nintendo Entertainment System.

But the technicians working on these primitive reading machines for the blind were skeptical that blind people would be able to learn an abstract code like musical print with any real efficiency, so in 1947, engineers at RCA, working on a more advanced version of the Optophone, developed a technology that didn't just indicate the shape of the letters, but could actually identify them—creating what (Mills writes) is "today widely considered to be the first successful example of optical character recognition (OCR)." This development paved the way for synthetic speech and machine reading, technologies that would have profound implications for the future of the internet.

• • •

In the late 1960s, Ray Kurzweil took an interest in the problem of machine vision. He was studying computer science at MIT with the artificial intelligence pioneer Marvin Minsky; at the time, OCR could recognize only specialized typefaces designed for testing in computer science labs. Kurzweil wanted to develop an AI that could recognize the type in any book or magazine, and after graduating, he founded Kurzweil Computer Products to do so, even though he says he wasn't sure what its precise application would be. In his futurist manifesto, *The Age of Spiritual Machines*, Kurzweil recalls that the purpose of the project came to him when he "happened to sit next to a blind gentleman on a plane flight, and he explained to me that the only real handicap that he experienced was his inability to read ordinary printed material." In this anonymous blind traveler, Kurzweil wrote, his solution had found the problem it was searching for.

In order to create a reading machine for the blind, he had to combine his machine-vision algorithm with flatbed scanning technology—the first of its kind—as well as more articulate synthetic speech. In 1976, his company released the Kurzweil Reading Machine, which claimed to be the first text-to-speech reader to recognize multiple typefaces.

The original KRM was the size of a commercial washing machine and cost $50,000 (the equivalent of more than $250,000 today). Kurzweil hired some of his collaborators at the NFB to travel around the country and train consumers on how to use it. Blind users recall the incredible slowness of the machine, which took minutes to process a single page of print before it finally began reading in a rudimentary synthetic voice that some people took hours to acclimate to. But it was also a game changer—for the first time, a blind person could take nearly any book off the shelf and have a computer read it to them, with no sighted intervention or code learning required, as long as they had access to one of these massive, exorbitantly priced machines. Kurzweil sold a few to public libraries and universities, and the NFB placed models for testing with blind executives and lawyers and in schools for the blind. But their first customer, according to Kurzweil, was Stevie Wonder, who heard about the machine in its initial publicity blitz on television. (Walter Cronkite ended his broadcast of January 13, 1976, by letting the KRM intone his famous sign-off in its robotic reading voice: "And that's the way it is.") Wonder loved his KRM, and in 1991 he bought a new model for Ray Charles on his sixty-first birthday.

The commercial applications for OCR were immediately apparent. The Kurzweil Reading Machine soon became the Kurzweil Data Entry Machine, and among its first customers was LexisNexis. The digital archive used Kurzweil's technology to scan reams of legal and news documents and became one of the earliest companies to make searchable databases of information available directly to researchers. This was a key step toward building the network that we know as the modern internet. Online repositories like Google Books and the Internet Archive—to say nothing of QR code readers and the synthetic voices of Siri and Alexa—all have the machine vision developed for the blind in their digital DNA. In 1980, the Xerox corporation bought Kurzweil Computer Products, gradually integrating OCR into its scanners and copiers. It took Xerox a few years to lay off the blind sales force it had inherited from Kurzweil.

Across the country, in Silicon Valley, Steve Jobs and Steve Wozniak spent the early seventies selling blue boxes—DIY hardware made from the newly available cheap electronic components one could find at a RadioShack. These devices produced tones and clicks that allowed their users—who called themselves "phone phreaks"—to make free long-distance calls, as well as poke around behind the scenes of the national phone network. Phone phreaking was rarely just about saving money on long-distance bills; instead, it was a playground for electronic experimentation, a foundational community of hacker culture. Before hackers built hardware and wrote code that allowed them to explore the backends of the internet, phone phreaks were soldering devices that let them travel the world through wires and patches, collecting visits to remote trunk lines like customs stamps in a passport. Years later, Jobs said, "If we hadn't have made blue boxes, there would have been no Apple."

And without blind people, there might not have been blue boxes. These devices had no screens or visual output: they were tactile buttons and audio output only. Their use required, among other qualities, an interest in spending large amounts of time messing with telephones—and thus a disproportionate number of these pioneering hackers were blind. In his seminal 1971 *Esquire* story, Ron Rosenbaum quotes one of these pre-digital hackers as saying that "the original granddaddy phone phreak" was Joe Engressia, "this blind kid with perfect pitch." Engressia was born blind, and from the age of three continually experimented with his family's phone. He discovered that he could mimic the tones the phone system used to initiate and end its connections by whistling a seventh octave *E* note—2,600 cycles per second, in telephonic terms. He later applied this skill (picking up the nickname "the Whistler" along the way) to make free long-distance phone calls. This party trick made him popular his freshman year at the University of South Florida, and he began an underground technical career that would eventually draw the attention of the FBI and land him in jail for a night. (Engressia deserves his own book-length biography, which would include a remarkable second act, when he legally changed his name to Joybubbles and declared himself a child, saying that because of the sexual abuse he experienced at a school for the blind in New Jersey, he never had a real childhood. The story of the phone phreaks, including Engressia, is memorably told in Phil Lapsley's 2013 book, *Exploding the Phone*, and Joybubbles is the subject of a new documentary film.)

One blind phreak recorded a library of telephonic tones (the sonic keys that offered entry into the phone trunks they wanted to explore) onto his Library of Congress–issue talking book four-track tape player. Others distributed hard-to-find 800 numbers (also helpful for their toll-free journeys into the underbelly of the system) and instructions for building blue boxes in samizdat braille directories. Decades before internet chat rooms, they linked their calls together into conferences, where they'd gather day and night, a free twenty-four-hour party line where there was always a blind phreak hanging on the line to chat, trade technical advice, or share their tale of a particularly epic chain of connections. They traveled around the world from their homes, across the continents, from circuit to circuit, just for the thrill of it.

• • •

At first I'd thought of blind techies as just another subculture, like blind skateboarders (definitely worth looking up on YouTube), or blind knitters, or blind birders. But the more I learned about blindness, the more I realized that tech-savviness was an essential skill for any blind person. Whether they're college students studying computer science or the crew of retired septuagenarians in my local blindness group, blind people of every persuasion are, to some extent, steeped in the lore of the listserv. They lurk on assistive-tech Facebook groups and keep up with the blind-tech podcasts. The life of a blind (or, really, any disabled) person can, in the most cynical view, also resemble one long troubleshooting session, punctuated by occasional moments of smooth operation. There's just so much trouble to shoot when you're blind.

Fifty years after the era of the phone phreaks, I traveled to the Bay

Area to meet their descendants. Staying with my dad in his apartment in Marin, I thought about how his own story is bound up with the history of the region: he cut his teeth in the counterculture, producing alternative radio and then TV in the chaotic anti-war underground media movement of the early seventies. Over the years, these interests pulled him into the Silicon Valley desktop computing revolution. He'd told me all about it. But now I saw that there was a third strand to recent Bay Area history that we hadn't discussed, but that nevertheless seemed directly connected with these other two radical Northern California traditions: the politically active, technologically innovative disability culture of the Bay Area—and Berkeley in particular. After he made me the same breakfast I'd been eating at his place since the 1980s—fake sausage on a thick slice of hippie bread—he drove me down the hill to the ferry, which carried me across the bay to the city, where I'd scheduled meetings with a few of the nation's finest blind troubleshooters.

• • •

The LightHouse of San Francisco occupies three floors of a commanding building on Market Street. It's a beautiful space, designed with Chris Downey, a blind architect who works with embossed building plans. The design firm Arup helps him to test the interior acoustics of spaces using software, in the same way a sighted architect might rely on a computer-generated model to understand how people will move through a building. "I tap my cane, they record that as a source file, and they put it inside the space," Downey told *Interior Design* magazine. "And you can hear how the sound evolves based on how the architecture shapes it. You can hear alcoves or openings—things you learn to listen for when you're using a cane." As I walked in, I noticed that there wasn't any carpet; the hard surface of the floor provided better audio cues—footsteps, cane taps. Approaching the front desk, I walked beneath a canopy of sound-dampening material, which meant that acoustically I could tell I was entering a new part of the wide-open lobby. (The LightHouse's director, Bryan Bashin, later told me that the canopy was made from "a German-made wood product that looked just like wood paneling but actually contained hundreds of holes and voids that soaked up the echo.")

I walked down a long hallway, my cane resonating pleasantly, to meet Erin Lauridsen, the director of access technology at the LightHouse. Her office was small, but it had an impressive view, up on the tenth floor, with plate-glass windows that framed the cityscape. As I gazed past her, it occurred to me that the view couldn't have been too different than one from the office of a mid-level programmer at Twitter, whose headquarters were just a few blocks down Market Street. Normally, a center serving the blind would be in an infinitely more modest space—more government facility than acoustically treated, space-age university—but in 2014, Donald Sirkin, a Seattle insurance magnate who'd lost his vision later in life and had never visited the LightHouse, left them a surprise bequest of $125 million. The donation, along with the leadership of Bashin and their Bay Area location, has made the LightHouse one of the most innovative blindness rehabilitation centers in the country. Along with the fundamentals that any such center offers—cane training, classes in braille and the use of screen readers, demonstrations of basic living skills like cooking and cleaning—the LightHouse also provides customized tactile maps, courses in soldering and programming, and frequent seminars with representatives from various Bay Area tech giants to test apps and advocate for better accessibility.

Erin told me that one of the things she loves most about the internet is that it gives her the ability to lurk. "I have this sense as a blind person that I can't blend in," she said. "I just feel *noticed*." One day she was waiting for an Uber at the airport, and a stranger came up to her and said, "You probably don't know this, but I take the train with you all the time." They meant it as a friendly gesture, but it just felt creepy. "The internet is a place I can observe things without being observed," she said.

Erin was born blind, and she grew up in a religious family in rural Oregon. When she was in high school, her mom didn't let her go to her school's sex ed class, inventing a story about how the school would produce tactile diagrams that would be too embarrassing for Erin to touch in front of the other students. Erin knew this was just a cover for her mother's religious objections—the school had no plans to produce tactile sex ed materials. Instead, she got her hands on a computer and found a sex ed book online, which she could peruse without her mother's permission.

This anonymity is a large part of the appeal of the internet to anyone who uses it. When e-commerce began to enter the mainstream, every other dot-com advertisement bragged about the pleasures of "shopping in your pajamas." But for blind people, shopping in your pajamas holds not only practical value (e.g., for those who live in rural areas, without access to public transportation) but also a psychic one—a relief from the weight of the sighted gaze.

A month into the COVID-19 pandemic, I did some online lurking of my own, attending a Zoom call for blind academics. I listened to them argue the merits of leaving their cameras on while they taught their classes, which had all suddenly moved online. A few refused to turn their cameras on at all, contending that it's an ableist assumption that everyone needs to be visible at all times. "I like being able to turn off their gaze," one professor said. "They don't need to look at me to learn the thing I'm teaching. This is a good time for them to be uncomfortable with that."

Internet culture also gave rise to the notion of the "life hack"—the idea that it's not just consumer electronics that can be tinkered with and perfected; everyday activities can be optimized as well. The web is now littered with instructions for how to hack everything from cooking polenta to jogging—and blind people are naturally eager to share their own strategies among themselves. Erin told me she hated waiting in the long line of BART riders that formed during rush hour at the entry points on the platform. Because she couldn't see the line move, she would often advance too slowly, and sometimes missed her train. So she'd started waiting just off to the side of where the door would be, and as soon as it opened, she'd charge in. She asked her friend, the blind technologist Josh Miele, if he'd tried this; when he told her that he did the same thing, she felt a huge sense of relief. "I'm not being a jerk!" she thought. Erin and Josh had hacked the BART system's train-boarding process.

At the end of our conversation, the sun had set, and Erin's office had grown dim. We said goodbye, and I made my way down to the street, where I leaned against a lamppost and communed deeply with my iPhone. Eventually I glanced up and saw Erin, leaving work and politely fielding questions about her guide dog from a homeless man, who held a dog of his own on a rustic leash. She made her way down into the BART station, which I was about to do, but I felt like I should wait a minute, as a courtesy. As I descended the escalator a few moments later, there she was, standing just as she'd described, off to the side of the spot where the incoming train's doors would open, next to a snaking line of commuters. The train arrived, and I watched her execute her subway hack, expertly sliding onto the train. I felt a little creepy observing her from a distance like this—like I'd become Gene Hackman in *The Conversation*, a spook surveilling persons of interest in downtown San Francisco without being seen. But then the doors of the train closed, and Erin escaped my gaze.

• • •

I'd also arranged to meet Erin's friend Josh, who had a reputation as the charismatic genius of the Bay Area blindness scene. (A few years later, he won a MacArthur "Genius" Fellowship for his work in digital accessibility.) He hadn't told me where he worked—the address he gave me was for an unmarked building not far from the LightHouse—but as he walked me inside, we stopped at a desk where a woman handed me a clipboard with an NDA attached. I saw the Amazon logo across the top, and only then did I realize where we were. Josh works at Lab126, the branch of Amazon that designs and engineers all of the company's devices—e-readers, smart speakers, and tablets. Josh's title is principal accessibility researcher, which means he makes Amazon devices easier (or simply possible) for people with disabilities to use.

One of the projects he was most excited about was a "show-and-tell" ability for Alexa, Amazon's voice-activated AI assistant. A blind person could hold a product up to their device's camera and say, "Alexa, what am I holding?" The artificial intelligence (a descendant of the same machine-vision technology that Ray Kurzweil used in the 1970s) would then try to identify it. Josh had programmed a series of contingencies for Alexa: If it failed to fully identify the object on its first try, the AI then looked for a brand-name indicator somewhere, so if it couldn't say, "That's a can of Amy's medium-spicy vegan chili," at least it could say, "It's an Amy's Kitchen product." (I wish I'd known about this technology when I was telling Lily we'd have to label all our cans of beans with braille.) Failing that—perhaps if the label was torn, or defaced, or held in the wrong direction—it'd fall back on identifying whatever text it could find on the object, in what Josh called a "graceful cascade of failure."

This is a perfect description of how many systems in robotics and computing are designed—failure as progress. Silicon Valley has long been obsessed with the innovative power of failure and breakage, co-opting Samuel Beckett's imperative to "fail better." It reminded me of the way I'd seen Josh navigate the lobby downstairs. His cane had collided with a trash can, and he corrected course, but veering into the trash can didn't seem like a real error. There was no embarrassment or confusion or even hesitation (the way there sometimes is for me when I bump into things in public), just a newly refined path. It was a collision in the same way, perhaps, that some biomechanical researchers have found that walking is a form of constant, unconsciously corrected falling. The collision gave Josh the information he needed.

Josh lost his sight when he was four years old, in a horrifying attack at his family's brownstone in Brooklyn. He'd run to answer the door, where he saw his neighbor's adult son, who was later diagnosed with schizophrenia. Josh opened the gate, and the man poured a cup of sulfuric acid that he'd extracted from a fire extinguisher over Josh's head, instantly blinding him. Josh learned basic blindness skills at the Industrial Home for the Blind in Brooklyn Heights, and then his parents sent him to a mainstream elementary school, P.S. 102, in Bay Ridge. His mother frequently took him to art museums, and encouraged him to touch sculptures and explore spaces that were clearly off-limits. "He would say, 'Mom, is this really all right?'" Isabella Miele told *The New York Times* in a story about the acid attack. She'd say, "It's OK. Do it." Josh wasn't interested in blindness as a kid, and he didn't hang out with other blind people. "My attitude was, 'I've met blind people, and they're losers,'" he told me. "Obviously I'm blind, I'm burned—I'm not trying to pass—but I wasn't embracing it."

Instead, he embraced machines. He developed a reputation as a tinkerer and a maker, and friends and family brought him their broken clocks, radios, and toasters, which he'd take apart to try to understand. Every birthday became an occasion for another kit: chemistry sets, model rockets, amateur radios. But these came with printed instructions that he couldn't read, and that his mom didn't really have the time or inclination to read and reread to him, describing the diagrams that explained which pieces went where. So he developed his own techniques, which might also be described as graceful cascades of failure, as he inferred how the pieces fit together.

It wasn't until Josh arrived at UC Berkeley that he says he met cool blind people. "They weren't ashamed of themselves," he said. "I became psyched to be blind." Berkeley had enough blind students—and enough of a history of disability rights activism—that they had their own study center. Nicknamed "the Cave," it was a suite of offices buried in the basement of the university's Moffitt Library. Cal's blind students all received funds to hire readers, whose function was primarily to read them their inaccessible textbooks and other school materials. These readers were usually fellow students, and they'd meet up in the Cave to make recordings of their handouts. "We had keys," Josh said. "Twenty-four/seven access. It was a den of iniquity. There's a millennia-long history of blind people and their readers sleeping together," he added, laughing.

In the fifties and sixties, Jacobus tenBroek, the founder of the NFB (and a Berkeley rhetoric and political science professor, as well as an alum), was a regular presence in the temporary trailer building that predated the Cave, using it as an office where he met with the blind students who congregated there. Over the years, Josh said, the space became "a hotbed of blind thinking." By the time he arrived, in 1987, it was also a cluttered assistive-technology archive. New devices entered all the time, but they almost never came out. It became a proving ground—and workshop—for blind tech. Josh and his cohort got to play with early screen readers, a Kurzweil reading machine, some of the first CCTVs, and even stranger gadgets like the Opticon, which translated ink print into a vibrating code. There was a thermoform machine that students used to copy pages of braille, but it wasn't long before Josh and his friends figured out that you could also use it to make grilled cheese sandwiches.

Josh declared a physics major, which required him to take a basic semiconductors lab. "Holy shit," he thought, "I've gotta build electrified circuits!" Soldering semiconductors was a very different proposition than the model-rocket kits he'd built as a kid. How could he manage serious electrical engineering without sight? A friend suggested he get in touch with Bill Gerrey, a blind engineer who worked across the bay in San Francisco, who had a lab at the Smith-Kettlewell Eye Research Institute (SKI). Gerrey taught Josh how to make his own accessible tools, analog meter readers, and continuity testers that gave audible rather than visual feedback. He also gave Josh his clearest sense yet that blind people were, by their very nature, makers. Gerrey published a blind-electronics newsletter; in its first issue, in 1980, he'd described this intrinsic aspect of blindness. "Visually impaired persons have adapted to their impairment by 'engineering' solutions to their difficulties," Gerrey wrote. "Whether a solution is an adaptive technique, re-allocating responsibilities in a job situation, or a modified monkey wrench, it is still engineering."

Josh hung around SKI for longer than he needed to just to pass his physics lab, and eventually Gerrey pushed a pile of components off a table to make a place for him. Josh has vivid memories of listening to Gerrey through his open office door, particularly as he fielded a certain type of phone call that came in about once a week. Usually they were recently retired sighted guys, pitching Gerrey their ideas for devices like laser-guided canes, or a phone that called 911 when you knocked it off a table. Gerrey was patient with these men, but Josh fumed at their condescension. Blind people had designed devices that unlocked the entire phone system, and yet these guys couldn't envision one of them managing to dial 911 on their own?

Studying physics at Cal, Josh decided he wanted to be a space scientist. After graduation, he got a job at NASA, but it was a far cry from the open world of experimentation he'd found hanging around Gerrey's lab, and he left after six months. "I will slit my wrists if I have to be a part of a bureaucracy like this," he said. He found himself at a crossroads: Would he keep pushing to work as an engineer in a mainstream STEM field, or would he return to the world of blindness and accessibility? "I didn't want to work in access," he said. "But I was the best person to do access. There were plenty of space scientists, but no one to make tech accessible."

Most accessibility operations, though, were run by sighted people; even when he worked at Berkeley Systems, one of the few tech companies producing screen reader software at the time, Josh was one of only two blind employees. Most of the blind people he knew in tech worked in sales—like the blind reps who worked for Kurzweil in the 1970s. The mainstream innovations that disability had inspired didn't seem to end up benefiting the technical careers of individual blind people. (The blind phone phreaks were largely thwarted in their desire to convert their illegal tinkering into work for the phone company, while many of their sighted peers—most spectacularly in the case of Jobs and Wozniak—went on to successful runs in tech.) Josh wanted to push back against the trend. "I wanted to be the blind person *inside*," he said. "Doing design, with authorship." Becoming a designer in blind tech was the best way to subvert the sighted inventors who wanted to build a phone that called 911 when you bumped into it.

Josh eventually made his way back to SKI, where he got his own lab, inventing technologies for tactile mapping and more intuitive ways for blind people to type on a touch screen. After twenty years in the nonprofit sector, when he moved from SKI to Amazon, it wasn't a move toward space science—he's still working in accessibility—but it was a move toward the mainstream. The crowdsourced YouTube audio description platform he built at SKI, called YouDescribe, had fewer than ten thousand users. The Amazon TV he's designing a built-in screen reader for, on the other hand, will be used by hundreds of thousands of people.

• • •

One of the most intriguing new technologies for the blind is the visual interpreter. The two major players in this space are Aira and Be My Eyes. Their users (Aira calls them "Explorers") aim their smartphones at whatever they need help identifying, and the apps transmit a video feed to a sighted person who can verbally interpret what they see. If you're blind and alone and want to know if your shirt matches your pants, or in which direction you need to walk to find your gate at the airport, or the results of an inaccessible pregnancy or COVID test, you can just hold up your phone and someone will guide you. (Within limits—for liability reasons, neither company will guide their users through traffic.) Aira received $35 million from VC investors, and Be My Eyes got more than $5 million. Venture capitalists don't put up this kind of money out of altruism: the expectation is that the tech will eventually have a wider application beyond the bounds of disability. Blind people using visual interpreters today are serving as R & D for a future of seamless video-chat tech support for everyone.

My mom has the Be My Eyes app on her phone, and she once helped someone read a recipe on a box of brownies. Another time, she helped a blind woman evaluate her outfit in the mirror. My mom was excited to talk with these people, thinking it was fun to have a random conversation about brownies with a blind stranger. But while she chatted at some length with the woman trying to match her clothes, the brownie lady was all business. Which makes sense—on the user's end, Be My Eyes isn't necessarily a social experience. They have a task they need done, and they're using this tool to help them do it. It's a bit like being an Uber driver: one fare will want to tell you her life story, while the next might barely acknowledge your existence.

Sighted friends, family members, and paid assistants of blind people have offered something analogous to these services for thousands of years. The apps, though, do it at a distance, in a way that can feel like it removes the human from the equation—or, at least, it creates that illusion of frictionlessness that so much of contemporary technology conjures. The feeling of computerized magic that accompanies ordering a product on Amazon and having it materialize on your doorstep later that evening obscures the chain of temporary workers who package and deliver it. For now, Be My Eyes guides like my mom are digitally present; advances in computer vision—the ability of a computer to distinguish a traffic cone from a toddler—have the potential to eventually render these intermediaries obsolete. The next generation of Josh Miele's show-and-tell Amazon device might be one that you can wear, and that will tell you not just how many people are in a room, but who they are, what they're wearing, even what their facial expressions are, and offer sonic spatial cues so you can walk down the street, weaving through a crowd and effortlessly finding the entrance to the store you're looking for.

The allure of any assistive technology is the independence it offers its disabled users. The blind Be My Eyes user doesn't have to rely on their family to read the brownie recipe to them—they can take care of it themselves, through their phone. There's a durable public perception that disabled people, by definition, need more help than everyone else, and that in the best cases, they might overcome their disability by finding self-sufficiency in a few basic daily living skills. But all technology is about extending human capability. We can't pound in nails with our hands, but holding a hammer, we become powerful building machines. Most of us can't comfortably travel hundreds of miles on foot, but with a car, we do so with ease. We don't tend to think of hammers or cars as assistive technology, but just as a cane or a braille menu does for a blind person, these tools give us abilities that wouldn't have been possible otherwise. It's the gap between what a disabled and a nondisabled person are expected to accomplish without technology that makes disabled people seem like they don't have independence. If you need a cane or a guide dog to safely cross the street, you're disabled; if you need glasses and a pair of shoes to get there, you're fine. But the relationship with the tools is the same.

Leaders in the NFB have been critical of the use of guide dogs for much of the federation's existence—dogs, they argued, with all their biological needs and vulnerabilities, were less reliable than canes, and thus went against their ultimate goal of true independence for the blind. Unlike a cane, a guide dog inevitably gets sick, or tired, or distracted. "If we are going to be first-class citizens in our society," one NFB leader wrote in the group's flagship publication, the *Braille Monitor*, in an issue devoted to the dog versus cane debate, "we must not mistake who is primarily responsible for our lives. We are." The NFB has tried to move past the contentious internal battles that accompanied its leaders' criticism of guide dogs, though the stigma persists among some old-school NFBers.

I feel this responsibility sharply in my own life—it feels infinitely better to call a Lyft than it does to ask Lily to drive me somewhere. But I also think it's important to make peace with the fact that to some degree, I am dependent on her. Just as she, in our life together, is dependent on me. It's possible to overstate the importance of independence, or to overlook what we give up to get there. Blind and sighted people can grow to depend on the very technology that's supposedly liberated them. If you structure your life around your ability to drive, or to videoconference with your employer, then the loss of a driver's license or high-speed internet is an instant, debilitating loss of agency.

Ray Kurzweil predicted that the unimpeded progress of the technologies he helped develop—machine vision, synthetic speech, artificial intelligence—would eventually lead to a future where "disabilities such as blindness, deafness, and paraplegia are not noticeable and are not regarded as significant." But Kurzweil's enthusiasm for this transhumanist future, where bodily difference gets absorbed into a kind of cyborgian democracy, erases much of what is interesting, powerful, and beautiful about disability. Blindness won't lose its unique phenomenological flavor once blind people can wear an implant that tells them where the exit is, or if their spouse is smiling. Disability is not, at its heart, a design problem—even if its lived experience requires daily feats of engineering and imagination.

When the blind sociologist Rod Michalko got a guide dog, an administrator at the training center told him, "It's really like a car for sighted people. You drive it for a number of years, and then get a new one." But Michalko's experience was radically different than this utilitarian view. He developed a profound bond with his dog, finding a "grace of independence" that he'd never felt trying to navigate the city with a cane. He and his dog, Michalko writes, have "achieved an identity which no longer depends on being alone and is not yet a complete togetherness of man and dog. It is an 'alone-together.'" With a living being, the possibility of interdependence arises: the needs of a guide dog that turned off many in the NFB—the grooming, rest, and bathroom breaks that they require—are all ultimately instances of the guide dog's need for *love*. This is the hybridizing relationship that drove the artist Emilie Gossiaux to sculpt herself as a human–guide dog mix, a "doggirl."

Many disability activists now emphasize interdependence over and above independence. They see strength not just in the heroic disabled person overcoming their limitations by adopting technologies that push their bodies closer to achieving what a "normal" body can do, but in coalitions and communities, sharing information and tools, as in the push and pull that created the curb cuts in Berkeley in the seventies, or the newsletter that Bill Gerrey distributed from his lab at SKI, connecting blind people with compatriots who could help them build the tools they needed.

In her writing and talks, the disability justice educator Mia Mingus expands the idea of access beyond accommodations like wheelchair ramps, captions, or audio description. Those are important, she says, but demanding them can make a disabled person feel like a burden.

Mingus advocates for what she calls "access intimacy." "Disabled people's liberation cannot be boiled down to logistics," she says. "The power of access intimacy is that it reorients our approach from one where disabled people are expected to squeeze into able bodied people's world, and instead *calls upon able bodied people to inhabit our world.*"

In this framework, access becomes something far deeper than a legal imperative, or even an act of inclusion. It becomes, Mingus says, an act of love. A gesture performed out of an intimate, vulnerable desire to connect with the other person on their terms. In 1967, shortly before he began working with Ed Roberts and the Rolling Quads to transform Berkeley's sidewalks, Eric Dibner worked as an attendant on the third floor of Cowell Hospital, which Berkeley had converted into a makeshift dorm to accommodate Roberts and others in the first cohort of severely disabled students at the university. Dibner's first job was with Scott Sorenson, who had myotonia congenita, a condition that, Dibner recalled, "caused his physical shape to be quite different from a non-disabled person's shape." At first, Dibner was uncomfortable: "I was dealing with something completely new to me in my experience," he said. But then he noticed that Sorenson was wearing a "psychedelic" button:

> It was this shocking green color and it had kind of an amoeba form and it said "mutate." And that just struck me as very—how can I say—it set my confusion aside, while placing me in a totally different realm of thinking.

This psychedelic amoeba was the nucleus of Dibner's successful career working as an attendant and a collaborator with people with disabilities without condescension or distance. It woke Dibner up to the fact that he and Sorenson were peers, part of the same countercultural milieu, and freed him up to dress and undress Sorenson without awkwardness. At their first meeting, Sorenson told Dibner, "I do all the training. We can explain what needs to be done. See, I need to be lifted and dressed." Dibner could relate to this work, he said, "because I knew how to dress myself. But the catch was, it required doing it from the disabled person's perspective." This is, I think, what Mia Mingus means by access intimacy—an interaction that accounts for the emotional and social nuances of the encounter, and that feels like an exchange rather than an accommodation. This kind of intimacy isn't generally sexual, though it can be: I recognize it in Josh Miele's stories from the eighties, of blind people in the Cave drinking and sleeping with their readers. The readers and their counterparts were simply fellow students, with all the libidinous, playful energy that goes along with that relationship.

I feel a budding sense of this dynamic with Lily, as she makes small, inconvenient, but important gestures we've developed together, like keeping her shoes off the stairs so I don't trip over them, or putting food back in the fridge according to our system, so I don't have to touch every bag and bottle to find what I'm looking for. (After I told her about Mia Mingus's idea, Lily now sometimes whispers "access intimacy" in a funny voice as she touches my back to let me know she's there.)

These are all acts of love. And love, by its very definition, always entails a surrender of independence.

Part III

Structured Discovery

8.

Against Blindness

Lily and I sat in a waiting room directly across from a woman wearing a beige double eyepatch and a black face mask printed with an elegant floral pattern. The combination of mask and eye bandages made her look like a person in the process of being erased, a Cheshire cat with just her hair and ears remaining. She chatted in a sort of desperate-casual tone with her friend, who sat two cordoned-off chairs away.

In the trough between the initial spike of COVID cases in April 2020 and the surge around the end of the year, I had booked another appointment at Mass Eye and Ear. I usually took a bus or train on my own, but even with cases dropping, mass transit seemed like an unnecessary risk, so Lily offered to drive. We left Oscar with my sister and headed to Boston. Even though it was morning, and we were visiting a hospital, it felt like date night, one of the only times we'd be together without Oscar in a year and a half. It was also the first time Lily had come with me to a medical appointment. She would've come earlier if

I'd asked her to, but I hadn't wanted to burden her with the torpor and anxiety I felt sitting all day in the hospital that treats my untreatable eye disease.

Lily and I looked away from this couple to a poster hanging on the wall. In letters arranged like those on the Snellen eye chart, it read ALWAYS LOOK ON THE BRIGHT SIDE OF LIFE. Speaking quietly, we agreed that this was a terrible decorating choice for an eye hospital waiting room, commanding a cheerfulness that few patients, we imagined, were willing or able to muster as they waited for news on their increasing inability to look at whatever remaining bright sides life might have to offer.

As I read the Snellen chart to a nurse, Lily sat beneath the letters, peering up and checking my work as I struggled. Afterward, she told me how struck she was by the experience of seeing the vision-measuring process from the outside. It was like she was visiting a movie set for the first time, impressed by her proximity to these famous letters on the chart—so close she could have touched them. When the nurse handed me a card printed with random words, to test my near vision—I had to hold it close to my face to read aloud: *"samovar, census, sword"*—I didn't have to look at Lily to know she shared my appreciation for this found poem.

As I took the visual field exam, squeezing the buzzer whenever I saw a pinprick of light appear in the chamber, Lily watched from behind the scenes. The technician marked the spots where I was able to see her light as she flashed it in slow loops around the field, eventually connecting the dots with a thin line, making a picture like a topographic map. Watching her draw these wobbly ovals, Lily didn't know what the baseline was supposed to be—that a normal visual field was the outermost ring preprinted on the page—and that what I could see represented a fraction of that. But once it was explained to her, she appreciated in a new way how narrow my visual field really was. I had about 8 degrees remaining in my right eye, less than 6 percent of a normal visual field, with slightly more in the left eye. These numbers had more meaning to her now.

At the end of the visit, we sat down to go over the results with my doctor. "The gestalt is the same," she told us—the total picture hadn't changed since my last visit, even if there were small changes in my vision. I'd mentioned my experience with the medical fellow from the year before, the one who'd breezily disabused me of my original prognosis: that my vision loss would accelerate as time went on. My doctor spoke carefully about the disconnect between what I'd reported to her—that it felt like I'd experienced another dramatic decline in vision—and what her tests showed, what she observed in her "gestalt." I'd lost more vision in my left eye than my right, but that eye had better acuity. We had to stay on top of a few related conditions—cataracts and a swelling in the center of my eyes—neither of which was disastrous, but that still warranted careful monitoring and treatment. My overall vision loss was, she said, "slow, subtle, and *present*."

Slow, *subtle*, *and present* is such a strange way to experience a phenomenon like blindness. It's so much easier to conceive of it as a binary—you're either blind or you're not; you see or you don't. Even degeneration is more easily apprehended within an either-or framework of collapse. Sure, things are crumbling, but what we all really want to know is, When will the dam burst?

Talking about the rate of my photoreceptors' death with Lily and my doctor, I was thrown up once again against the perverse feeling of wanting her to tell me I was going blind more quickly than I was. Let's just go all in on the catastrophe, shall we? A graver prognosis would justify my feeling that seeing had in fact become dramatically more difficult. My friend Will Butler told me that during the period in college when he lost the bulk of his vision, he got a "rush" whenever his sight took a new precipitous decline. Calamity can be intoxicating. I thought again of his injunction to me, over burgers at the NFB convention, that at some point I'd need to just have my "going blind" moment, and then be done with it. But looking around the room with my porthole of good vision, I knew I wasn't ready to let it go quite yet.

"What about my original prognosis?" I asked the doctor, already knowing the answer. I made her tell me everything again, and I pushed back again, and she had the final word, again. "I'm not seeing an acceleration or a degree of change, especially over four years, that makes me think you're at some kind of precipice with your vision," she said.

Still, I wanted more. I wanted her to admit that things were falling apart, and I wanted to know what would happen when they fell apart, even if the answer was simply that things fall apart. She acknowledged that despite her sense that there was no reason to expect an imminent decline, there was also no way of knowing for sure, and the clinical fact remained that RP "inherently changes."

"I also think that as RP gets advanced, or people live with it longer," she added, "it takes a little less structural change for it to have a bigger day-to-day functional impact for them, in terms of how they experience their vision." I told her that I'd found a financial metaphor useful for thinking about this—the way the rate of decay could feel like it's accelerating even if it wasn't. Say you have $100,000 in the bank: a loss of $100 a month doesn't feel like a big deal, even if there's no income coming in. But once you're down to $1,000, each monthly withdrawal comes as a catastrophic blow. "How did you go bankrupt?" a character in *The Sun Also Rises* asks his friend. "Two ways," the friend says. "Gradually and then suddenly."

There have been advances toward a treatment for RP since I was diagnosed, but none has ever had any direct bearing on my case, and my eyes glaze over when I try to follow the research. The bottom line has remained, for me and for most people with inherited retinal disease, that no treatment is available. Every conversation I've had with a retinal specialist on the subject goes the same way: a semi-apologetic confirmation that at present, there's still nothing to be done, followed by some muted enthusiasm about the incredible work occurring in clinical trials, and the sense that by the time I've lost a lot more vision, there could even be something on the market that could help me. The field seems to be in a permanent state of promising development, and I feel more or less resigned to the fact that if this promise is ever realized, it will be long after it's of any use to me.

• • •

The cells in the retina that die from RP—rods, and eventually cones—are, like brain cells or teeth, typically thought to be incapable of regenerating on their own. We get what we're born with, and they're meant to last. But scientists have figured out a way to extract stem cells—the kind of cell that serves as the base from which all specialized cells in the body can emerge—and use them to grow a healthy retina in the lab. The goal is to insert these healthy growing retinal cells into the eye, and hope that the body accepts and reproduces them, filling the eye back up with healthy photoreceptors. But the body tends to reject foreign biological material (which usually enters in the form of a virus), and the retina in an advanced RP patient often becomes an inhospitable place. There's also likely a narrow window of applicability—implant the stem cells too soon, when the patient has too many healthy retinal cells, and there's no point. Too late, and the retina has become a hopelessly toxic wasteland, with no chance of regeneration. For the treatment to be effective, the patient will have to be in a sort of Goldilocks zone. In 2021, a phase-two clinical trial injected six million of these stem cells that had partially developed into healthy retinal cells into the eyes of RP patients, with promising results. Participants experienced improvements in vision, reading new letters on the eye chart and reporting improved sensitivity to contrast. But the trial excluded patients with visual fields smaller than 20 degrees, whose paltry number of remaining rod photoreceptor cells gave them "a low potential for restoration of their cone function." I'm a member of this ineligible group.

"If I could pull out my wishful prescription pad," my doctor said, "and prescribe something for you right now, it wouldn't be stem cells." She acknowledged that the research was promising, but that she got most fired up about gene therapies. Since they'd found the particular mutation that caused my RP, scientists could now theoretically develop a targeted, personalized treatment that would replace my misspelled gene with a corrected version. These therapies have already been developed for other genes—the first FDA-approved, gene-specific therapy for any inherited disease was administered in this very clinic, by one of my doctor's colleagues, in 2018. That therapy, Luxturna, wouldn't do anything for me, but for those whose RP is caused by a mutation on the RPE65 gene, the effect is transformative. Researchers described scenes that called to mind New Testament miracles: children putting away their canes, reading print with comfort, seeing starlight for the first time.

Developing gene-replacement treatments is incredibly expensive—if the stem cell approach is like shopping at a furniture warehouse, where the same couch could fit in any number of homes, targeted gene therapy is like buying a handmade, custom sofa. Researchers estimate that between one and two thousand people in the US have the RPE65 mutation, and Spark Therapeutics priced Luxturna at $850,000; as one CNBC financial analyst astutely observed, that's $425,000 per eye. Researchers hope that a single treatment—one very expensive tenth of a milliliter in each eye—will last a patient's lifetime, but the treatment is so new that there haven't been any studies on its long-term efficacy.

My doctor said she'd love to be able to offer me a Luxturna for MAK, my particular mutation. But this is also a distant possibility. There are dozens of genes whose mutation causes RP, and new ones are discovered every year. Every genetic subgroup wants its own Luxturna, but very few of us are likely to see one developed for our tiny cohort. The largest MAK study to date had only twenty-four participants: it determined that one in fifty-five Ashkenazi Jews are carriers, but the disease only manifests if two of those carriers happen to have a child together.

At the University of Iowa, where the MAK mutation was discovered in 2010, a fund known as Project MAK supports a group of scientists led by Dr. Edwin Stone. Amid their other work on inherited retinal diseases, these scientists are developing therapies for my form of RP. The project's funding is spearheaded by Theodore Hersh, a retired physician with the mutation. As nice as it would be for Project MAK to find a breakthrough, there's also something that turns me off about the idea of focusing on this tiny group, of which I'm a part. It feels like the most solipsistic charity imaginable. I wish them luck, but fighting this narrow slice of blindness doesn't strike me as the best way to help blind people. I'd sooner increase my recurring donation to Bookshare, the accessible digital library for people with print disabilities.

My doctor seems most excited about a technology called CRISPR, whose developers shared the 2020 Nobel Prize in Chemistry. In explaining how it works, she compared a single gene with a chapter of a book. The MAK chapter of my genetic book—more of an instruction manual—has a misspelling that results in a few key errors that make my photoreceptors degenerate over time. Gene-replacement therapy, like Luxturna, inserts a clean copy of the entire chapter, so the degeneration stops and healthy photoreceptors are produced. This pause in degeneration is why gene replacement is most appropriate for early stages of the disease, and Luxturna has mostly been administered to children with RP. In some cases, though, a gene is too large to be replaced outright—it doesn't fit in the viral delivery truck the therapy deploys. CRISPR is more precise: the treatment sends a pair of molecular scissors—enzymes called Cas9—that finds the misspelled gene, cuts it open, and actually edits the typos in the genetic sequence directly. But research into treating RP with CRISPR has yet to reach clinical trials.

• • •

I have a Google alert set for "retinitis pigmentosa," but I've been deleting the alerts I receive without really reading them for nearly twenty years. When I do bring myself to scroll through one, it offers a revealing, dispiriting cross section of how the world thinks about disease and blindness. Most of the links lead to biomedical investment blogs, written in the artificially intelligent style of search-engine-optimized content and geared toward potential investors, about the earning potential of various publicly traded biotech and pharmaceutical companies developing experimental treatments for rare eye diseases.

Nestled among these reports, there's often a new scientific paper, along with the halo of summaries that attend its release. These are written either in the hyper-technical jargon of medicine or the gushing language of the corporate press release. Every once in a while, I'll try to read a scientific paper closely, mustering a determination to care about what it says. "A hypomorphic variant in EYS detected by genome-wide association study contributes toward retinitis pigmentosa," I read, before blinking a few times, and then impulsively smashing the Delete button. How about a press release, then, to cleanse the palate? These documents promise breakthroughs, making leaps toward "curing blindness" and "saving sight," while in the next paragraph the legal department swoops in with an elaborate, almost gymnastic series of caveats whose absurdity makes me appreciate the elegance of my doctor's thoughtful hedges by comparison. They all essentially say, This breakthrough technology will cure blindness and you should invest everything in our company, but you can't sue us if we fail spectacularly and the only blindness we cure is that of a few mice in our lab.

The last element in the Google alert digests—and the only part I read with any regularity—is the human-interest stories that appear every week in local newspapers from around the world. These are stories about people with RP who take painting classes, run triathlons, or start small, often disability-oriented organizations with sight-punning names like Insightful Visionaries. (If the organizations don't adopt a visual pun in their name, the newspaper's headline writer picks up the slack, titling the story something like "Finding Her Focus.") These profiles almost always describe the blind person as one who "suffers" from RP—a "blinding disease"—but who's managed to devise a way to "overcome" their blindness, either through riding tandem bicycles, fundraising, or starting their own small company. They've found their way toward, if not a normal life, then at least something that isn't suicidally terrible, as it presumably would be without these leisure activities or business opportunities. The piece often ends with a guide dog doing something cute.

I find all of this extremely depressing, so I largely avoid it, and as a result my sense of the state of the research with respect to RP treatments tends to be years out of date. As my doctor spoke about clinical research possibilities, I mentioned a prosthetic retinal technology I'd heard about, the Argus II, which has always struck me as a kind of RoboCop treatment for blindness. She smiled. "That's like the clamshell cell phone," she said. Artificial vision had made strides since I last bothered reading a Google alert about it. In the 1970s, RP researchers like Eliot Berson focused on vitamin supplements and the nascent field of genetic therapy. But Berson and his colleagues also employed a surprisingly mechanical approach to vision restoration. Berson was the founding director of Mass Eye and Ear's lab for studying inherited retinal diseases (funded in part by Gordon Gund, who lost his sight from RP in his thirties and, with his siblings, inherited the billions his father made from the Sanka decaf coffee company and a major stake in Kellogg's). Berson developed an optical device—all these machines resembled different species of cumbersome, futuristic goggles—that expanded a low-vision patient's field of vision using magnifiers and mirrors. To me, it seemed like something that belonged to the realm of braille displays and synthetic speech processors, not medicine. But of course, if a clinical researcher is concerned above all with saving sight, and biological interventions aren't getting them anywhere (as they weren't for decades), devices like these were at least a way to offer a concrete form of help. Today you can pay $5,000 for a field expander: a pair of goggles fitted with cameras that take the image of the world around them and adjust it to capitalize on their wearer's residual vision, allowing them to see more than they otherwise could, while an onboard processor algorithmically corrects the image for contrast, brightness, and scope.

In the 2000s, this wearable technology began to bleed into the biological. In 2013, the FDA approved the flip phone–grade device I mentioned to my doctor, the Argus II. It requires an ophthalmologist to surgically implant a microchip into the retina of a patient with RP; the chip then wirelessly communicates with a giant pair of goggles they wear. Cameras in the goggles send encoded visual information to the chip, which uses an array of electrodes to artificially stimulate the cells at the back of the eye. The Argus II is a prosthetic retina, and unlike the field-expander goggles, it allows people who've lost all of their sight to see basic shapes. Years ago, when I watched the demonstration video, I was impressed (and a little horrified, though I couldn't have quite explained why) by the image of a woman who had been totally blind from RP for years tracing a glowing white *X* on an otherwise black TV screen in a darkened room.

But the Argus II doesn't restore sight in any traditional sense, and ophthalmologists warned patients that, as with cochlear implants, the distance between what a healthy sense organ provides and what an artificial one can give you is vast. This is why my doctor compared the device with a flip phone: in spite of its medical miraculousness—demonstrable, usable artificial vision!—the results are, in practice, underwhelming. "The vision generated by the Argus II device is very different from sight," a paper offering guidelines for implementing the device warned, "and the patient must be ready to learn a new 'language' of sight." The paper went on to provide a list of tasks that patients with the Argus II prosthesis have been able to perform: "locate doors, windows and elevators; use a crosswalk to cross a street; locate coins; locate utensils on a table; locate but not identify people; and track a ball or players on a field." Most blind people I've met are able to do all these things without a prosthetic implant, using their orientation and mobility skills, hearing and touch, residual vision (if they have it), or occasionally the help of an app on their phone. The irreversible electronic intervention into the sensorium itself, along with the potential complications, hardly seems worth the low-res experimental vision the prosthesis provides. (That's easy for me to say, of course, with my scrappy core of good central vision still hanging in there. I might feel differently when that's gone.) The chance that the device could become exposed in the eye and muck things up is real, and the paper warned of the potential for the implant to erode or even burst.

These solutions are all subject to the whims of the bioengineering industry. In 2020, Second Sight, the company that produced the Argus II, was close to bankruptcy, and stopped supporting customers who needed replacement parts, upgrades, or consultation. It was like having an old-model laptop that's no longer supported, except instead of a laptop, it's a device that's been surgically implanted in your eyeball. In 2022, Second Sight merged with Nano Precision Medical (NPM), an "emerging biopharmaceutical company." None of Second Sight's leadership survived the merger, and the CEO of NPM told *Spectrum* magazine (in a harrowing investigative article called "Their Bionic Eyes Are Now Obsolete and Unsupported") that their priority going forward would be NPM's drug delivery device, not bionic vision.

A more promising avenue is being developed using optogenetics, a new branch of neuroscience that uses light to activate neurons in the brain and elsewhere in the body. Dr. Sheila Nirenberg at Cornell University's Weill Medical College claims to have "cracked" the brain's neural "code" for processing images, and her device aims to stimulate the optic nerve with the same set of encoded impulses that a healthy retina would. Unlike the Argus II or similar devices, which talk to the retina through electrodes, Nirenberg's device inserts light-sensitive proteins into the eye that directly stimulate the optic nerve itself, what

Nirenberg calls "speaking to the brain in a language it can understand." (Her research into deciphering the neural code of the eye won her a MacArthur "Genius" Fellowship in 2013.) If her device works, it promises blind users vision that's far closer to a complete image than the low-res pixels that the Argus II or its more sophisticated descendants offer. After testing it in mice (researchers screened little movies for the mice, and then recorded their eye movements), the device went into clinical trials in 2020. In preliminary results, completely (and near-completely) blind RP patients experienced a twenty-fold increase in light sensitivity, and those with a higher dose of the therapy experienced a hundred-fold increase. These results don't translate to patients seeing the faces of their loved ones, and they're not a lot better than what the previous generations of artificial retinas have accomplished: while they wore their VR-style goggles, this handful of patients could detect light, motion, and, in two cases, the direction of motion, but it was still basically white lines on a black screen. The ganglion cells (which translate images from the retina's photoreceptors into the brain), unlike our auditory nerves, are far from uniform, and they fire in a complex, interrelated series of on and off channels that even sophisticated optogenetic switching has difficulty reproducing with precision. But this trial was primarily designed to test the safety of the therapy in humans, and in subsequent trials, Nirenberg will up the dosage even higher.

Nirenberg named her prosthetic retina Bionic Sight, and in interviews, she's said that her vision for the device extends even beyond its purported goal of restoring acuity and a full visual field to blind users. "There's a potential to enhance it," she told NBC, "so we could also include ultraviolet light, or infrared light. We could make blind people actually have *better* vision in some ways than *we* do. And I like the idea that if you've been blind, and so you're always on the side of being the 'challenged' person, that now you'd be the *bionic* person, now you'd have all these extra advantages—you could see things that regular people couldn't see." Then she added, as though she were considering this idea for the first time, "Seems fair."

But what value would the ability to see ultraviolet or infrared light have for anyone? Would it be a kind of medical cosplay, the private pleasure of watching a phantom stream burst out of the remote control and leap toward the television, like Harry Potter's wand-fire? Nirenberg's research has powerful implications not just for restoring sight in people, but for enhancing machine vision in robots, from assembly lines to self-driving cars. (She is also the founder of Nirenberg Neuroscience LLC, "an artificial intelligence company with proprietary software that allows us to develop powerful new computer vision technology.") Her notion of giving people superhuman vision (while simultaneously contemplating its remunerative applications in the commercial sector) recalls the transhumanism of Ray Kurzweil, with his vision of a techno-utopia where humans and machines become indistinguishable from each other, funded by technology startups that begin with disabled consumers before entering the mainstream. But her comment also belied a kind of medical hubris, glorying in her ability to bestow bionic powers on a blind person in order to compensate for their experience of disability. I see her fanciful idea less as a source of empowerment, as she seems to intend it, than as a way of preserving the image of blind people as separate from sighted people, even after they've been cured of their blindness.

Contemplating these treatments, I run up against a basic contradiction: I've been searching for blind mentors, people who in their inhabiting of blindness make it seem not just like something that can be overcome, but like something that's intellectually productive, interesting, even cool. But the medical world is by definition positioned *against* blindness—in a way that makes it hard to conceive that some blind people (particularly those blind from a young age) might *want* to remain blind, or that being blind has any value in and of itself. Does having pride in one's blindness mean letting go of a hope for a cure?

Many Deaf people say they'd prefer to be Deaf than hearing, and intentionally find partners with the same genetic cause of deafness to ensure that their children are Deaf, too, celebrating the large Deaf family trees they're a part of and the linguistic and cultural community and traditions they pass on. But while I've encountered plenty of proud blind people—nearly everyone I met at the NFB convention fits that description—it's comparatively rare to find a blind person who looks at research into curing their disability with the same animus that Deaf activists do. The prevailing view—and one that resonates with my own experience—is well expressed by the disabled feminist scholar Alison Kafer, who writes, "As much joy as I find in communities of disabled people, and as much as I value my experiences as a disabled person, I am not interested in becoming more disabled than I already am." Disability has likewise become a rich new source of knowledge, community, and experience in my life, and yet I have no interest in courting, extending, or preserving it.

• • •

The adversarial idea of blindness is visible right in the name of the primary engine of research behind many of its treatments: the Foundation Fighting Blindness, the largest retinal-disease charity in the US. Deborah Kent Stein, the blind writer I met at the NFB convention, told me, "When I hear 'the Foundation Fighting Blindness,' I hear 'the Foundation Fighting *me*.'"

I share some of Debbie's antipathy to the tragic air that the FFB projects. Not long after the Ice Bucket Challenge went viral, the FFB's marketing team sought out a way to imitate the ALS Association's fundraising success. The "How Eye See It" Blindfold Challenge encouraged people to post videos of themselves blindfolded (wearing sleep masks distributed by the FFB, custom printed with the #HOWEYESEEIT hashtag) while performing basic tasks—the foundation's suggestions included activities like baking, cutting hair, going out to lunch, and even minding a toddler. The campaign was featured on the *TODAY* show, and hundreds of people posted their responses online.

The backlash came swiftly. Imagining that a blind person experiences their entire life with the fear and disorientation that come in the first minute or two after a sighted person puts on a pair of sleep shades is a dangerous error. It reinforces the idea that blindness is scary, and that a blind person is necessarily fumbling and incompetent. (Blindness has reliably appeared at or near the top of the list of "most-feared disabilities" in polls and surveys for decades.) The FFB had explicitly played on these stereotypes in order to raise money: *Look how terrifying and impossible blindness makes your life*, the campaign suggested. *Wouldn't you want to help to put an end to it?* The NFB was scathing in its response, pointing out cases of children who'd been separated from their blind parents by social workers, based solely on misconceptions about the ability of a blind person to care for their child. As part of their campaign, the FFB posted an ominous video called "What Would You Do If You Couldn't See Your Child?" that showed a silent image of children playing as the focus got progressively blurrier. Such fearmongering could lead, the NFB argued, to further family separations.

The FFB's methods of promoting its research initiatives may (on occasion) be ableist and retrograde, but I still sometimes feel seduced by the promise of a cure. How could I not be, even if the vacillation between acceptance of blindness and hope for its defeat (or delay) is painful? When my rod cells deteriorate to the point that the cones start to go, too, and my central vision collapses, I might feel differently. If Bionic Sight or any of the other artificial vision technologies have advanced to the point where a surgery will allow me to see the faces of my family again, along with everything else—wet forests, printed matter, good paintings, and on and on—it will be difficult to justify resistance to treatment, even if that vision retains (as it likely will) distortions and interference and doesn't really feel like vision at all.

As a heavy iPhone user who reads science fiction, listens to electronic music, sometimes wears a Fitbit, and spends all day interfacing with my computer, I ought to be excited by the prospect of life as a cyborg. But when I imagine the future—Oscar's high school graduation, ten years from now, has become a kind of landmark, the backdrop that I most frequently see when I picture the future—I'm a lot more comfortable with the image of me as a standard-issue human blind guy,

Lily whispering the visual highlights of what's happening on the graduation stage into my ear. That's a much happier image, somehow, than one where I'm wearing massive optogenetic goggles and watching the proceedings like a proud, fatherly RoboCop, or Predator, as though I'm viewing it on a security camera broadcast through a weak transmitter.

Most days I really do feel like my growing blindness is not to be feared. It isn't a death sentence. Reading braille is marvelous, and blindness opens up interesting hermeneutic and epistemological questions that I could spend the rest of my life exploring. A full and joyous blind life is indeed possible. But this attitude is instantly and entirely shaken whenever I'm forced to consider the possibility that Oscar might have RP. Lily has admitted that she was reluctant to get tested because she was worried I'd read her anxiety about the outcome as a rebuke—as though she were telling me, "I'm so distraught that he's going to grow up . . . *to be just like you!*" As though I'd shout in reply, "And what's so bad about *being like me*, may I ask?"

But I would probably be at least as distressed as she was. Mixed in with the anguish, of course, I'd feel confident in my ability to guide him through the experience, offering him the blindness mentorship that I never had, at his age. I'd also probably become one of the parents I've encountered through the Foundation Fighting Blindness. The most vocal component of the FFB's membership is sighted parents whose children have been diagnosed with a retinal disease. The prospect of blindness seems far more devastating to a sighted parent of a blind child than it does for the child themselves.

Still, I've gradually come around to Lily's view: What would genetic testing actually change for us? Would it benefit Oscar in any way?

There's nothing practical we could do differently if we learned that Lily was a carrier, besides steering Oscar away from careers that require sight. The idea of my saying "Forget about the air force, son" is repulsive and absurd. In all likelihood, a positive genetic test now would just add an unnecessary layer of anxiety over our daily lives. Better to leave it as an unknown question, lingering in the far distance.

• • •

Lily hadn't really learned any new information from my ophthalmologist—I'd told her all of it before. But my explanations had always been variable, fuzzy, and mired in the day-to-day, always coming with an interruption from Oscar, or as she was trying to get dinner on the table, or while we were exhausted and capable of little more than watching twenty minutes of TV and falling asleep. The trip had stripped all that away, and afterward, her relationship to my blindness changed. I had worried that having her there would feel like being a child accompanied by my FFB parent, who would speak to the doctor as I passively listened. But that's not how it felt. She'd carefully watched the visual field exam being drawn, she'd considered the tiny holes of remaining sight in the center and the tough little strip of peripheral vision still hanging on, and she'd thought about the prospects for how long they'd remain. Perhaps most important, she had begun to wonder more seriously what it would be like for me—and her—when they did contract further.

In part because of the power of medical authority, coming with me to the hospital had a profound impact on her understanding of how I saw the world. This felt like an extension of the classic marital dynamic, where I make a determination about something—like what could be wrong with our sink—and she won't believe me, but when the plumber comes and says the same thing, it's suddenly true. But I think the experience of seeing me in the medical theater, under the bright lights of the ophthalmoscope, also restored me to the status of patient, of disease sufferer. It restored the flavor of medicine and illness to my blindness, which in our day-to-day had stopped being legible to her. I don't necessarily want to be medicalized in her eyes—I want her to see past my blindness, through to the core person she married. But at the same time, this awakening felt like a necessary step toward her acceptance and comfort with it.

Strangest of all, I felt like I understood my vision better. I hadn't learned anything new at the eye doctor either—the "gestalt" and even the diagrams of my eyes had looked the same as they had the year before. There had been some melt, but the ice on the whole was holding its shape. But now I was returning home with someone who had a new, up-to-date, in-depth, and clinical appreciation for what I could see, and what I might expect to see in the near future. In the kitchen, when she materialized without warning in front of the fridge, and I knocked gently into her, I felt a new softness in her body's response. My vision hadn't changed, but I was seeing what I saw through her eyes, through the Goldmann perimetry, that chart the nurse made of my visual field. In the past my sense of my vision was much vaguer, and more pessimistic: *I didn't see that because I'm going blind—because my vision is shit*. But in the days after Lily came with me to Boston, my blind spots felt clarified: *I didn't see because I only have 5 percent of my visual field left*.

The day after we got back, there was an electrical storm in the afternoon. By evening, the storm had passed, but the sky was still patched with clouds. The light was surreal—I'd never seen anything like it. It was as though the glass enclosing the sunset had cracked, and a viscous orange dusk-light leaked its way down into the yard. Lily said it was like standing in a photograph. Neighbors texted one another to come outside. You could see, in the distance, patches of blue, which made the oozing haze look even stranger. Lily's skin glowed orange. I let my vision bathe in this light.

9.

Lady Justice

In 2020, after the murder of George Floyd, the NFB held a series of open Zoom meetings. The goal was to provide a forum for Black Federationists to discuss their experiences of racism within the organization, and for other (mainly white) NFBers to listen and ask questions. Like most large virtual meetings, these calls were filled with moments of confusion, with people interrupting one another, veering off topic, and blasting incidental sound from their kitchens. (Blind Zoom meetings are also notable for occasional bursts of hyper-speed synthesized speech—people sometimes forget to mute their screen readers, and so the entire group tries to talk over an iPhone as it reads someone's email aloud, at three times the rate of normal human speech.)

These calls soon became spaces for painful, searching conversations. One person told a story of his time at the national convention in Orlando. He was riding an elevator from the hotel rooms down to the convention floor, along with a group of other blind people. One of them got off on the mezzanine, and as the doors closed behind them, a blind guy said, "I'm glad the [n-word] got off the elevator."

"Well, you left one on," the man said. The group rode the rest of the way down in silence. I heard numerous anecdotes like this on the calls, along with stories of Black Federationists who felt blocked or discouraged from attaining positions of leadership within the NFB.

A white NFB leader from Texas inserted herself into the conversation. She began by saying that she felt it was important for her chapter to address the protests, and to make sure its members knew that the NFB believes in diversity and inclusion. But then she sort of blurted out, "I just don't see color! Of course, *literally*, I don't. . . . But . . . I really don't notice." A number of blind white people spoke out along these lines, offering their support and solidarity, but also, it seemed to me, trying to absolve themselves of any wrongdoing by using their disability as an alibi.

Later in the same call, a Black member said that he'd been speaking with a white blind person he knows, who told him the same thing: "I'm blind; I don't see color."

"*I'm* blind," he responded to his white acquaintance, "and I don't see color either—*but I hear ignorance vividly*. You can't replace four hundred years of oppression and injustice by saying 'I don't see color.'"

Blindness, as a metaphor, is almost never good. It usually connotes obliviousness and incompetence: *blind fool*, *blind drunk*, *blind spot*, *robbed blind*, and on and on. *Justice* seems to be one of blindness's few positive metaphors. Lady Justice traditionally looks like a cousin of the Columbia Pictures lady whose torch illuminates the opening credits of thousands of movies: a beautiful, berobed, sighted white woman, wearing a carefully tied blindfold around her head. She usually holds scales, doubling down on the image of her impartiality: she just weighs the evidence, without distraction from superficial visual judgments.

In the US legal tradition, justice's blindness has been invoked most frequently and forcefully around race. As the law professor Osagie K. Obasogie has observed, color blindness is often held up as a progressive legal ideal, but in reality it reflects an unwillingness to engage with the inequities of race. When Homer Plessy boarded a whites-only train car in 1892, he passed as white. But when a train conductor asked if he was white and he said he was not, on account of his one-eighth African American ancestry, he was arrested by the train detective. In a segregated society, his one-eighth Blackness was all that counted. When his case was brought before the Supreme Court in 1896, all but one of the justices ruled against him, saying that while the Fourteenth Amendment aimed to treat all citizens equally, arrangements like segregated train cars, which were "separate but equal" with respect to whites-only cars, didn't constitute a violation of the law. In the court's only dissenting opinion, Justice John Marshall Harlan called on the color blindness of the law to support his argument against segregation. "In the view of the Constitution, in the eye of the law, there is in this country no superior, dominant, ruling class of citizens," Harlan wrote. "There is no caste here. Our Constitution is color-blind and neither knows nor tolerates classes among citizens."

For Justice Harlan, blindness in the eye of the law is a good thing, the very reason that Lady Justice wears her blindfold. It provides an objectivity that's the only possible corrective to prejudice. If you want equality, Harlan suggests, the law must remain blind to racial difference.

In his 1932 poem "Justice," Langston Hughes reimagined the classical image of Lady Justice as the victim of a terrible act of violence, wearing not a blindfold but medical gauze around her head:

> That Justice is a blind goddess
> Is a thing to which we black are wise:
> Her bandage hides two festering sores
> That once perhaps were eyes.

Hughes's poem subverts Justice Harlan's notion of legal color blindness: achieved through gory, violent means, Lady Justice's blindness is what makes her fail to see the oppression that marks the Black American experience. Ralph Ellison's Invisible Man seems to disappear from view as a result of this same kind of white blindness: "I am invisible," he says, "simply because people refuse to see me."

• • •

The NFB's founder, Jacobus tenBroek, like all of its presidents, was a white man. But tenBroek was deeply interested in the rights of marginalized groups; as he led the NFB through its first few decades of political action, he simultaneously pursued his career as a constitutional scholar, publishing work on the rights of Japanese Americans imprisoned in American internment camps during World War II and the "antislavery origins" of the Fourteenth Amendment's equal protection clause. (This latter work would bring him into contact with Thurgood Marshall, then a lawyer for the NAACP, who cited tenBroek's scholarship in his arguments before the Supreme Court in *Brown v. Board of Education*.) In 1966, at the height of the Black civil rights movement, tenBroek published a legal journal article called "The Right to Live in the World: The Disabled in the Law of Torts." In the article, tenBroek makes explicit the connection between civil rights for disabled people and racial equality. "As with the black man, so with the blind," he wrote. "As with the Puerto Rican, so with the post-polio. As with the Indian, so with the indigent disabled." As Angela Frederick and Dara Shifrer have pointed out, tenBroek's article was published shortly after the passage of the Civil Rights Act, which notably excluded disability from the list of characteristics (sex, race, color, religion, national origin) to which it offered legal protection.

Two months after the protests sparked by the murder of George Floyd, the news media carried a day or two of stories pegged to the thirtieth anniversary of the Americans with Disabilities Act (ADA). One afternoon I listened to a woman named Judy Heumann talk on the radio about her work as a disability rights activist during the transformative years between the passage of the Civil Rights Act in 1964 and the enforcement of laws protecting disabled civil rights more than a decade later. Heumann grew up as a white Jewish kid in Brooklyn, and was part of the last generation born before the advent of the polio vaccine. When she contracted the virus at eighteen months, she became quadriplegic, with limited use of her arms. When her mother brought her in her wheelchair to public school to start kindergarten, the teachers told her that they couldn't accommodate her daughter—she'd be a fire hazard. At the time, before the passage of Section 504 of the Rehabilitation Act of 1973 (and the adoption of regulations to enforce it in 1977), this exclusion was perfectly legal. Heumann called Section 504, which prohibits discrimination based on disability in any federally funded setting—followed, seventeen years later, by the ADA, which extended the same legal protections to the private sector—"an Emancipation Proclamation."

When I heard her say this, I paused. Heumann wasn't exaggerating the effect that these laws had: they were responsible for the opening up of schools, buildings, jobs, and transportation to millions of disabled people, whose lives were transformed and enriched as a result. The varieties of marginalization and oppression that disabled people have historically experienced, from forced sterilization, language deprivation, and euthanasia to denial of education and work, are unforgivable. Well into the 1980s, people with intellectual disabilities were sent to notorious institutions like Willowbrook, on Staten Island, where children were subjected to nonconsensual medical tests (doctors reportedly fed them stool samples that had been infected with hepatitis in order to study the effects of the virus) and decades-long sexual and physical abuse. To this day, at one residential school in Massachusetts, autistic and other disabled children must wear shock collars to correct "aggressive or self-injurious behavior" (as the DC Court of Appeals put it, overruling an FDA ban on the devices in 2021). But I still felt hesitant to accept Heumann's analogy. Was she suggesting that the injustices levied against disabled people, as terrible and widespread as they are, were commensurate with chattel slavery?

"Though my life wasn't marked with the little 'Whites Only' signs that signaled segregation in the South," Heumann wrote in her memoir, "the life I lived was also a segregated one." After years of fighting the

New York City Board of Education, Heumann's mother finally got her placed in a program for kids with disabilities at P.S. 219. But as delighted as Heumann was to get to go to school, what she found there was hardly an equal education. Students from ages nine to twenty-one were all mixed together; they had nap time, even the teenagers; and the amount of actual instruction they did get—far below what Heumann, who was reading at a high school level, needed—was a fraction of what the nondisabled kids upstairs received. "Since we'd been left out of the Civil Rights Act of 1964," Heumann wrote, "we needed our own Civil Rights Act."

Heumann wanted to be a teacher, and after graduating from Long Island University, she began the process of obtaining a New York State teaching license. In addition to written and oral exams, the state required a routine physical to ensure she didn't have any medical conditions—like communicable diseases—that would endanger the students in her classroom. But at her exam, the city's doctor ran her through a humiliating series of questions, asking her to demonstrate how she went to the bathroom and how she walked, even as Heumann explained again and again that she'd never really been able to walk and that she got around fine in her wheelchair. Three months later, the city rejected her application for a credential.

She reached out to the ACLU, which threw up its hands. "You've been denied your license for medical reasons," the ACLU's lawyer said, "which is not discrimination." This response captures the stubborn durability of the widespread view of disability as a fundamentally medical problem; even progressives working on the civil rights of other marginalized groups have tended to view disability as a basic physical defect that falls into a different category than race, gender, or sexuality. Nineteenth-century American medical literature is full of racist arguments for the biological inferiority of African Americans and their physiological suitability for slavery; as the historian Douglas Baynton argues, people justified the subjection and exclusion of African Americans, women, and immigrants by aligning those identities with disability. Anti-suffragists pointed to the supposed temperamental instability of women, suggesting that they lacked the intellectual aptitude to vote. And US immigration policy, Baynton writes, aligned ethnicity and disability to a nearly inseparable degree. In 1907, the commissioner general of immigration in the US wrote, "The exclusion from this country of the morally, mentally, and physically deficient is the principal object to be accomplished by the immigration laws."

As a result, the progress of the movements that advocated for the rights of women, African Americans, and immigrant communities all entailed a disassociation from disability: these groups had to prove that they were just as capable as nondisabled white men. As the formerly enslaved abolitionist Frederick Douglass believed, "The true basis of rights was the capacity of individuals." Baynton follows the unspoken inverse of Douglass's assertion, with its implication that if an individual had a different set of capacities, they might also be entitled to a different set of rights, offering a "justification for political inequality."

By 1970, Heumann had harnessed her experience fighting the New York Board of Education (and the massive publicity it garnered) to build a career as a disability rights organizer. With a group of other activists, she founded Disabled in Action, which addressed a range of issues across disabilities, from advocating for accessible public transportation to ending sheltered workshops (which grew out of the first schools for the blind, paying a fraction of the minimum wage to blind and, later, developmentally disabled adults for industrial work that rarely offered opportunities for career advancement or any hope of financial independence). Not long after, Ed Roberts, the former UC Berkeley student who founded the Independent Living Movement (and got curb cuts installed on corners across the city) cold-called Heumann—her actions had made headlines across the country—and asked her to move to Berkeley to help run the Center for Independent Living. Heumann's move put her at the center of the most visible and active disability rights organization in the country.

In 1977, the CIL (in concert with other disability groups from around the country) organized a sit-in at the Federal Building in San Francisco's Civic Center, where the offices of the Department of Health, Education, and Welfare (HEW) were located, to protest the government's failure to enforce Section 504. That protest, coordinated with sister actions in cities across the country, was a foundational episode in disability rights history, often described as the first moment that disability rights entered the national consciousness. (It's memorably documented in the 2020 film *Crip Camp*.) Disabled activists occupied the Federal Building for twenty-six days, sleeping on the floors and discussing strategy in meetings that lasted deep into the night. When HEW shut off the phone lines, Deaf members of the group communicated in ASL to their comrades on the street. When HEW closed off the building in an attempt to starve out the protesters (as they'd successfully done at sit-ins in other cities), the Black Panthers broke in with hot meals and continued to deliver food every night for the length of the protest.

Among the activists occupying the Federal Building were Bradley Lomax, a wheelchair user, and his caregiver, Chuck Jackson—both members of the Black Panthers. Dennis Billups, a blind activist who's been described as the "spiritual leader" of the sit-ins, later became a Panther as well. But the protesters were predominantly white. In an interview with the Black Panther newspaper during the occupation, Billups called out for a more diverse movement: "To my brothers and sisters that are Black and that are handicapped," he said, "get out there, we need you. Come here, we need you."

At a victory rally after the HEW director finally signed the regulations that would enforce Section 504, the Black Panther Party leader Ericka Huggins expressed a kind of radical liberatory color blindness, connecting the largely white group of disabled people with the experience of Black marginalization in stark terms. "The United States has always had its [n-words]," she told the crowd.

> And they come in all sizes, shapes, colors, classes, and disabilities. The signing of 504, this demonstration, this sit-in, this beautiful thing that has happened these past few weeks, is all to say that the [n-words] are going to be set free.

• • •

Activists like Judy Heumann, in demanding equal rights, have to make the argument that disabled people are essentially the same as everyone else. (The title of her memoir, *Being Heumann*, makes this point by punning on her wonderfully apt surname.) This argument, which seems so self-evident on its face—*we're people too!*—nonetheless raises complicated questions of identity that have obsessed me since I began thinking about what it means to join the amorphous entity known as "the disabled community." How central should my identity as a blind person be? Disability rights activists argue that blindness is a non-defining characteristic. But they make this argument, that disability is incidental at best, from within organizations with names—Disabled in Action, the National Federation of the Blind—that suggest the contrary, that disability is the primary marker of their identity. How to account for this paradox? How can the law treat everyone equally, while at the same time recognizing the imbalances that tip the scales away from certain groups?

The bioethicist Adrienne Asch, who died in 2013, spent her life actively wrestling with the ways that disability can be both central and incidental in a person's life, and the importance of recognizing its presence in some instances and ignoring it in others. Before Asch was set to start kindergarten in 1951, her parents moved to New Jersey because it was one of the only states that allowed blind children to attend mainstream public schools. By the time Asch was in high school, in the early 1960s, she was passionate about politics and the Black civil rights movement, but she hadn't yet developed a political consciousness around her own disability. In a magazine called the *Jewish Braille Review*, she encountered the speeches of Jacobus tenBroek, but as she read his fiery diatribes about the discrimination blind people faced, she thought it couldn't be true—she'd never experienced anything like that. She vividly recalls another article in the magazine, by a blind historian, that posed the question of whether it was easier to be Black or blind in the

US. "I remember being horrified," Asch recalled. "Of course it's harder to be black in this country. This is ridiculous. What are you talking about? I'm not lynched. Nobody's stopping me from doing anything I want to do."

Asch had encountered discrimination, however, and would continue to do so. When she applied to college, one of the schools that accepted her told her that—because of her academic record, and because they were a state school—they had to accept her, but they didn't want to. They were afraid she'd hurt herself crossing the busy main thoroughfare of campus, they explained. But she'd also gotten into Swarthmore, which hadn't given her any paternalistic traffic-safety warnings, and so she brushed off this incident as she had all the others: the barriers were temporary, and could be worked around.

At Swarthmore, she met other blind students, and other disabled students, but she didn't feel any particular allegiance to them. "I didn't either like them or not like them," she said. "The person who had polio was someone I actually liked quite a lot. The person who was of short stature I didn't particularly like." She thought of them the same way she thought of herself—just another person, not defined by disability or any one of the constellation of other identities.

After college, Asch's attitudes shifted. She applied to dozens of jobs, most of which she knew she was qualified for, and started experiencing blatant discrimination in response. This time, there was no work-around. A manager at Lincoln Center told her she deserved an interview, but his supervisor would have to conduct it; that supervisor nixed the idea of a blind person in the job, and when Asch demanded a meeting with the center's vice president, she was refused. Like Judy Heumann, who later became a friend and an ally, Asch tried to find legal recourse, petitioning the city's human rights commission, and quickly discovered that they had no interest in helping. There was no state or federal law protecting her from discrimination either. "It was the first time I realized that disability was a political issue," Asch said, "and that I wasn't going to solve my problems if I didn't get political." She'd learned some tactics from her involvement in the anti-war and civil rights movements in college, and she grudgingly accepted that she needed to apply them to fight the oppression she was facing herself. A friend joked, "Adrienne's twenty-three, and she's just discovered that she's blind."

She joined the NFB with some friends, and they formed their own New York City chapter. Around the same time, she met Heumann and joined Disabled in Action, the cross-disability activist group Heumann founded in 1970. She also became involved in a similar group, the American Coalition of Citizens with Disabilities. Then she pulled together these two worlds—the single-issue-oriented NFB and the cross-disability coalitions—to lobby New York State to pass a law that prevented workplace discrimination based on disability. A demonstration of hundreds of people she helped organize brought together blind people from sheltered workshops and her NFB connections, as well as people with other disabilities, to picket in front of the capitol in Albany. But this work got her into trouble with the NFB. After the law was passed, people from the New York affiliate chided her for representing herself publicly as an activist for not only the NFB but also other disability groups. Later, the NFB's president, Kenneth Jernigan, openly criticized Asch's actions at a national convention.

Asch believed that the NFB's resistance had to do with fear of losing the benefits they'd fought for if the law applied to a wider group. Blindness is a relatively low-incidence condition compared with other disabilities and comes with particular needs. If someone needs a wheelchair, Asch said, a state agency can buy them their chair and close their case. But a newly blind person needs months of braille instruction, cane lessons, home management skills, and so on. The fear was that if blind people didn't have their own place in the tax code, with their own separate state commissions, they'd lose the specialized services they'd fought so hard to win.

Asch didn't leave the organization after the NFB scolding, but she reduced her involvement. She admired the effectiveness and clarity of the NFB's fight for the rights of blind people, but as a radical East Coast liberal Jew, she felt a fundamental clash of cultures. Jernigan's administration had criticized her for being open about living with a boyfriend. "You just didn't do that—you certainly didn't do it publicly in the National Federation of the Blind," Asch said. "This was not Berkeley."

> This was run by people from Iowa and South Carolina, who were as mid-American and Republican—in all of the ways you could be—as you could imagine. They were fabulous on blindness discrimination, but they were not part of the counterculture. . . . They didn't want people picketing the Vietnam war. They didn't want to talk about abortion.

But Asch also resisted fully aligning herself with more radical disability organizers like Heumann, who in a very different way resembled the NFB's leadership in her "twenty-four-hour-a-day, seven-day-a-week absolutely unstoppable commitment." Asch had been blind her whole life, and felt passionately about her activism, but she held on to some of her high school attitude: if blindness isn't relevant in the moment—if there's not an immediate injustice to fight—she'd just as soon let it fade to the background, in ways that the 24-7 disability activists seemed incapable of doing.

• • •

Unlike the NFB, the disability justice movement begins from a premise of intersectionality—the idea that the oppressions people experience because of their race, sexuality, gender, class, and disability are all linked. The movement began in the Bay Area in the early 2000s, with a group mostly comprised of queer disabled women of color. Earlier generations of activists had tended to focus on the most visible disabilities: sensory disabilities like blindness and deafness; physical and developmental disabilities like spina bifida or Down syndrome. But the disability justice movement, in addition to calling out the whiteness of previous generations of activists, also expanded the kinds of disabilities they included in their community. They added *sick* and *mad* to *disabled* in their lists of self-identifiers. In their book *Care Work: Dreaming Disability Justice*, Leah Lakshmi Piepzna-Samarasinha holds up figures not historically associated with the disability rights movement as their spiritual and intellectual forebears, celebrating the lives of "second-wave queer feminists of color" like Audre Lorde, who survived breast cancer with a mastectomy, and later died of liver cancer. (She was also so nearsighted that she was legally blind.) Figures like Lorde, they write, "are marked by bodily difference, trauma-surviving brilliance, and chronic illness but . . . mostly never used the term 'disabled' to refer to themselves."

Piepzna-Samarasinha describes the disability justice movement as a haven for those who have been excluded from traditional disability-activist spaces, including those with chronic or mental illness whose "disability the state never approves of—so it's not 'real,'" they write.

> Some of us are in the in-between of needing some care but not fitting into the state model of either Total and Permanent Disability or fit and ready to work—so we can't access the services that are there. Many of us are familiar with being genuinely sick as hell and needing some help but failing the official crip exams because we can still cook, shop, and work, only slowly and when there is no other choice.

Members of the blindness groups I'd been hanging around and the proponents of this newer, more intersectionally minded movement seemed to be speaking different languages. The NFB spoke the language of civil rights, fighting the power in the name of a single cause. Race or other identities existed as analogies to disability, but the NFB rarely considered how these identities interacted. The disability justice movement, on the other hand, spoke the language of transformative justice, arguing that racism and ableism and sexism and transphobia were all inseparable forces that needed to be fought together. In their manifesto, the disability collective Sins Invalid lays out their mission to dissolve the barriers that have traditionally divided these battles, in an impressive litany of cross-movement solidarity. Disability justice, they write, must align itself with "racial justice, reproductive justice, queer and trans liberation, prison abolition, environmental justice, anti-police terror, Deaf activism, fat liberation, and other movements working for justice and liberation. This means challenging white disability communities around racism and challenging other movements to confront ableism."

By contrast, the NFB's resistance to aligning itself with other disability groups has a long history. When the ADA was being drafted in 1989, the NFB came out against the bill. "So-called accommodations may often themselves be discriminatory," Kenneth Jernigan, the former NFB president of nearly twenty years, wrote in the *Braille Monitor* six months before the bill passed. For Jernigan and the NFB, cross-disability coalitions had brought harm to blind people. After wheelchair users (including Judy Heumann) had put pressure on airlines to create accommodations (providing wheelchairs, offering assistance while boarding, and allowing them to fly without attendants), Jernigan complained that a "generic" approach to disability had created "new and unwarranted restrictions" on the blind in air travel. After the airlines created these accommodations, blind people were suddenly forced to ride through airports in wheelchairs they didn't need. This practice remains common today: nearly every blind person who flies regularly is repeatedly asked, if not compelled, to sit in a wheelchair at some point in their travels, an experience many describe as humiliating.

When they got wind of the NFB's opposition (formalized in a resolution at its 1989 national convention in Denver), members of the Bush administration and Congress who were working on the ADA met with

NFB leadership at the White House to negotiate an amendment. Even after this meeting, which was cordial and productive, Jernigan wrote that if their amendment wasn't included, "we will do anything we can to slow it down and block its passage. . . . Simply because a thing calls itself civil rights, that does not mean that it is civil rights."

In the end, Congress added an amendment stipulating that the accommodations the ADA required were, in fact, subject to the choice of the disabled person. I'm grateful that the law protects me from being forced to sit in a wheelchair I don't want or need, but I feel a deep ambivalence about accepting Jernigan's insistence that blindness is not a disability. On the one hand, there's a profound sense of liberation in his assertion that blindness is merely a characteristic, and that after learning "alternative techniques" (like cane travel), the blind person remains perfectly capable and independent. This philosophy reassures me that my sense of myself as a normal person will survive blindness, and that all of my privilege won't be stripped from me as my last few degrees of vision drain away. But he goes too far in suggesting that while the blind aren't really disabled, other groups, like wheelchair users, are. What's the difference between an "alternative technique" (like browsing the internet with a screen reader, which requires web developers to design their sites with accessibility in mind) and an "accommodation" (like a wheelchair ramp)?

With the NFB's amendment, the ADA makes it illegal for a bus driver, for instance, to demand that a blind person sit in one of the seats designated for the elderly or people with disabilities. "Some may regard disputes about seating as quibbling," Jernigan wrote, "but Rosa Parks and others brought the entire civil rights movement to a national focus by exactly this type of issue." But Rosa Parks and the Black civil rights movement could argue that the capacities of Black people are identical to those of whites. Can blind people make the same argument about their abilities in relation to sighted people? What's at stake in admitting that a blind person has a different set of capacities than a sighted person does?

• • •

Anil Lewis is the highest-ranking Black leader in the NFB. I didn't hear him in any of the Black leadership Zooms I attended in the weeks after George Floyd's death, but in July 2020, Lewis published a searching, surprisingly self-critical essay in the *Braille Monitor* called "Being Black Helped Me Be Blind and Being Blind Helped Me Understand That #BlackLivesMatter." Lewis took the NFB's slogan—*live the life you want*—and repurposed it in the context of BLM: "I have realized that I have not exercised the same degree of dedication to address the systemic racism that prohibits black people from living the lives we want," he wrote. He had been too focused, he seems to suggest, on the NFB's single-issue orientation, the blind part of Jacobus tenBroek's equation: "As with the black man, so with the blind."

In his essay, Lewis sounded angry with himself. The commitment he'd made to the organized blind movement had, he wrote, prevented him from recognizing the need to join the movement for Black lives. Earlier that year, before the Floyd killing, in a video he recorded for the National Disability Rights Network, Lewis had suggested that the discrimination he faced as a blind person was in fact more difficult than what he faced as a Black person. Racism, he said, "is based on ignorance—through hate and dislike." But the discrimination he dealt with as a blind person "was ignorance—but through *love*. The hardest part for me was to fight the custodialistic value system that was placed on me as a blind person." When I spoke to him later, over the phone, he told me that strangers' perceptions of him as a blind person tended to "supersede" his racial identity. Before blindness, he said, as a six-foot-two, 230-pound Black man, he appeared as the stereotypical "super-predator"; people "crossed the street and locked their car doors" when they saw him coming. But now, as a blind man, "I'm walking down the street," he said, "and even this frail little white woman is stopping on the corner trying to help me cross the street." Without the white cane, he concluded, "she would have not been at that corner when I got there."

The more blind I become, the more I understand the sort of discrimination that emerges out of love (an impulse, Lewis later told me, that could less charitably be called *pity*). I recently offered to carry a large plastic crib down a flight of stairs for a family member. They told me not to worry about it, that they'd take care of it. I was confused—why didn't they want me to help? "You won't be able to see where you're going," they said. "Just let me do it." Coming as it did as a gesture of accommodation—a gesture of love, even—this was a far more confounding type of prejudice than a more blatantly dismissive or intolerant remark would have been. But it seemed that in the wake of 2020's Black Lives Matter protests, Lewis had to recalibrate the hierarchy of pain that these two varieties of prejudice created for him.

Lewis's essay ended on a note that read to me like the usual NFB banquet address, with its exhortations toward unity and resilience on behalf of blind people fighting against oppression everywhere. But the message of the Black Lives Matter movement was present as well. "We realize that blind lives matter," he wrote at the essay's conclusion, "and require specific intervention and action to eliminate the discrimination blind people face. . . . Reinforcing that #BlackLivesMatter will help you #LiveTheLifeYouWant." Lewis had written himself into a tricky rhetorical position: he was trying to present an intersectional message without altering the language of the group's original, single-issue approach.

The NFB's 2020 convention, which was held only online in July, included remarks by a handful of younger people who seemed more comfortable dwelling at the intersection of race and disability. The most striking voice I heard connecting these two worlds belonged to Justice Shorter, who appeared in the LGBTQIA+ Zoom session—incidentally, only the fourth of its kind. For years, members had tried to organize an LGBT meetup at the national convention. Federation leadership always deflected them, though, telling them to focus instead on the blind part of their identity. But the NFB had numerous other interest groups, from Jewish and other faith-based meetups to "home cooks" and "members of the Masons." How was sexual orientation or gender identity any different from religion as an acceptable identity that intersected with blindness? To the meetup proponents and their allies, this rejection felt more like a function of the social conservatism that Adrienne Asch had identified in the NFB in the 1970s. At the 2006 convention, an NFB member had written an announcement inviting members to discuss the formation of an LGBT group and submitted it for president Marc

Maurer to read from the podium at the convention assembly. According to several NFB members I interviewed who were in attendance, Maurer made a show of tearing up the announcement onstage. (Maurer told me he didn't recall this particular incident, but confirmed his position against the meetup. "I wouldn't have done it publicly," he said, "though I would have done it.")

Justice Shorter began her talk as a guest speaker at the 2020 NFB LGBT Zoom meetup by offering a quick image description. This is a practice that's becoming more common, particularly in activist circles and in some corners of the academic humanities; speakers describe themselves for any blind people in the audience who may be curious about their self-presentation.

"In terms of how I look," Shorter told the LGBT Zoom, "I have my hair natural; I kinda look like I have a mohawk. It's one of those funky things Black women are doing with their hair." Shorter said she felt a deep connection with the fact that Alicia Garza, one of the founders of BLM, specifically named disability as part of that group's statement of purpose. (This acknowledgment came only after the protests of the Harriet Tubman Collective, a group of Black Deaf and disabled organizers, who pointed out that the original BLM statement had failed to mention disability.)

When the George Floyd protests began, Shorter said, she didn't feel comfortable heading out alone into the protests near her home in Washington, DC; Keri Gray, a friend who walks with a prosthetic leg, agreed to join her. When they arrived at a demonstration a few blocks from the White House, the sight of two disabled protesters marching together turned heads. People recorded Shorter and Gray on their phones. "We were so odd to them—an anomaly," Shorter said. "There was no way to separate our Blackness from having a disability. Reporters came up, like, 'What are you doing here?' As if we're not also Black." She pointed out to these reporters that between 30 and 50 percent of those killed by police are disabled.

Shorter urged the NFB members in the meeting to refocus their activism around the disability justice movement's principles. "If your main thing is blindness," she told the group, whose main thing was, on the whole, blindness, "think about how you can focus on Latinx immigrants who are blind—whatever your area of expertise is."

Shorter works as a disaster protection adviser for the National Disability Rights Network, where she gives presentations to government agencies and nonprofits on disability issues that arise during emergencies like pandemics or fires. At one of these presentations, she talked about how agencies like FEMA, looking to connect with disabled people, need to search outside the usual disability organizations. "I'll talk to some government folks," she said, "and they'll say, 'Listen, we contacted the local department on aging, we contacted the local blind group.'" Shorter applauded these efforts, but added that people with disabilities often operate outside these traditional disability spaces. "For example, in my life, I've never formally been part of a blindness group," she said. "But you can certainly catch me in Black lesbian circles." NFB leadership often speaks of representing blind people everywhere—whether they're dues-paying members or not—in much the same way that elected politicians are fond of saying they represent all their constituents regardless of their political affiliations. But Shorter's presentation belied the diversity within blindness, not just in terms of race or sexual orientation but within blind people's relationship with disability solidarity itself, which is often far more complex than a simple, direct affiliation with other blind people.

• • •

As I looked over the agenda for the 2020 general sessions—the NFB national convention's main event—I didn't detect a lot of overlap with Black lesbian circles. Unlike the LGBT meetup, the general sessions were attended by thousands of blind people and featured voices more in line with the NFB's traditional values. After a brief introduction from President Riccobono, a woman named Laura Wolk gave a short talk on her legal career—the week before, she'd just finished clerking for Justice Clarence Thomas, making her the first blind woman to clerk on the Supreme Court.

Wolk has been a member of the NFB since she was a young child—her father founded the Pennsylvania affiliate of the NFB's Organization of Parents of Blind Children, and she attended her first convention at seven years old, in 1994. The following year, Wolk and her father attended a meeting with Pennsylvania's governor, Tom Ridge, to advocate for braille instruction in public schools. Like Adrienne Asch, Wolk insisted that her blindness wasn't a central part of her identity, and grew up balancing awareness of her need to advocate for herself with a sense that she was no different than anyone else. "I maintain a stable circle of friends," she wrote in an NFB magazine when she was in the eighth grade, "who treat me so equally that they sometimes forget they have to describe movies to me."

Like Asch, Wolk was blind from infancy, attended mainstream schools, and then ended up at Swarthmore. But her college experience was very different than Asch's. Asch was delighted to immerse herself in the college's liberal-leaning intellectual climate, but Wolk, who entered college as a largely "cultural" Catholic who was politically center-left, underwent a conversion. She became increasingly devout and increasingly conservative. Asch treated her Jewishness the same way she treated her disability—she didn't deny it, but she also resisted the way that some Jews felt like they had to stick together based on their shared identity alone. Even as she taught at Wellesley, a women's college, and then Yeshiva, a Jewish university, Asch was critical of both—she thought that students should be exposed to cultures and identities beyond their own. "You don't need a blind role model," Asch said. "You need a role model."

Wolk's faith, on the other hand, exerted a powerful influence on her thinking. When she was nineteen, at a routine oncology appointment, her doctor asked if she was sexually active, and what her plans for having children were. The oncologist told Wolk that if she got pregnant, she could have embryonic screening to determine if her baby would be affected with retinoblastoma (a cancer of the retina, and the cause of Wolk's blindness). The doctor added that with IVF she could also be implanted with an embryo that lacked her genetic predisposition for the disease. Wolk heard her oncologist's comments, which she said came out of nowhere, as a clear suggestion that "obviously the only rational thing to do is to make sure you don't have a child who has retinoblastoma," and that if she did become pregnant with a child who would be born blind, an abortion was the best option.

When she was a sophomore in college, she met Asch (who at the time was a professor at Yeshiva) at an NFB convention. Asch was by then immersed in her research in the field of bioethics, and she told Wolk about a volume she'd coedited, *Prenatal Testing and Disability Rights*, which Wolk read soon afterward. While the book presents the case both for and against prenatal testing for disability, all of its contributors write from a pro-choice perspective. Asch herself was "staunchly pro-choice," but she had a habit of rattling her feminist colleagues by insisting that it was unethical for a woman to have an abortion based solely on their desire to avoid having a disabled child. Asch argued that the screening process sent a message to disabled people that their lives were inherently less valuable than nondisabled lives. She pointed out that most people would agree that it's unethical to abort a fetus once a mother learned it was female, for instance, because of the message it sent that women's lives are less worthy or desirable than men's. But few had qualms about the practice of screening for nonlethal disabilities like Down syndrome. Genetic counselors and obstetricians frequently discussed these screenings in terms of the "risk" of acquiring "devastating defects," in many cases actively encouraging or assuming mothers will decide to abort if the fetus is found to have the extra chromosome that causes the disability.

Asch never argued for the criminalization of aborting fetuses that would grow into disabled infants. Her solution was to advocate for the reform of the way that doctors and genetic counselors talked about disability. She encouraged an "informed choice" approach, urging doctors to provide information to parents about the rich and regular lives that disabled people (like her) lived.

When Wolk found Asch's book, she read into the arguments about the value-judgment prenatal screening sent to people with disabilities to justify her own burgeoning pro-life ideology. For Wolk, it wasn't just that prenatal screening sent a message about the value of disabled life, as Asch argued, but that *every* abortion sent a message about the value of *all* life. "And so in a weird way, and not the way she was intending, I'm sure," Wolk said, "that whole experience—meeting Asch, and reading her book—really helped me come to terms with what my own beliefs on abortion were." After college, Wolk moved to Philadelphia and worked at a Center for Independent Living, helping adults with physical and intellectual disabilities. She also began waking up before dawn to join the Helpers of God's Precious Infants, who prayed in front of the entrance to the Philadelphia Women's Center, the first outpatient abortion clinic in Pennsylvania.

• • •

After college, Wolk attended a bioethics conference at Notre Dame, where she met O. Carter Snead, a pro-life law professor at the university. Snead was impressed by Wolk's passion and intellect and recruited her to attend Notre Dame Law School. In her first semester, Wolk took a class with Amy Coney Barrett, who quickly became a mentor and ally. After President Trump nominated Barrett to the Supreme Court, Wolk testified on her behalf at Barrett's confirmation hearings. Reading off her braille display, Wolk described the practical and emotional support that Barrett had offered her through various disability-related challenges. Notre Dame had promised Wolk they'd purchase backups of her assistive technology but failed to do so, and in her first semester, her laptop broke down. Wolk approached Barrett, whose ability to listen with "deep attention" allowed Wolk to let down the "mask" of self-assurance that a disabled self-advocate must wear. "I poured out all my concerns," Wolk told the Senate committee, "my worries about failing classes, having to choose between completing my assignments and figuring out how to get to the grocery store independently, and feeling as though the energy spent troubleshooting these issues was preventing me from forging friendships." Her professor's response, Wolk said, was measured and full of conviction. "Laura," Barrett said, "this is no longer your problem. It's my problem."

At the confirmation hearings, Wolk presented blindness as at once a handicap and a neutral characteristic. She led with the hardships she faced as a blind law student—her reliance on assistive technology, the time it took her to map a route to the grocery store. But ultimately Wolk held Barrett up as an advocate whose support helped her participate "on equal footing with [her] sighted colleagues." This is the same tension that the NFB wrestled with in its early resistance to the ADA, and every time it negotiates the administration of government assistance: Are blind people disabled and in need of accommodation? Or are they equals, who simply go about their business in a specialized, blind way? As Adrienne Asch asked herself again and again throughout her life, is blindness really relevant here?

"It's like I can't acknowledge that my blindness imposes actual difficulties on me," Wolk said when we spoke on the phone in the summer of 2022, the week after Justice Barrett had joined the majority in issuing the Supreme Court's decision in *Dobbs v. Jackson*, the landmark case that overturned *Roe v. Wade*. "Even if we lived in an ideal world," she said, "with everything accessible, the fact is, I still can't see. And that's going to impose limitations and difficulties on me that it doesn't impose on a sighted person. In some ways, life would be easier for me if I were sighted," she continued. "And I can hold that idea simultaneously in my mind with: I have equal value and dignity as a person who is sighted."

I reject the conclusion that Wolk draws from this observation—that because there is value in disabled life, and indeed in all life, abortion should be illegal, and women's reproductive autonomy must be regulated by the state. But I do share her sense that even if blindness is a disability, this doesn't preclude the possibility that it's also, as Asch insisted, a neutral characteristic.

After Asch's death from cancer in 2013, the legal scholar Dorothy E. Roberts wrote an appreciation of her life in the science journal *Nature*. "As feminist scholars who wrote about the bioethics of reproduction and inequality," Roberts wrote, their paths crossed frequently. She added that Asch's "cogent arguments helped me to incorporate disability studies in my own writing on genetic selection and the devaluation of black women's childbearing." Roberts's first book, *Killing the Black Body: Race, Reproduction, and the Meaning of Liberty*, documented the ways in which the reproductive rights of Black women had been harshly regulated by the state, from laws designed to prevent women on welfare from having children to coerced sterilizations.

Both Roberts's and Asch's arguments run counter to the more widely told story of women's rights, which, as Roberts points out, is consistently linked to the right to an abortion. Both scholars write against the grain of this account, which centers white, nondisabled women. In different ways, they each point out how preventing or discouraging women from having children can also be a loss of reproductive justice.

And just as Wolk used Asch's work as a justification for a pro-life ideology, there are African American women who point to the brutal history of Black eugenics in the US as a framework for arguments against abortion. But in both cases, regardless of one's position on abortion, the underlying source of oppression remains the same. The problem arises, as Asch observed, when "a single trait stands in for the whole, the trait obliterates the whole." Disabled people, like African Americans or any other marginalized group, are dehumanized and oppressed by being reduced to a single, devalued trait; the path to justice must be driven by the rehabilitation of that characteristic.

But that rehabilitation can't be so strenuous that it blocks out the rest of a person's qualities. Asch's philosophy offers a way out of the paradox of identity that's confounded me—this question I keep asking: How can this new identity I've taken on be at once central and incidental? I aspire to Asch's answer, though it's far more easily articulated than enacted: that everyone ought to ignore blindness, including the blind themselves, until the prejudice and discrimination of the sighted world forces us to pay attention to it again. Dorothy Roberts wrote approvingly at the end of her obituary for Asch, "Adrienne wanted mainly for us to see her and others with disabilities as unremarkable. As she put it in a 2006 interview: 'I'm neither unhappy nor proud. I just am.'"

10.

Half Smiling

Even though the twenty-four units at the McGeorge Mountain Terrace apartments are all occupied—music often blasts from a window on the second floor, and laughter wafts up by the picnic tables—there isn't a single car in its parking lot. This is because none of its residents have driver's licenses.

The McGeorge apartments are in Littleton, a suburb of Denver, less than two miles from the Colorado Center for the Blind, one of the NFB's three residential training centers; they house nearly all of the CCB's students. At 8:41 a.m. every weekday, a dozen or so residents holding long white canes and wearing backpacks loiter around the bus shelter at the curb below the apartments, awaiting the bus to the center, where they learn how to be better at being blind.

When I tell people how I'm writing about blindness, they sometimes accuse me of overintellectualizing my situation—using my interest in the ideas and history that surround blindness as a shield against what they see as its more urgent emotional demands. I'll admit that I do enjoy thinking about the philosophical questions that blindness raises, the way it opens doors into fundamental ideas about how we perceive and experience the world. It's also comparatively easy for me to immerse myself in blindness the way I have been for the past three years: interviewing blind people about their lives, reading disability history, even documenting my own trials in vision loss as I pass by its first milestones. At some point I began to think of the process of writing this book—like the process of gradual vision loss itself—as a journey that starts in the shallow end of blindness and moves by icy degrees into the deep end. But I still felt like I hadn't experienced the real immersion I'd need. Even with my cane sweeping the road in front of me, I was still mostly living in my eyes, clinging to my residual vision, and trying to maintain a sighted relationship with the world.

So it seemed important to confront what real blindness feels like—and not in the problematic way that the Foundation Fighting Blindness's Blindfold Challenge offered, where the mask goes on and you experience a few minutes of fumbling meant to scare you into coughing up a donation. I needed something more intensive, more sustained. The best way to find it, I surmised, was to spend time at one of the NFB's residential training centers.

These centers require their students to wear sleep shades for seven or eight hours a day, for an average stay of nine months. They're run almost entirely by blind people, who teach residents how to read braille, use screen readers, cook meals, sweep floors, cross busy streets, even use power saws in on-site woodshops—all using nonvisual techniques. Students in the adult programs range from recent high school graduates to retirees, those who've been blind from birth to those who've just lost their sight, people with no light perception to folks with more vision than I have. The three NFB centers, in Colorado, Louisiana, and Minnesota, had been closed or offering virtual instruction for most of the pandemic, but in early 2021, they were beginning to welcome small groups of students back to their campuses. I wrote to the directors of all three, and got the most immediate and affirmative reply from Julie Deden, the director of the CCB. Impulsively, I booked my travel for a two-week stay. Julie asked if I wanted to spend some time under sleep shades while I was there, supplemented by other periods when I'd conduct interviews or observe the classes visually. Though I'd only be staying for two weeks, I told her I wanted the full student experience: Whenever students are under sleep shades, I said, I want to wear them too. When they're cleaning the kitchen, that's what I'll do too.

On my first morning in Littleton, Isabella, a staff member at the center, gave me a ride from my room at the nearby apartment complex to the center itself. Another CCB student, Sienna, who had a mobility disability in addition to her blindness, rode with us. On the drive, Sienna told me she'd had major surgery on her legs and her brain when she was three, which had left her nearly blind and in need of mobility aids like her walker. When we arrived, I helped get her walker out of the trunk. As she was pulling herself out of the car, she dropped her coffee, which landed in a brown explosion across the asphalt. She mourned the loss of her coffee with a low-key "I hate Mondays"–style resignation, and angled her long white cane over her walker like a pool cue. She made her way toward the center, a low-slung concrete building framed by picnic benches and trees. A few days earlier, Denver had been through a historic blizzard, and I watched with concern as Sienna plowed her walker into one of the icy piles of snow that ran the length of the sidewalk.

Isabella urged me not to wait. "Go ahead," she said. "There's a handicap button on the door she can press." I felt torn; it didn't seem right to leave Sienna out there in the snow. But Isabella, seeing me hesitate, said again, more firmly: *Go ahead.* The day before, on our drive from the airport, she'd told me that she'd been reminded a few times by the CCB's director not to be so helpful to the students. Several staff members later said that they'd received similar admonishments—the center's goal was to raise expectations for its students, and refrain from intervening in the ways that parents and teachers likely had for most of their lives. I looked back once more, as Sienna made her way slowly around the snowbank, then left her there.

Isabella was one of only two sighted employees at the Colorado Center. Inside, the receptionist heard me enter and asked who I was, her gaze not quite meeting mine. When I identified myself, she called out to Martin, who emerged from his office and opened a wardrobe along the wall filled with long white canes. These canes were different from the one I'd received from my state vocational rehabilitation counselor back home; that one was aluminum, folded down to the size of a baton, and had a large white ball at the end that I rolled along sidewalks in a clatter. The NFB centers don't allow their students to use any other style of cane than their own. The NFB cane was originally produced by a fishing pole manufacturer, and it shares a fishing rod's flexible, lightweight footprint. Every aspect of the design has its source in NFB philosophy: it doesn't fold up, because the NFB (and its training centers) don't want their students to do what I and so many others did—stash it in a bag as soon as it doesn't feel absolutely necessary. A sixty-inch-long, unfoldable white cane is impossible to hide. And that's a good thing, because blindness isn't something to be hidden! Wield your cane with pride! Its length, too, has philosophical origins: the longer the cane, the more quickly and confidently its user can walk. With a sixty-inch cane, you're getting feedback at least three feet ahead of your step, so you can move through the world with speed and confidence. No more mincing and shuffling for the blind! Stride toward your goals with purpose!

Along with the cane, Martin handed me a pair of sleep shades, the kind I'd first seen NFB-center trainees wear back at the national convention. He paged another staffer, Charles, over the center's intercom, and soon my new travel instructor arrived, wearing a sleeve of tattoos on each arm and a beard visible through his bandanna-style face mask, which made him look like a train robber who'd watched a lot of skateboarding videos. Charles walked with a white cane, too, though as he greeted me I thought he could see a little. He must be a high partial—a blind person who retains a decent amount of vision, like me. He trailed behind me as we walked to his office, giving me directions: "At the bottom of these stairs, take a one-eighty," he said, guiding us into a hallway that ran in the opposite direction of the stairs we'd just come down. Even though I hadn't yet put on the sleep shades, my travel instruction had begun.

After the initial shock of entering a building that's staffed and populated almost entirely by blind people, I soon recognized the feeling I'd gotten when I was at the NFB convention: I had entered a blind space. It's a powerful feeling, full of relief and liberation, when one is no longer the outlier and the seemingly indelible stigmas of blindness are lifted. I noticed it everywhere I went on my first day: people knocking into one another, for example, and jokingly saying, "Hey, man, what'd you bump into me for?" in a tone that made it clear it was totally fine. If anything, they were mocking the idea that someone could ever be put out by a blind person accidentally jostling them. People also announced themselves constantly, and I soon felt no shame responding to a greeting with a casual "Who's that?"

Even so, Julie Deden, the director, told me early in my stay that it was important to leave blind spaces eventually; the center is, like any school, designed to push its students out of the nest once they've graduated. Program leaders reminded students that the reason they immersed themselves in blindness was to learn to navigate the sighted world with independence. It was a ticket to rehabilitation—a return to the mainstream, not a refuge from it. But the power of blind spaces, and blind solidarity, was seductive.

It didn't take me long to recognize the incredible insularity of the CCB, a reality that seemed directly connected to this solidarity. Nearly every blind staffer at CCB is married or in a relationship with another blind staffer (or ex-staffer or alum), and almost all of them are former CCB students. Students and staff told me that the population of Littleton includes a disproportionate number of blind people, many of whom graduated from CCB and then stuck around. Alums sometimes showed up at the apartments to drink with the current students. When I was out later that evening with Charles and his fiancée, Stephanie—another CCB grad, now teaching home management there—they casually asked, as they strolled down the street ahead of me, hand in hand, their canes swinging in unison, if my wife was blind too. It was an entirely friendly question, but it also contained, I thought, a suggestion that this was something for me to consider, a good way of doing things. When I said no, they followed up by asking if I had many blind friends back home. I told them I was working on it, but that in my small city, most of the blind people I'd met were at least thirty years older, and felt more like an affectionate klatch of honorary blind moms than peers. Charles and Steph listened to me in silence; I felt (perhaps unfairly) like they were judging me a little—like I'd revealed my desire to cling to life in a sighted world, when an immersion in blindness had so much more to offer.

• • •

Half an hour into my first day there, Charles told me it was time to put on the sleep shades. The shades' stretchy Velcro strap attached to a flexible hard-shell mask, which was padded around the edges with a generous slice of soft foam. I folded up my glasses, gingerly slid them into my breast pocket, and pulled the shades over my head. The black foam pressed softly into my face. I was surprised by how completely the shades blocked out the light—I saw only blackness, even around the edges.

"OK," Charles said, "follow me." I stood up and set my new cane in front of me, following the sound of his voice and soft footsteps across the carpet. He helpfully knocked his cane against the door to his office. "How are you with angles?" he said. "You seemed to handle that one-eighty all right. Make a forty-five-degree turn to the left here." I made a hard left. "That's more like ninety degrees, but OK." Embarrassed, I corrected course. When I'd made the one-eighty earlier, without shades, it had been obvious what he meant: I saw that I needed to walk through the doorway to my right and then head back in the direction we'd come, down the adjoining hall. With the shades on, "forty-five degrees" felt abstract; I was a blue dot on a black map, with no sense of where I was in relation to anything around me. It took an extra minute or two to make it upstairs, where Charles guided me to the room where my next class was about to begin.

Home management is normally held in the center's kitchen, where students learn to cook and clean; the final assignment, after nine months in the program, is to prepare a meal for the entire student body and staff—in non-COVID times, about sixty people. But since it was Friday, that day's class was taken up by a mostly good-natured argument between the teachers and the students about how home inspections were graded. Students have to clean their apartments while wearing their sleep shades, and once a month the home management instructors—both of them totally blind—come and run their hands over everything, marking off points for showers that feel slimy or crumbs they discover under the fridge.

After class, my mentor, Cragar, came to find me. Every new student is assigned a mentor—a fellow student who's been there longer—to help them get oriented, find the bus, and integrate into the community. The center's teachers offered formal instruction, and the peer mentors—like assistant blindness tutors—provided informal reinforcement of those lessons. Cragar and I had met the day before, at the apartments, where no one wears sleep shades. As we'd regarded each other, there was an odd moment of sizing up each other's vision—I'd thought I could see him actually looking, and I felt him observing the same ability in me. We were a pair of high partials, scoping each other out.

The tour Cragar gave me at the center, both of us under sleep shades, was lively and efficient—I could tell right away that he was a star student. He'd fully adopted the NFB's style of hands-off help—which they call "structured discovery"—asking leading questions like *What direction do you think we're facing? What do you notice about this wall? Do you remember which way we go from here?*—rather than just feeding me information or pulling me along by the elbow. But by the end of the day, I still wouldn't be able to get around on my own. I felt a special shame, later, when I was forced to tell Cragar that I had to use the bathroom again, and he gamely guided me there.

We finished our tour in a small meeting room, where we waited for lunch. A student nicknamed Jackie was graduating that day and would be cooking his final meal, which he'd been planning and practicing for weeks. He had a high voice, and I'd spent most of the day thinking he was a woman. But people kept calling Jackie *man* and *buddy*, and with some effort I finally reworked the mental image I'd drawn of him. I didn't actually see him until close to the end of my trip, where I found that my revised image was fairly accurate—though it's hard to be sure; as soon as I saw him, the mental picture I'd made was destroyed, instantly overwritten with the impression I'd gathered with my eyes. It was like seeing a film version of a favorite book, the actor irrevocably replacing the face of the character you've been imagining for so long.

As a COVID safety measure, everyone broke out into small groups to eat in separate rooms. (Masking was required, but with sleep shades on, and an almost entirely blind staff, enforcement was spotty.) I found a seat with what sounded like the teenage cohort of CCB students. Over the next two weeks I'd learn more about the social organization of the student body, which Cragar compared with high school cliques: cool kids and nerds. The wide age range made for some unlikely friendships; a few teenagers became drinking buddies with people pushing fifty. The most common time for a person to come to the center for training was just after high school, for a gap year, to sharpen one's blindness skills before living on one's own for the first time. Other students, like Cragar, had taken time off during college, having realized that they didn't quite have the skills they wanted to succeed at a university as a blind person. And there were a number of older adults in the program, whose lives and careers had been diverted by sudden blindness.

In my first few days, I met students who'd been blind from birth and others who'd lost their vision recently, from an astonishing range of causes. There were all the greatest hits of eye disease (Stargardt, RP, retinoblastoma) as well as a few ultrarare conditions I'd never heard of. Several people I met had traumatic brain injuries from gunshot wounds. Alice, a bright and hilarious woman in her forties, told me the first time I met her that after her husband shot her, her doctors woke her up from a drug-induced coma to remove her ventilator, informed her she was permanently blind, and then asked her for her permission to remove her eyeballs. Then they put her back under. "I never mourned the loss of my vision," she told me one day as we made our way around the sidewalk next to the bus loop, looking for the bus that went back to the apartments. "I just woke up and started moving forward." She told me she'd had a number of "shenanigans" at the center, her word for falls she'd taken, including a visit to the emergency room after she slipped off a curb during her travel class and slammed her head into a parked truck. She discovered after this ER visit that she'd been living with significant hearing loss; after she got fitted with hearing aids, her balance improved, and the number of shenanigans she endured declined.

At one point a few days into my stay, as I sat in the lunchroom listening to the chatter around me, an obvious but nonetheless powerful idea dawned on me: *How strange,* I thought, *that I'm still myself, even under sleep shades.* I'd built up blindness so much in my mind, heard stories of people not being able to handle total occlusion for the first few days, but now this felt surprisingly normal. It felt doable. I felt encouraged.

To be fair, I reminded myself, I wasn't actually blind. At four p.m. I'd tear off the shades and return to my luxurious patch of usable central vision. There were a number of high partials like me at the center, who with sleep shades off could see if another student had wandered off course on their way to the bus stop (which happened every day on the way home—usually the same two guys, who Cragar always hung back to help). Another high partial I met played his Nintendo Switch with the screen pressed literally to his nose. But many students had no useful vision, just smears and shadows, and those few with no light perception whatsoever weren't required to wear sleep shades at all.

As I acclimated to life under sleep shades, I began to notice a shift in the way I inhabited and experienced the world. A new sort of patience settled over me. I felt content to just sit and listen, whereas without the shades I'd be more inclined to look at my phone, to scour the room, to restlessly, visually roam about. My attention under sleep shades felt like it had taken a different shape.

A new voice entered the room and said, "Aw, man, why am I in *here?*" Everyone instantly responded: "*Alice!*" Alice had wandered into the small meeting room by mistake and, after saying hi, headed off toward wherever she'd meant to go. This was another change I noticed in my experience of the world under sleep shades: a good-natured acceptance of ending up somewhere other than where I'd intended. I'd be searching for the bathroom or a classroom, but ended up in Isabella's or Martin's office instead. He was always friendly about it—"Hi, Andrew," he'd said with an audible smile, instantly understanding that I hadn't meant to come visit him. Everyone who worked in the building was accustomed to new students wandering into their offices by mistake, exchanging a few pleasantries before heading off to their intended destinations.

Over the intercom, we were called to lunch. I felt a little apprehensive about eating under sleep shades for the first time—would I make a mess? I followed Cragar to a little rectangular window where Jackie and a few helpers were passing through plates of food. Jackie had made arroz con pollo for his final meal, which I discovered in a paper bowl sitting on the plate, along with two mystery items. I tasted the first—a homemade plantain chip. I picked up the second, figuring it was a roll, meant to be dipped into the chicken and rice, but after a tentative bite, I was sweetly surprised to find that it was an orange-flavored cookie. I ate carefully, but found that after nearly forty years of bringing utensils from my plate to my mouth, I was pretty good at it. Only once did I raise an accidentally empty plastic fork to my lips; a few times I used my fingers to gently maneuver some food onto my fork. All in all, I don't think I looked too different than I do when I eat with my eyes.

The notion that blind people have better hearing than the sighted is a fallacy, but relying on one's ears does change one's relationship with sound. At lunch, Cragar's wife, Meredith, who was visiting from Houston, came into the room carrying their fifteen-month-old daughter,

Poppy. The teenagers quieted down as Poppy started babbling, and I was struck by the toddler's powerful sonic presence. The sounds she made—cooing, laughing, simple words—cut through the room like washes of color. I didn't quite hallucinate these colors, but I came close. My visual cortex was still switched on. Over the coming weeks, I had several mildly psychedelic experiences like this, synesthesia and visionless visualizations.

I was also struck by the vividness of my tactile impressions. In the art room, a teacher showed me how to pull a wire with two loops on either end through a mound of wet clay in a plastic bag, lopping off a hunk I could take back to my seat. Later that evening, as I described the experience to Oscar and Lily on a video call, I had to forcefully remind myself that I'd never actually seen this tool, or the clay, even though my memory of it was overwhelmingly visual. The tableau was utterly clear in my mind's eye.

My entire sense of space felt like it was gradually transforming. Walking the carpeted halls of the center's lower level, I could see a faint black-and-blue minimalist landscape, a virtual-reality environment lit by some psychic, unseen light source. More than once I peeled the edge of my shades up just to confirm that this other blue world was a fiction. Each time, it was remarkable to realize that the shimmering shadow vectors I'd been traveling through were all in my mind, and that there was in fact a stingingly bright, permeating yellow shine filling the rooms of the center instead. It was a relief to let the shades snap back into place and return to that cool, dark landscape.

Sometimes my cane penetrated one of these velvety black-blue walls that I felt I could see before me, and I had to redraw my mental map. My mind struggled with the effort of this recalibration; it was actually easier to continue to believe that there was a wall there, even when my cane gave me solid feedback that it was empty space. At other times I felt dizzy, especially when I was out in the city with Charles, who informed me in his West Coast deadpan of my errors—that what I thought was Alamo was actually Prince Street, and that I wasn't facing east as I'd been so sure I was. In those moments, I had to lift the entire landscape up in my mind, rotate it 90 degrees, and gently set it back down. I could almost feel my mental muscles trembling under the strain.

After lunch, everyone called in to Zoom—audio only—to attend Jackie's graduation. A few people put the call on speakerphone, and as we listened to teachers and students pay their tributes, we could hear their voices bleeding through the doorways and walls and phones all around us, creating an effect like a loudspeaker at a ballgame, an echoing broadcast. At the end of the toasts, Julie handed Jackie his Freedom Bell, which all CCB graduates receive as a symbol of their newfound independence as blind people. It was emblazoned with the motto TAKE CHARGE WITH CONFIDENCE AND SELF-RELIANCE! When the bell rings, Julie explained, it represents not just Jackie's independence, but that of blind people everywhere. Jackie rang his bell, and then Cragar and I headed downstairs to braille class.

• • •

Rehabilitation services tend to fall into the gravitational pull of the low expectations that so many sighted people have for the blind. In his landmark 1969 study *The Making of Blind Men*, the sociologist Robert Scott visited dozens of public and private agencies for the blind in the US, most of them modeled after the rehabilitation centers for veterans that the US government established in the wake of World War II. Scott concluded that the vast majority of these agencies took an "accommodative approach," by which he meant that they assumed that blind people are incapable of real independence, and that any exceptions to this rule are modern miracles rather than realistic models. Scott saw evidence of this attitude everywhere in the agencies he visited, observing bells installed over their front doors, so the blind could easily find the entrance from the street; cafeterias that served only precut, manageable foods, and those only with spoons, to avoid any unpleasant awkwardness with a fork or knife; and bingo nights "played with the aid of a corps of volunteers who oversee the game, attending to anything the blind person is unable to do himself." Scott saw the workers at these agencies celebrate their clients for the tiniest accomplishments, with the result that "since anything they do is praised as outstanding, many of them come to believe that the underlying assumption must be that blindness makes them incompetent." Per his book's title, Scott's conclusion was that this treatment more than any other factor was responsible for the making of blind men. Blind people in a state of vulnerability—recently injured, or attempting to push beyond sheltered lives—came to internalize the low expectations that much of the sighted world had for them.

Scott found a handful of agencies that took an alternative approach. He saw the clearest expression of what he called the "restorative" approach in the writings of Father Thomas Carroll, a Catholic priest who had worked with blinded World War II veterans at the army's experimental rehabilitation centers, where many innovations in blindness rehab—including the long white cane—were first developed. Carroll eventually established a residential training center of his own at the site of the Catholic Guild for All the Blind, in Newton, Massachusetts. After his death in 1971, it was rededicated in his name, and the Carroll Center remains one of the best-known residential blindness training centers on the East Coast. In *The Making of Blind Men*, Scott praised Carroll's belief that the average blind person is fundamentally capable of achieving independence. I approached Carroll's own book, *Blindness: What It Is, What It Does, and How to Live with It*, with optimism, held up as it was by Scott and others as a positive vision of blindness rehabilitation. But it turned out to contain some of the darkest and most depressing writing on blindness I've yet encountered.

Carroll's book begins with the observation that "loss of sight is a dying." For the blind man, he continues, this loss is "a blow almost to his being itself." Carroll spends the first section of his book going into exquisite detail on all the ways in which blindness is a death: loss of physical integrity, loss of confidence in the remaining senses, loss of the "visual perception of the pleasurable," and on and on. Along the way, Carroll casually but firmly dismisses any possibility that blindness might have something positive to offer. The point of this immersion in blindness's deprivations is to justify the program he goes on to expound in the rest of the book, emphasizing psychological care alongside cane travel and "techniques of daily living," and dedicated to restoring all the losses the blind person has incurred. But in Carroll's description, these techniques will always be substitutes for the superior advantages that sight once provided.

Carroll's philosophy met its sharpest critic in Kenneth Jernigan, the second long-term president of the NFB, who rejected Carroll's Freudian sense of blindness as castration and death in favor of the civil-rights-oriented view of it as merely a characteristic, limiting in the way that all characteristics are limiting. A blind person can't be sighted, he said, in the same way that a white house can't be blue, and so what? Jernigan, blind from birth, was an early, active member of the NFB, and eventually he moved to Northern California to work with the NFB's founder, Jacobus tenBroek, on codifying a blind-positive philosophy of vocational rehabilitation centered around this idea: that blindness is a neutral characteristic, with its own limitations as well as advantages, just like intelligence, income level, or hair color.

In the late 1950s, tenBroek, Jernigan, and their associates in the NFB proposed an experiment: they'd take control of one of the state agencies for the blind (of the custodial, accommodationist variety that Robert Scott had described) and refashion it according to their own principles. When a director position opened up soon afterward at the Iowa Commission for the Blind—an agency that a federal study had just rated as one of the worst in the country—they seized the opportunity. Jernigan got the job, and moved to Des Moines, transforming its training center into a prototype for the independent centers—like the one I was staying at, in Colorado—that the federation would establish more than twenty years later.

In the early 1960s, Carroll and Jernigan engaged in public sparring matches at blindness conferences, articulating tensions that still play out within the blind rehab system today. The NFB remains at odds with the organization that certifies orientation and mobility (O&M) instruction, criticizing the custodialism of their methods, their disinclination to train and hire blind mobility instructors, and their emphasis on skills like memorizing routes and counting steps over the more flexible and exploratory "structured discovery" method the NFB advocates (and that I'd experienced on my first walk with Cragar at CCB). Julie Deden told me that when she and the leaders of the two other NFB training centers visited the Carroll Center a few years back, she tried to go with an open mind. But, she said, she was shocked by the degree to which the center sheltered its students. She described the staff's lack of trust in their students to not injure themselves—they received permission only after a few weeks to even enter the kitchen, whereas at the NFB centers, you're working in the kitchen from day one. "Everything was on guide rails there," a blind graduate of the Carroll Center told me. "Everyone was being guided to their seats."

The NFB centers all have woodshops, where students can design cabinets and learn how to use power saws; putting blind people in front of such tools would be an unthinkable arrangement at most agencies for the blind. When I told people I was going to Colorado to wear sleep shades all day every day, most people sounded excited for me—crossing streets, cooking on the stove, good for you! But when I added that they had a woodshop, almost invariably, people's excitement dampened. For the NFB, though, there is unparalleled empowerment in activities that the average sighted (or blind) person would find unthinkably dangerous. It's another part of their larger program of raising people's expectations for the blind, and blind people's expectations of themselves.

Depending on who you ask, the NFB centers are famous—or notorious—for their radical approach to training. One non-NFBer, when I told her I was going to Colorado, said, "People come back from those programs *loaded for bear*"—ready to hunt the big game of living with blindness. That's the image that the NFB cultivates: a sort of Navy SEAL blindness training, grueling and immersive, whose graduates are prepared for anything blindness might throw at them. Among the requirements for graduation is the Independent Drop, where you put on sleep shades (required of all students with any degree of light perception) and someone drives you around the city in circles, before letting you off, alone, at a mystery location. Without using your phone, and asking only one person one question, you have to find your way back to the training center. Some students begin their training having barely crossed the boundaries of their own front yards without assistance, and so it takes a lot to get them to this point. Instructors have a reputation for tough love: *This is what you signed up for. This is why you're here. Push yourself.*

There is real power in the NFB's philosophy of blindness as a nonlimiting characteristic, and deep ableism in Father Carroll's insistence on a blind person's fundamental incompleteness. But sixty years on from these debates, it's clear that aspects of the NFB's teaching philosophy have failed some of the blind people it was meant to serve. A few months before I arrived in Denver, the NFB centers had been the subject of a huge wave of criticism. Dozens of people shared stories of sexual abuse they experienced or witnessed in the NFB, including at the training centers. At the end of 2021, the *Colorado Sun* reported out shocking stories at CCB, building on the findings of the external investigation the NFB commissioned in 2020. These allegations included "the alleged sexual assault of a 13-year-old girl by a summer youth camp counselor in 2001, of which police have no record; a teacher accused of sexually harassing students in 2019 who was hired despite school leadership allegedly knowing he had faced accusations of unwanted sexual contact at another school; and a teacher who admitted he engaged in a sexual relationship with a 19-year-old student in violation of school policy." According to the *Sun*, none of these allegations are currently being investigated by police; in two cases, the accusers declined to report the incident to the police because of the emotional toll such a proceeding would incur. (At the CCB's sister center in Ruston, Louisiana, however, a Ruston grand jury voted to indict a former employee with eighteen counts of child molestation by an educator; he pleaded not guilty and was released on bond in December 2021.) The NFB has declined to speak publicly about any specific allegations beyond the findings of its official investigation, which outlined a series of general recommendations for reform. These included increasing resources and oversight for overburdened staff at the training centers and overhauling the response protocols for future sexual-misconduct complaints. While I was in Colorado, the staff and students all took a mandatory half-day training with the Rape, Abuse & Incest National Network—the first time anyone in the organization had been required to take sexual harassment training of any kind, despite the fact that the NFB had been running residential centers since 1985.

This sort of institutionalized abuse is hardly limited to the NFB—similar stories have emerged from schools for the blind around the world. Part of the problem is certainly, as the NFB's current president has argued, societal; these sorts of abuses happen everywhere, from tiny colleges to giant corporations, and a blindness training center is no exception. But it's also true that disabled people are disproportionately affected by sexual abuse. A US Department of Justice study of data from 2009 to 2014 found that people with disabilities were two and a half times as likely to experience violent attacks—including rape and sexual assault—as nondisabled people.

Graduates of the NFB centers also shared stories of racist and ableist microaggressions, which they explicitly connected to a broadly retrograde culture at the NFB. Many students at the centers had, in addition to blindness, a range of other disabilities: hearing loss, mobility impairments, mental health issues, cognitive disabilities. Blind students with learning disabilities reported being mocked for having poor orientation and mobility skills; their spatial impairments made the intense mental mapping that blind cane travel requires a particular challenge.

In an open letter in the wake of the sexual abuse allegations, a group of blind activists and allies outlined their demands. "What blind consumers want in the year 2020 is not what they may have wanted in previous decades," they wrote. "We don't want to be bullied or humiliated or have our boundaries pushed 'for our own good.'"

For generations, the NFB has fought against custodialism, downplaying or reframing the vulnerability of blind people. In his rebuttals to Father Carroll, Kenneth Jernigan seemed to mock the notion that a blind person needed emotional support as a part of their rehabilitation. According to Carroll, Jernigan wrote with seeming derision,

> what the blind person needs most is not travel training but therapy. He will be taught to accept his limitations as insurmountable and his difference from others as unbridgeable. He will be encouraged to adjust to his painful station as a second-class citizen and discouraged

> from any thought of breaking and entering the first-class compartment. Moreover, all of this will be done in the name of teaching him "independence" and a "realistic" approach to his blindness.

But the reckoning of 2020 has forced the federation into an uncomfortable confrontation with the reality of the tremendous vulnerability and pain of many blind people. As part of its response, the NFB no longer dismisses therapy—as Jernigan seemed to in his public comments—and it now maintains a fund that pays for counseling for its members who are survivors of sexual violence that occurred within the organization. Would an NFB more attuned to the vulnerability of disability have been able to protect its members from harm?

• • •

I felt most emotionally overwhelmed in Colorado during a moment when my sleep shades were off, in a conversation I had with a sighted woman on a warm Saturday afternoon. For the first time that spring, students fired up the grill that stood lopsided next to the parking lot and brought out some burgers and drinks. After a week at the center, I felt like I'd begun to make a few friends. I'd enjoyed hanging out with Ahmed, who also had RP. Though he was ten years younger than I was, the disease had already destroyed his useful vision. He often left his sleep shades on at the end of the day when the other students tore them off, mostly because they cut the glare of the sun that he found so painful. After a long, slow decline, he'd lost the bulk of his residual sight during his last year at law school. With a little help from his state vocational rehabilitation agency, he'd managed to figure out how to use a screen reader and a cane and still graduated on time, but his progression into real blindness took a deep emotional toll. After he passed the bar exam in DC, he moved to Tulsa, where he had what he describes as a lost year. He deflected most of my questions about what he actually did during his time in Oklahoma, only gesturing toward its bleakness. "But why Tulsa?" I asked.

"Because it was cheap," he said. He just needed a place to go and be alone with his new blindness. With all apologies to a city I've enjoyed visiting in the past, after listening to Ahmed, I began thinking of Tulsa as the depressing place one goes when one confronts that final loss of sight. When would I move to Tulsa? Right now, I'm still on the highway, a few states away, but the city has started to show up on road signs, with decreasing distances next to its name.

Ahmed's wife, Hend, a psychiatrist, had moved to Littleton to be with him while he went through the program, and I pulled away from the gaggle of blind bros to introduce myself. I asked her if she thought Ahmed had changed while he was in Colorado.

"I like that he's cooking so much now," she said, alluding to the endless series of meal-planning assignments the home management team gave its students. "But honestly, after he went blind in law school, he figured most of this stuff out on his own, just to survive. The thing I think he's gotten out of the program the most," she said, "is the camaraderie. He's never had blind friends like this. It means a lot to him."

Until she pointed it out, I hadn't realized how moved I'd been by the care I'd seen the students show one another. Later that weekend, Amelia, who'd only been at the center for a few weeks, came out of her room to socialize outside of school hours for the first time. Cragar, ever the mentor and tour guide, pointed out to me how interesting it was to see unexpected friendships develop at the center, gesturing at Amelia and Hank, an impassive guy in reflective Oakleys I'd met in Charles's office on my first day. They were sitting side by side on a couch in one of the apartments, each wearing dark sunglasses and facing straight ahead, like they were in a parked car. They passed a weed vape back and forth, and I overheard Hank say, "When I first lost my sight, I didn't leave my bed for a month."

That night, Hank, Amelia, and Ahmed—all totally blind, and, aside from Ahmed, still beginners in their O&M training—wanted to make a liquor store run. As the three of them made their way down the apartments' empty parking lot toward the busy road that led to the shopping center, Cragar and Tony, another experienced student, consulted each other on whether someone should go with them. If Cragar and Tony weren't blind, or if they had said it any differently, I think I would have found it patronizing. But the way it went down, it felt like a gesture of love, of care. Cragar and Tony didn't want to guide them, barking commands to stay back from the curb—they just wanted to make sure a more experienced traveler tagged along, to be there in case they got lost. "I'll go," I offered, figuring my residual vision qualified me as a suitable helper. But as I followed the group, my presence felt unnecessary. Ahmed didn't even drink—he was just out with his friends, and he knew the route backward and forward. He literally walked backward for part of the trip, cracking jokes as he steered Amelia and Hank away from a loading dock at the back of the shopping center that he'd heard them wander into.

The single most important skill for blind travel, Ahmed later told me, is that "you have to be willing to get lost, and be confident in your ability to figure it out." In the early days of his blindness, he once took three hours to traverse a route that would have taken him five minutes with a sighted guide. Eventually he got better at navigating Washington, DC, learning the direction of traffic, the patterns of certain stoplights, the way the sound of another person's footsteps changes as they begin descending a set of stairs. In Colorado, he learned to use cardinal directions, and can now often figure out which way he's facing from the feeling of the sun on his face. But, he added, "it's not like once you leave CCB, you'll never get lost again." This is useful practical advice for any blind traveler, but also points to a larger idea that blindness can offer anyone: the experience of being lost, like the experience of loss itself, need not be an occasion for pity and tragedy, panic and disaster. Like Josh Miele's "graceful cascade of failure," missteps can be fruitful. Getting lost is not always comfortable, or pleasant, but it is an organic and fundamental part of the human experience. The more one is able to accept it, rather than fight it, the more skillful one becomes in one's travels.

The Colorado Center had provided a road out of Tulsa for Ahmed. I'd only known him for a week by that point, but I still thought he seemed a little depressed, in the wary way he talked about his past and in the pained reserve with which he sometimes spoke about blindness. But when I watched him out with these two other students—walking backward, making jokes—I could see what Hend meant: this camaraderie was gradually transforming him. Was it restoring him to the man he was before? Or had that man vanished in Tulsa, to allow Ahmed to be rehabilitated into a new person, reborn into blindness?

I also thought that this camaraderie suggested an alternative model of care, and of blindness, one that synthesized the contradictory visions of Kenneth Jernigan and Father Carroll. A blind person who's not broken, but who's still vulnerable; blindness itself as at once a non-defining characteristic and a serious disability; and a path to rehabilitation that doesn't mean accepting deprivations, but that still demands an acknowledgment of the pain that one must pass through to arrive at blindness's full joy and humanity.

• • •

I'm not sure I'll ever return to Colorado for the full nine-month program. As much as I know I'd benefit from the immersion—particularly the travel instruction—I can't stand the idea of being away from Oscar and Lily for that long. It's also an ego-stinging proposition, moving in with mostly teenagers who are learning how to do things—cook, clean, format a Microsoft Word document—that I've been doing effortlessly for most of my life. I know I'll need to relearn those skills, but the idea of pausing for nine months to focus on them is hard to fathom.

As I continue my blindness training at home—walking different routes around my city under sleep shades; making my family dinner without letting myself waste time visually scanning for the spatula—I'm struck by the mindfulness that blindness requires. In these moments, as I stand on a corner through several stoplight cycles trying to decode the traffic pattern, or run my hands up and down the counter in search of the garlic, blindness doesn't feel at all like the death of the sighted person that

Father Carroll insisted it was. Rather, it feels like a cultivation of what the Zen teacher Shunryu Suzuki called "beginner's mind." I may be a middle-aged man with a master's degree, but I'm still going to have to take a deep breath in, let it out, and try one more time to find the door to the men's room, even if I know all my friends can see me groping around in the dark from their perches at the bar. Bryan Bashin, the director of the San Francisco LightHouse, described "the Zen of blindness" in an interview. "Having been both sighted, low vision, and blind," he said, "I can say that savoring the world as a blind person is often a bit slower and can often be beautiful in rich and unexpected ways."

When I walk around town with my cane these days, I can still see the effect it has on strangers: people will literally cross to the other side of the street when they see me coming, and parents yank their children aside when I'm still half a block away. Literature is full of evidence of such reactions to blind people in public. (Baudelaire: "Like mannequins, vaguely ridiculous, / Peculiar, terrible somnambulists, / Beaming—who can say where—their eyes of night.") This experience—every day, on every block—of appearing as a *peculiar mannequin* adds up. I can feel my face beginning to harden into a permanent grimace, and I catch myself regarding every stranger as a hostile, judgmental adversary.

This is no way to move through the world. So I've recently added a technique to my cane-travel practice that has transformed my experience of being blind in public. In addition to all the usual O&M tricks—how to hold my cane, paying attention to cardinal directions—I also try to cultivate a half smile. This is an idea I first encountered in an interview with the artist Helen Mirra, whose work often takes her on long walks and hikes through the wilderness. She found herself walking around Cambridge, where she lived, wishing she were still in the unpeopled forests and mountains she frequented. But she realized this desire was preventing her from being present in the city. "Then I started practicing half-smiling," she said, "exactly as described by Thích Nhất Hạnh," a Buddhist monk whose teachings she'd studied. The practice itself is very simple, as Mirra explains on her website. "The half-smile is slight, just enough, barely apparent." Wearing a half smile, she told her interviewer, means "meeting absolutely everything and everybody, always, with equanimity and friendliness."

I was initially turned off by this idea, which I found precious. You walk around town with a little smirk on your face and that makes everything better? But the idea of the half smile has stayed with me, and gradually changed my life. It's not a smirk, or fake cheerfulness; the partiality of the smile is important. *Half* is enough that even if you're faking it, forcing a frown into a half smile, it works. And in times when I feel overwhelmed as a blind person—a crowded line I can't figure out my place in, people moving and jostling and rattling heavy unseen hand trucks inches from my ankles—I'll begin to shut down and anxiety about my place in space takes over. But as soon as I put on the half smile, my grimace softens, and I'm no longer the embattled blind guy, the terrible Baudelairean somnambulist. I'm restored to the status of one person encountering another, "with equanimity and friendliness."

In his teaching on the half smile, Hạnh writes, "We seem to move forward, but we don't go anywhere; we are not drawn by a goal. Thus we smile while we are walking." My walking still has a goal—I'm going to pick up Oscar from school, or meet Lily for lunch, or whatever—but that goal has been emptied of meaning. Walking becomes a form of meditation. If I take longer than I intended (as I do more and more these days, adjusting to the pace of blindness), if someone seems confused or angry or heartbroken by the sight of my cane, if I get briefly but totally lost on a block I've walked down a dozen times before, it doesn't matter. I'm still here, still alive, making my way down the path I intended.

Conclusion: Endgame

Sitting on a bench near the Hayden Planetarium at the American Museum of Natural History, Oscar and I watched a blind mom approach a four-foot-tall metal model of the moon. It was as tall as her daughter, who she was chasing around the museum. They stopped long enough for the mother to run her fingers briefly along the moon's surface, feeling the shape and scale of its craters. I had the urge to approach her and say something, to give her some kind of solidarity from a fellow blind parent at the AMNH on a Sunday afternoon, doing the same thing she, and really most of the adults, was up to: trying like hell to keep track of our kids and enjoy ourselves in the process. It can be hard for blind people to find one another in public. A few blind friends have told me that when they hear the tap of a cane or the babble of a phone's screen reader on a bus or street corner, it's a rare delight; they'll usually approach the person to chat with them. But the blind mom I'd spotted quickly ran off after her daughter, and then it was my turn to resume chasing Oscar around the museum.

My experience that day was hyper-visual, even as I felt my blindness acutely. I searched for Oscar with constant vigilance, read the large print on the exhibits, and marveled at the astonishing fact that walruses exist. In the Hall of North American Mammals, bighorn sheep gazing proudly across the peaks of the Rockies stirred some kind of weird naturalist-patriotic feeling in me. But large swaths of the museum had become inaccessible since my earlier visits. I relied entirely on Oscar to find our seats in the planetarium's theater, and the movie itself was largely a sonic experience for me—I occasionally caught a glimpse of a passing planet or satellite, but for the most part, it was too dim.

Near the end of the day, we stopped in front of the owl diorama. It looked empty, like it might be closed for restorations, but Oscar said, with wonder in his voice, "Look at *that*." I told him I couldn't see anything, but if he wanted to, he could describe it for me. Without hesitation, he told me the owl's wings were spread wide, and it looked like it was about to capture a rodent. "The talons are like this," he said. With a pang of frustration I realized I couldn't quite see his hand either. I instinctively reached out to find it instead; his fingers had taken the shape of the owl's attacking claws.

There was something so natural in this exchange, and in our whole day together, that I felt like I'd unlocked a new, airy chamber in my life as a blind person. Oscar and I were in far greater touch with each other than we normally are—we walked hand in hand, or with my hand on his shoulder. Much of this touch was practical, but it was also affectionate. Standing in the crowded subway on our way home, I put my arm around him to keep a tactile eye on him, but as I did, he leaned his head into me, and the gesture was at once a functional accommodation for my blindness and a moment of love. The border between these two kinds of touch had dissolved. The day was wonderful not in spite of my blindness, or because of it, but merely alongside it.

• • •

It's striking how repetitive my journal entries are when I write about my experience of vision loss. I record the same short sequence of observations again and again, micro-variations on a theme. "I had a slight drop in vision in the last few days," I write—I'm not sure exactly *when* it happened, just that I started to notice it sometime in the last week or so. I express hesitation, ambivalence—could this just be a bad day? No, it's been a full week—this new low seems like a permanent feature of the landscape. I try to record what it looks like, how it manifests, and that's always the same too: I've lost something I've just put down—a mug, my cane, a pair of boots—that I should've been able to find more quickly. I start knocking into doorframes and tables that I'd never knocked into before. Reading, even with the assistive tech I've been using, has become more difficult. Everything is qualified by this sense that what I'm experiencing is happening "more and more," but not *too* much more—always "little by little." In a kind of Borgesian hall of mirrors, I conclude by pointing out the very sameness of the journal entries that I'm writing about now: *This is near identical to what I wrote a few months ago, including this observation about its sameness. It's so hard to make any new decline sound any different than the last one*. I always write about how I always write about the experience in the same way.

I try not to talk about my new-blindness anxieties around Oscar, but he's our house detective, listening acutely to everything we say, demanding clarification if anything is unclear, and so he's generally aware of where I'm at, whether I want him to be or not. His default response is usually matter-of-fact analysis. "Wow, you really *are* going blind," he said to me one day as I stared at the ground, trying to find a chopstick that was, for him, directly in my line of sight and, for me, swallowed into another dimension. More recently, he asked, "*When* did you go blind?" That one stumped me. *Wait,* have *I gone blind?* I thought. It didn't feel that way, as I sat there on the couch, gazing at him—even as I also knew that blindness had seeped into nearly every aspect of my life.

This experience of relentless, minor cataclysm, folded into the banality of everyday life, makes me feel like I'm in a Samuel Beckett play. I imagine a scene where a man is being buried alive, a shovelful at a time, over the course of decades. "Another shovelful of dirt, landed," the man could say from his hole, and then lie there in mordant thought for a month or two. "Another one, not quite a shovelful," he'd eventually add. "More a handful, generous dusting."

But I don't need to invent this Beckett play, because he wrote *Endgame*, which perfectly captures this experience of confoundingly slow decline. "Finished, it's finished, nearly finished, it must be nearly finished," Clov says at the beginning of *Endgame*, and this opening line might appear in any number of my journal entries. Clov, half blind, spends the play grudgingly but obediently serving his adoptive father, Hamm, who is totally blind, and who sits in a makeshift wheelchair. "Grain upon grain," Clov continues, "one by one, and one day, suddenly, there's a heap, a little heap, the impossible heap." The ancient

Greek paradox of the heap, to which this line alludes, has become for me the best way to explain the paradoxical experience of gradual vision loss. If one places rice or millet or quinoa or whatever on the floor, one grain at a time, at what point does it become a heap? One grain isn't a heap. Neither is three. Where is the threshold? The world is most easily apprehended when one conceives of it in binaries—you either have a heap of quinoa or you don't; it's day until it's night; it's the beginning until it's the end. But Beckett's play sits with the pain and ambiguity of the in-between, a world in which the sun has set but it's not night, where the sky is not simply gray but "light black." This is precisely my experience of blindness: a long decline in vision that will almost certainly end with the disappearance of form and detail, but with a paradoxical sense that even as the decline continues, it might never quite arrive at its terminus. I'm living in this infinite endgame, a frozen twilight where I've gone blind but still can see. Then another grain of blindness is added to the heap. At what point will the pile I've collected finally become equal to the sum of its parts?

The leader of a retinitis pigmentosa support group once told me that every five years she'd say to herself, "I thought I was blind then . . . now I'm *really* blind!" And then, five years after that, she'd have the same thought again. At sixty-nine, she's still going through it—she has no visual acuity at all, and is totally blind in one eye, but she still speaks of the fuzzed-out perception in her good eye with reverence—it allows her, under favorable conditions, to glean some basic high-contrast visual information about her surroundings, deducing where, for instance, the bright sidewalk becomes the dark asphalt. Even though, compared with me, she's quite blind, she still sets herself above other, even more blind people, who don't have that fogged-over patch of residual vision she can sometimes use to orient herself. "I don't know how they do it," she said. "I know they get good training, and they manage, but . . ." She trailed off, gobsmacked by the challenge of what real blindness must be like.

One has to laugh at the absurdist slapstick that arises from blindness—the spills, the mishaps, the cases of mistaken identity. ("Nothing is funnier than unhappiness," a character in *Endgame* says from inside the trash can she lives in.) There are instances, too, of what some call "disability gain": new vistas opening up from the experience of physical difference. I've felt it in the strange beauty of reading braille, as the tableau of my imagination blooms with word images gleaned through the patterns I feel through my fingertips brushing across a page. I recall the synesthetic exhilaration I felt under sleep shades, listening to the colorful stream of a toddler's babble, or the uncanny immediacy of feeling a wire slice through a mound of wet clay—the majesty of the tactile and audible worlds. I've even felt inklings of gain in my frustration at running into inaccessible products or services—a sense that blindness is nudging me toward a deeper social and political consciousness.

William Loughborough was a sighted technologist and artist who worked alongside Bill Gerrey and Josh Miele in the Bay Area, developing assistive technologies for the blind for more than thirty years, and put a tremendous amount of energy toward understanding how blind people experienced the world. He referred to his own sight as "blindlessness"—inverting the idea that blind people are merely sightless, and insisting that blindness has a rich set of affordances all its own that all those blindless people don't have access to.

• • •

One of the most surprising discoveries I've made is how absolutely ordinary blindness can be. It's hard for nondisabled people to appreciate this—that something as radical as not being able to see can fade into the background. Adrienne Asch, for all her involvement in the disability rights movement, remained adamant that her blindness wasn't the most salient thing about her; she insisted that disability wasn't "formative" to who she was. It's only when someone mistreated her because of her blindness that her disability rushed into the foreground. Asch is far from alone in this view. "When everything works, my blindness is just a fact of life, not an insurmountable obstacle blocking my path," Georgina Kleege has written. "I work around it. I ignore it. On a lot of days, it matters less than the weather." The writer Elizabeth Sammons told me that blindness is hardly the "main character" in her life.

The fact that I'm still in the midst of my degeneration makes it harder for me to let blindness fade to the background in this way. Two students at the Colorado Center who both lost their vision suddenly told me that they thought that going blind slowly over years sounded much harder than what they'd gone through. They'd had the shock and trauma of abrupt and total vision loss, but they'd also been forced to confront it all at once, and thus (they imagined) come to terms with it more quickly. I had trouble believing them—their lives sounded so much harder than mine, in ways that extended far beyond the causes of our blindness—but I do sometimes wonder how much easier it would be if I lost my vision all in one go.

I'm beginning to experience the stirrings of this sort of blind normalcy. At first, I used my computer's screen reader with an almost occult trepidation and seriousness—I wasn't just word processing or web browsing, I was doing special, challenging, embarrassing, interesting, *blind* versions of these activities. The trappings of blindness all felt unimaginably novel—writing an essay with this babbling voice instead of the voice I hear in my head; using the screen reader to collate all the headings or links on a website into a navigable list instead of just visually scanning the page. But the process eventually became transparent, a normal part of my daily workflow.

And as blindness becomes more familiar, I also experience the discrimination and marginalization that temporarily make it the painful focal point of my existence. I'm used to being the customer who mainstream society imagines and prepares for and accommodates—spaces and products and processes have always been built with people like me in mind. Classrooms, cities, websites, checkout lines, consumer electronics—I've spent my life comfortably navigating all of them. But as I get used to life under the canopy of blindness, I can feel my centrality—as a customer, a citizen, and even as a *person*—begin to erode. The more I use a screen reader, the more apps and websites simply don't work. The more I need to use my cane to find curbs and doorways, the more patronizing and intrusive (and sometimes hostile) strangers become.

As I approached a crosswalk on my way to pick up Oscar from school the other day, I saw that I'd drawn the attention of an eccentric-looking woman in an ankle-length brown coat. When the cars slowed to let us pass, we both began making our way across the street. Suddenly, in a quiet, tentative singsong—in case I was somehow unaware of where

I was—she announced, "Crossing the street now!" I reacted by pretending that she was totally unhinged, as though she was just announcing what she was doing to herself. "So am I!" I replied, sounding 40 percent angrier than I'd intended to.

• • •

Exploring the world of blindness feels like digging through a field of paradoxes. Blindness is at once central and incidental. I'm blind, even as I can see the room number on my hotel room without touching the braille beneath it. The process of retinal degeneration has turned out to be one of the most generative experiences of my life. And I've begun to realize that mourning the loss of my vision also entails accepting, and even enjoying, the vision that remains.

Walking around with severe tunnel vision, you have a choice: you can keep your eyes on the ground, scanning for obstacles, or keep your head up, and trust the cane to catch the curbs. The DeafBlind poet John Lee Clark, who was born Deaf and then became blind from RP in early adulthood, has written beautifully about his decision to stop looking down. "I'd taken up a blindfold, only the blindfold itself involved a kind of vision," Clark wrote. "My blindfold wasn't black. It was the scenery with which I wrapped around my eyes." His decision to stop using his vision for navigation freed Clark to visually appreciate the world around him. "Vision was a bonus," he told me. In this way, Clark took agency over when he went blind, even if it meant it happened before the last of his vision had disappeared. "The way I would live the rest of my life had already arrived," he said. "I chose the calendar date. I made that date arrive for me, instead of waiting for it. My sight could go all out overnight, or drain out slowly over thirty years. Makes no real difference."

There's a powerful medical or even commonsensical impulse to keep fighting, to hang on to my vision, to preserve it (as another blind mentor put it to me) "down to the last photon." But that no longer feels like a productive fight (if it ever did). It's a losing battle, and one that sets me up against myself. These days, I feel ready to follow John Lee Clark's path, to stop using my eyes for the basic visual functions I'm straining so much to hang on to—scanning the ground, reading large print, trying to find the spatula with my eyes instead of with my hands—and just let go.

When James Joyce was in the worst throes of his vision problems, he needed surgery to prevent one eye from going permanently blind. Facing this prospect, and continuing to work on *Finnegans Wake*, he wrote to a friend, "What the eyes bring is nothing. I have a hundred worlds to create, I am losing only one of them." This comment, for all its bravado, still captures, I think, the reality of vision loss: one is indeed losing an entire world, a planet's worth of images, all those dioramas plunged into darkness. And yet the worlds that persist after blindness—in the remaining senses, in the imagination, and in the depth of feeling that has nothing to do with visuality—far exceed what's lost.

• • •

I'm surprised to find solace in a play as bleak as *Endgame*. But even though Samuel Beckett has no interest in redemption or salvation, his technique of glazing calm onto terror (as Stanley Cavell put it) provides, if not a way out (for Beckett, it should go without saying, there is no way out), then at least a path through. At one point, Hamm tells Clov the story of how they came to be in their present situation, beginning when Clov was a child. Hamm trails off as his story reaches the present day, and Clov asks, "Will it not soon be the end?"

"I'm afraid it will," Hamm says.

"Pah!" Clov answers. "You'll make up another." As I write from this same place, where the story of my visual life seems to be coming to an end, I get the sense that, having ended, it will be in my power to continue, and make up another. "The end is in the beginning," Hamm says as the play reaches its finale, "and yet you go on. Perhaps I could go on with my story, end it and begin another." What feels like death, and loss, and finality—it's never really the last word.

I remember the realization I had under sleep shades: even in total darkness, I was still myself. I went on. This is something blind people have said (but really shouldn't have to), over and over, to the sighted world around us: we're still people. We don't see, or see very well, but aside from that, we're just like you. The failure to appreciate this basic fact, that someone's difference does nothing to alter their humanity, is the wellspring of all discrimination, alienation, and oppression. It ought to be obvious, but if you're not disabled, it's stubbornly easy to forget. It's as though, with regard to blind people, the sighted lack any sense of object permanence, the understanding a baby develops when her father hides his face behind his hands: she knows he hasn't really gone anywhere. He's still there.

I began this book with the idea that I existed with one foot in the sighted world, and the other in the blind one, and that I'd immerse myself in blindness, exploring all the radical, frustrating, innovative, weird, and wonderful things going on in this foreign land, to understand where I was headed. And, like H. G. Wells's Nunez, I did discover a country of the blind, with blind ways of living, blind modes of thinking and perceiving, blind traditions and technologies and subcultures and habits. I found that the experience of blindness encompasses both tragedy and beauty, the apocalyptic and the commonplace, terror and calm. This is true of most of human experience: the same can be said of the process of aging, or of dying. In the end, I found that the separation between the blind and the sighted worlds is largely superficial, constructed by stigma and misunderstanding rather than any inherent difference. If we could remove the misperceptions people have about blindness—the image of it as a place of fear, claustrophobia, infantilization, and fundamental otherness—the landscape would begin to look very different. The two worlds would cease to feel so distinct, and their overlapping zones would grow. Ultimately, they'd have to yield and concede and share territory. The blind belong to our world, and we belong to theirs. It's the same world.

One night, my eyes felt totally spent, and I lay in bed with my glasses off. Lily was watching a video I was interested in, and I felt a surge of exclusion—I wanted to watch with her, but I just couldn't bring myself to push my eyes to do any more looking that day. I started to feel a rising panic about the blindness to come, when I'll no longer have the luxury of resting and resetting my vision. Before the feeling grew too large, I fell asleep. Early the next morning, I half woke as Oscar climbed into bed between us. I still couldn't see much—my eyes take longer and longer to clear after I wake up these days. But I wasn't in any rush to see; I found I already had in full the intimacy and unmediated experience of being wrapped up in blankets and bodies, our morning breath rolling in and out, laughing and murmuring as though we were a single human-blanket organism with three voices and a lot of legs. I had no desire to see anything. My love for Lily and Oscar and the life we shared felt in that moment full, unbroken, and utterly complete. I didn't reach for my glasses until they'd both already gone downstairs.

Acknowledgments

I spoke with hundreds of people during the years I worked on this book, and cannot thank them all here, but I want to acknowledge a fraction of them by name: Jennifer Arnott, Robert Baran, Bryan Bashin, Edward Bell, Charles Bennett, Ahmed El Bialy, Barbara Black, Rick Boggs, Pamela Bortz, Brett Boyer, Sandra Burgess, Will Butler, Fanny Chalfin, Kim Charlson, John Lee Clark, Kevin Cosgrove, Maliea Croy, Ann Cunningham, Chris Danielsen, Julie Deden, Robert Englebretson, Brian Fischler, Chancey Fleet, Serena Gilbert, Haben Girma, Dan Goldstein, Cragar Gonzales, Tony Gonzales, Emilie Gossiaux, Antonio Guimares, Jen Hale, Mary Haroyan, Michael Hingson, Rachel Huckfeldt, Mike Hudson, Chip Johnson, Millie Kapp, Áine Kelly-Costello, Gene Kim, Tina Kurys, Erin Lauridsen, Anil Lewis, Will Lewis, Maren Tova Linnett, Bec Loomis, Barbara Loos, Ramona Manzanares, Marc Maurer, Tom McClure, Josh Miele, Laura Millar, Helen Mirra, Deirdre Nuccio, Cheavon Otto, Josh Pearson, Eliza Portugal, Lauren Race, Mark Riccobono, Delfina Rodriguez, Amy Ruell, Hend Salah, Elizabeth Sammons, Meredyth Sauter, Connor Scott-Gardner, Matthew Shifrin (whose podcast, *Blind Guy Travels*, will be of interest to any reader of this book), Justice Shorter, Darien Simmons, Chris Snyder, Logen and Jim St. Leger, Deborah Kent Stein, Tai Tomasi, Giorgio Vickers, Maddie Williams, Laura Wolk, and so many others.

Working with editors at several publications sharpened my thinking about disability during the writing of this book: Delaney Hall, Roman Mars, and Avery Trufelman at *99% Invisible*; Willy Staley, Vauhini Vara, and Bill Wasik at *The New York Times Magazine*; Nimal Eames-Scott and Michael Luo at *The New Yorker*; Matt Kielty, Lulu Miller, Latif Nasser, Maria Paz Gutiérrez, Pat Walters, and many others at *Radiolab*; Claire Boyle at *McSweeney's*; Emily Watlington at *Art in America*; Britta Greene and David Krasnow at *The New Yorker Radio Hour*; and Rob Walker and Joshua Glenn at *Significant Objects*.

I wouldn't have the confidence to call myself a writer without the selfless support and encouragement of Gideon Lewis-Kraus, who told me in 2003 to pull myself together, and has been helping me to keep it together every year since.

A number of friends read drafts of this book at various stages in its genesis, including Gideon, whose notes were so encouraging they tricked me into thinking I was finished two years before I actually was. Eli Horowitz read every chapter as I wrote it, like an editorial Tour de France pacer van; his affectionate skepticism and crinkled enthusiasm gave me energy and guidance at crucial junctures throughout the long race; I owe him acknowledgment for support he's given me far beyond the bounds of this book. Catherine Kudlick's notes on an early draft were so bracing they came with their own trigger warning; I'm grateful to her for pushing me to move past the comfortable shores I'd been hugging. Alex

Kitnick and Andrea Gadberry, both hilarious and warmhearted philosophers, read early drafts of different chapters and offered deeply useful and encouraging notes. Annika Ariel read the manuscript so carefully that Penguin Press should poach her from her current job; her notes were brilliantly precise and made this book quantifiably better. Sheri Wells-Jensen's notes on a late draft of this manuscript were themselves worthy of publication; while I didn't profile her in these pages, our conversations about blindness, ableism, and humanity infuse every paragraph.

Jordan Bass has been a stalwart long-distance parallel writing partner; I value our shared Golgotha spreadsheet with the same ardor I bring to family heirlooms. Late in the game, he came through with a line edit I can only describe as heroic: generous, encouraging, but mercilessly precise, comprehensive, and wise. I owe him more than I'll ever be able to repay.

Working at *The Believer* from its beginnings put me in close contact with most of my favorite writers, and felt like an eight-year MFA program where I didn't write much but still learned how to write (and read, and edit), under the unparalleled mentorship of Dave Eggers, Heidi Julavits, Ed Park, and Vendela Vida, along with that magazine's contributors and all of my colleagues at *McSweeney's*, including Barb Bersche, Emily Doe, Brent Hoff, Laura Howard, Dave Kneebone, Adam Krefman, Brian McMullen, Heidi Meredith, Ethan Nosowsky, Angela Petrella, Michelle Quint, Oscar Villalon, Alvaro Villanueva, Chris Ying, and many others.

In 2016, I proposed a project that would become the seed for this book as an audio series for *Triple Canopy*'s "Vanitas" issue. I bailed on that project, but I remain grateful to *TC* editors past and present for the totally undeserved patience and generosity they showed me: thank you, Sam Frank, Lucy Ives, Alex Provan, and Matthew Shen Goodman.

KCRW's *Organist* podcast was a crucial forum for developing my writing and research into blindness, which I did with the encouragement and collaboration of my brilliant colleagues there: Jenny Ament, Ben Bush, Jonna McKone, Niela Orr, Ross Simonini, David Weinberg, Myke Dodge Weiskopf, Nick White, and many others, including honorary *Organists* such as Sam Greenspan, Rob Rosenthal, and Julie Shapiro.

Invitations from Patty Gone and Jon Ruseski at the PLATFORM reading series in Northampton, Massachusetts, and Julie Beth Napolin at the University of Pennsylvania, provided generative opportunities to talk about the intersections of art and disability. Early interest from Reyhan Harmanci, Max Linsky, and Jenna Weiss-Berman added fuel to the fire that eventually ignited this book.

Many friends, colleagues, and mentors have helped me in ways large and small: Alex Abramovich, Lucas Adams, Sandy Allen, Sari Altschuler, Mary-Kim Arnold, Robin Beck, David Berman, Alix Blair, Katie Booth, Will Butler (again for good measure), John Lee Clark (once more with feeling), Josh Cohen, Bojana Coklyat, Adam Colman, Georgia Cool, Chris Cox, Matthew Derby, Rodney Evans, Kelly Farber, Ezra Feinberg, Isaac Fitzgerald, M. Leona Godin, Daniel Gumbiner, Greg Halpern, Kayla Hamilton, Ben Brock Johnson, Phyllis Johnson, Rachel Khong, Jina Kim, Robert Kingett, Jason Klauber, Georgina Kleege, Ryan Knighton, Jim Knipfel, Andrea Lawlor, Allison and Christian Lorentzen, Hai and Youme Nguyen Ly, Sarah Manguso, Frank Marotta, Mara Mills, Kevin Moffett, Ryan Murdock, Sam Nicholson, Stacey Novack, Sheridan O'Donnell, Emilio Oliveira, Sarah Orem, Nat and Jacob Otting, Richard Parks, Lindsay Patterson, Ahndraya Parlato, Nicole Pasulka, Ben Pauley, Jason Polan, Sumanth Prabhaker, Matt Roberts, Matthew Rubery, Ben Rubin, Emily Schlesinger, Molly Shea, Andy Slater, Jason Strother, Paul Sturtz, Jessica Tam, Justin Taylor, Aaron Thier, Sarah Trudgeon, Dave Weimer, David Wilson, and many others.

While I wrote this book I had to learn how to become a blind reader, writer, and researcher. I can't fathom how I would have pulled this off without access to Bookshare, the accessible book repository for people with print disabilities. Instead of donating your car to NPR, you might consider giving it to Bookshare, a Benetech company. The Internet Archive was also an invaluable resource and must be supported. Thanks also to David Kingsbury of the Carroll Center for the Blind, whose book, *The Windows Screen Reader Primer*, helped me make the switch to JAWS at a late stage of the revision process when I could no longer avoid MS Word (which is shockingly inaccessible on the Mac).

Thanks to Michael Gorra, Michael Thurston, and the Smith College English Department for inviting me to teach a class on the literature of blindness, and to the students who took that class, whose curiosity and intelligence pushed my thinking in new directions.

I'm also grateful for the patience and support of Kathy Roberts Forde, Brian McDermott, and the UMass Amherst Journalism Department, along with the talented, empathetic students I worked with in that program.

I was supported throughout the last few years of adaptation to vision loss by various online communities, including the Blind Academics listserv, the Pioneer Valley Blind Group, the erstwhile Monday Night blind meetup, and the MetroWest FFB RP Support Group. Not blindness-related (or online), but thanks, too, to Pagan Kennedy and Karen Brown for whatever our group is called, and to Matt Abramovitz for strengthening the radio community in the Happy Valley.

I'm grateful for the training I've received from the Massachusetts Commission for the Blind, and I particularly benefited from the ambulatory pedagogy of Mr. Michael Dionne.

Claudia Ballard, my agent, entirely deserves her reputation as a model of generosity, intelligence, and skill; I feel immensely lucky to have the chance to work with her. This book wouldn't exist without many of the people thanked here, but it *really* wouldn't exist without her. I'm also grateful to Ann Godoff, Scott Moyers, and everyone at Penguin Press for their faith in this book and my ability to write it. Victoria Lopez, Randee Marullo, and Ryan Sullivan deserve special thanks for their careful reading (and rereading) of the text. Kyle Paoletta fact-checked the manuscript with astonishing rigor, intelligence, and grace; any errors herein remain my own. Thanks to Ilya Milstein and Christopher King for the perfect cover illustration and design. Thanks to Juliana Kiyan and Lauren Lauzon for their care in helping this book find its way to readers, blind and otherwise.

I'd always had the image of a book editor as someone who gives you one close read, and the rest of the time they're sending you straight to voice mail. Emily Cunningham, by contrast, has astonished me with her willingness to read a seemingly endless number of drafts, each time coming at them (and me) with grace, patience, and perspicacity, from the sentence level to large-scale restructuring. I owe her a tremendous debt of gratitude for the immense energy, intelligence, and care she brought to this project, and for helping me to stop spinning out of control without holding me rigidly in place.

I offer my infinite thanks to Ellen Simon, my mom, whose unconditional love has been a prerequisite of any accomplishment I've achieved. Love and thanks to Jon Leland, my dad, who taught me so much from the very beginning, including two of the most central activities of my life: the production of electronic media and the practice of seated meditation. One only needs to look at the canvases that my sister, Nicola Florimbi, produces to appreciate the depth of her feeling and talent. Thank you for the tactile painting; I love you. Love and thanks to the rest of my family, too: Nancy Simon, David Florimbi, Sofia Florimbi, Marsha Mason, Rae Slater Vermeulen, Elaine Joyce, Nanny Baim, Joan Simon, Neil and Danny Simon, Marjorie and Maurice, Bryn Martyna, Matt Bruss, Miles Leland, Bill Leland, Sky Esser, Ginny Winn Hafiz Leland, Wendy Martyna, Deb Leland, John Hunter, all Lelands, all Simons, Gary Wachter, Carol Ott, Laura Gurton, Alan Greenhalgh, Anna Gurton-Wachter, Ian and Lev Dreiblatt, all Gurtons, all Wachters, everybody.

I'm unspeakably proud of Oscar Leland, whose colossal intelligence is matched only by his immense compassion, sweetness, and hilarity. I love you with every atom of my being.

Lily Gurton-Wachter read multiple drafts of this book even as she lived through it. I'm inexpressibly grateful to her for letting me write with such candor about our life together (and for her brilliant prepositional solution to the problem of the subtitle). It would have been enough for her to have been as kind, intelligent, thoughtful, and patient as she is (*dayenu!*)—but on top of that, she also somehow gets to be beautiful, hilarious, penetratingly insightful, and sublimely attuned to the uncanny pleasures that language gives rise to. There's no one else I'd rather spend the rest of my life with, beneath the canopy of a romantic-municipal building constructed of clay, wood, cloth, feathers, language, and natural stone.

Notes on Capitalization and Sources, and Image Descriptions

A Note on Capitalization

The decision to capitalize the word *braille* when it's referring to the writing system (as opposed to the person) engenders surprisingly strong emotions among some blind people. The proponents say that *braille* ought to be capitalized, since it, like Morse code, derives from the proper name of its inventor. Furthermore, they argue, it does a disservice to the man who transformed the lives of so many generations of blind people to strip him of the honorific the capital provides. Those on Team Lowercase argue, to the contrary, that a capital letter is less honorific than exoticizing: braille is too often held up as a strange, arcane, language-like phenomenon, rather than an everyday communicative system like print, or hieroglyphics, or texting. This is the position that the Braille Authority of North America, which formalizes the rules governing the system on this continent, has adopted.

As an amateur braille reader who feels a need to push back against the rising alienation I feel in my own life as a novice blind person, I've opted to lowercase *braille* here, smoothing down its hair, as it were, in an effort to domesticate it into my own life, and perhaps that of the readers of this book. (I'm indebted to Jonathan Mosen—the captain of Team Uppercase, it might be said—whose podcast introduced me to this debate, and to Robert Englebretson and Sheri Wells-Jensen, who were generous with me in their thinking about why they so strongly prefer the lowercase styling.)

Notes on Sources

INTRODUCTION: THE END BEGINS

The epigraphs to this book come from Hannah Arendt, *Men in Dark Times* (1968), and Theodor W. Adorno, *Minima Moralia: Reflections from Damaged Life* (1951), translated by E. F. N. Jephcott (1974). I encountered the Hannah Arendt quote via Tanya Titchkosky's *Disability, Self, and Society* (2003). I first encountered the Adorno quotation in the title and introduction to Martin Jay's *Splinters in Your Eye: Frankfurt School Provocations* (2020). (It bears mentioning that Jay's related 1993 study, *Downcast Eyes: The Denigration of Vision in Twentieth-Century French Thought*, offers a useful—and highly influential—account of the "ocularcentrism" of Western culture.)

The name of my introduction, "The End Begins," is borrowed from the first chapter of the British sci-fi writer John Wyndham's 1951 novel *The Day of the Triffids*. The conceit of that book—the population of the world mysteriously gone blind, with a few sighted travelers roaming among them—makes it an unlikely precursor to José Saramago's 1995 novel *Blindness*. Both novels depict a pandemic of blindness as an apocalyptic threat to humanity. (In Wyndham's case, the threat is amplified by homicidal plants.)

The title of this book is borrowed from H. G. Wells, as discussed in the introduction, but I also owe a debt to Stephen Kuusisto, whose similarly titled 1998 memoir, *Planet of the Blind*, is as lyrical as the writer's poetry, which likewise has engaged in the aesthetics and phenomenology of blindness. The essayist Edward Hoagland, who went blind in his fifties, then recovered his sight, only to lose it again in his seventies, published an essay and, later, a novel, both under the title *In the Country of the Blind*. In the essay, written after he regained his sight, he recalls, "Goodness knows, I hadn't wanted to be blind, but neither had I wanted to be young forever, and some of the changes I was now undergoing were amusing in their way, or curious, and an adventure." But after he lost his sight again, he painted a more desperate picture: "Blindness is enforced passivity," he wrote in 2016.

My limited understanding of Deaf culture comes from conversations with Deaf and DeafBlind writers and scholars such as John Lee Clark and Carol Padden. Clark's essays, collected in *Where I Stand: On the Signing Community and My DeafBlind Experience* (2014) and his forthcoming essay collection from Norton (2023), as well as Padden's, including *Inside Deaf Culture* (2005), written with Tom Humphries, and Susan Burch's *Signs of Resistance* (2002), were all useful guides.

The quotation from Greg Tate is from the introduction to *Flyboy 2: The Greg Tate Reader* (2016), and Susan Orlean's quotations are from *The Orchid Thief* (1998).

1: SEEING STARS

The public perception of blindness as a binary is stubbornly durable, and its debunking is commonplace in blindness memoirs (which are, themselves, superabundant in literary history). In 2021, Elsa Sjunneson published a memoir, *Being Seen: One Deafblind Woman's Fight to End Ableism*, in which she observes, "There are a million different ways to be blind"; that same year, M. Leona Godin wrote in *There Plant Eyes*, her "personal and cultural history of blindness," that "there are as many ways of being blind as there are of being sighted." Stephen Kuusisto begins his memoir with a similar observation, adding that he stares at the world "through smeared and broken windowpanes." This idea is also beautifully expressed throughout Georgina Kleege's work (her 1999 memoir *Sight Unseen* is a classic, and served as an abiding inspiration as I tried to write about blindness from a cultural and social as well as a personal perspective). Kleege has written of "imperfectly blind people," which she invokes to describe the majority of blind people who see something other than complete darkness (a category in which she includes herself; the line appears in her 2018 study *More Than Meets the Eye: What Blindness Brings to Art*).

The remark about "visual tinnitus" comes from Damon Rose, "Do Blind People Really Experience Complete Darkness?" *BBC News*, *Ouch* (blog), February 25, 2015.

Jorge Luis Borges's lecture on blindness was translated by Eliot Weinberger, and appears in his 1999 *Selected Non-Fictions*, also edited by Weinberger.

RP's emergence in the "teen age, at evening parties" comes from

Christian Hamel's entry on retinitis pigmentosa in the *Orphanet Journal of Rare Diseases* 1, no. 40 (October 11, 2006).

While they are dated and unreliable in places, I learned a great deal from prewar and midcentury American histories of blindness, including Richard S. French's *From Homer to Helen Keller: A Social and Educational Study of the Blind* (1932), Harry Best's *Blindness and the Blind in the United States* (1934), and Gabriel Farrell's *The Story of Blindness* (1956).

For information on the lives of blind people in ancient Greece, and their presence in classical literature, I relied most heavily on Martha L. Rose's *The Staff of Oedipus: Transforming Disability in Ancient Greece* (2003). Felix N. W. Just's 1998 Yale dissertation, "From Tobit to Bartimaeus, from Qumran to Siloam: The Social Role of Blind People and Attitudes Toward the Blind in New Testament Times," provides a rich index of biblical representations of blindness, as does Moshe Barasch's *Blindness: The History of a Mental Image in Western Thought* (2001).

Henri-Jacques Stiker's *A History of Disability* (published in French in 1982, first appearing in English in 1999) provides a wide-ranging overview of the lived experience of disabled people throughout Western history, as well as a genealogy of the attitudes that people and institutions have held toward them.

For more on the "Homeric question"—the scholarly debate over the evidence for a single blind bard named Homer who might or might not have authored a huge range of poetry, see chapter 1 ("From 'Homer' to the Homeric Poems") in Suzanne Saïd's *Homer and the Odyssey* (1998), and Barbara Graziosi's *Inventing Homer: The Early Reception of Epic* (2002).

Plutarch's story about Timoleon comes from volume VI of the Loeb Classical Library edition of Plutarch's *Lives*, translated by Bernadotte Perrin (1918).

My historical account here is geographically narrow; part of this has to do with the pervasive Eurocentrism of disability studies itself. Leah Lakshmi Piepzna-Samarasinha is one of the most persistent voices calling out academic disability studies for its whiteness; in *Care Work: Dreaming Disability Justice* (2018), they offer the beginnings of an alternative history of disability, including the observation of disabled Cherokee scholar Qwo-Li Driskill that "in precontact Cherokee, there are many words for people with different kinds of bodies, illnesses, and what would be seen as impairments; none of those words are negative or view those sick or disabled people as defective or not as good as normatively bodied people."

Just as this book was entering production, the University of Michigan Press published Wei Yu Wayne Tan's *Blind in Early Modern Japan: Disability, Medicine, and Identity* (2022). Disability studies is a rapidly expanding field, and I'm hopeful that scholarship like this—which expands readers' access to histories of blindness beyond the historically European, Western, and white orientation of disability studies' first decades—will continue to flourish.

2: NATIONAL BLINDNESS

The quotation on the economic conditions of blind people in France comes from Catherine Kudlick and Zina Weygand's introduction to *Reflections: The Life and Writings of a Young Blind Woman in Post-Revolutionary France* (2001). Material on the Quinze-Vingts and the lives of the medieval blind

French is from Zina Weygand's comprehensive history, published in English in 2009 as *The Blind in French Society from the Middle Ages to the Century of Louis Braille*, translated by Emily-Jane Cohen.

The NFB maintains a page on their website, "Blindness Statistics," that assembles a fairly up-to-date collection of figures from a range of studies and surveys of blind people. The statistics I cite here are all derived from William Erickson, Camille G. Lee, and Sarah von Schrader's 2017 article "Disability Statistics from the American Community Survey (ACS)," online at disabilitystatistics.org, or from more recent census data from 2019, also available at that site.

The NFB's sprawling official history, written by a highly subjective federation insider but still rich with primary sources and detail, is Floyd M. Matson's 1990 *Walking Alone and Marching Together: A History of the Organized Blind Movement in the United States, 1940–1990*. Matson is also the author of a thorough (if hagiographic) biography of tenBroek, *Blind Justice: Jacobus tenBroek and the Vision of Equality* (2005), based on many of tenBroek's papers, which are archived at the NFB's headquarters in Baltimore. TenBroek's own writings, particularly his banquet speeches (online at nfb.org), scholarly writings, and books (particularly *Hope Deferred: Public Welfare and the Blind* [1959]), provide an excellent sense of his legal thinking, philosophy, attitude, and style. In 2015, the NFB published a collection of historical articles commemorating its seventy-fifth anniversary, called *Building the Lives We Want*, edited by Deborah Kent Stein, updating and expanding upon Matson's history. I particularly benefited from reading the contributions of Brian R. Miller, Deborah Kent Stein, and James Gashel.

The American Council of the Blind published its own sprawling official history, *People of Vision* (2003), written by James J. and Marjorie L. Megivern, two sighted researchers friendly with the ACB, which (like Matson's book) contains a useful overview of blind history going back to ancient times to frame its deep dive into institutional minutiae.

Frances Koestler's *The Unseen Minority: A Social History of Blindness in the United States* (1976) is also, technically speaking, a biased official history—commissioned by the American Foundation for the Blind to commemorate its fiftieth anniversary and document the story of that organization's founding and development. But Koestler goes far beyond her mandate to provide a sweeping account of the major milestones—legislative, institutional, educational—of blindness in the US; nearly fifty years after its publication, it remains one of the most useful histories available.

Will Butler's writing is well worth looking up online, including his work at *The New York Times* and *VICE*.

Elisabeth Gitter's *The Imprisoned Guest: Samuel Howe and Laura Bridgman, the Original Deaf-Blind Girl* (2001) elegantly parses a great deal of archival material produced by Howe and the Perkins School.

The quotations from Newel Perry come from UC Berkeley's indispensable collection of oral histories at the Bancroft Library, all of which are freely available online.

Maggie Astor's reporting offers a helpful overview of the fight to update disability benefits rules; see "How Disabled Americans Are Pushing to Overhaul a Key Benefits Program," *The New York Times*, July 30, 2021.

My understanding of the NFB's midcentury legislative battles was greatly enriched by the historian Felicia Kornbluh's article "Disability,

Antiprofessionalism, and Civil Rights: The National Federation of the Blind and the 'Right to Organize' in the 1950s," from *The Journal of American History* 97, no. 4 (2011).

Few general histories of disability cover the clash between the ACB and the NFB, but Doris Zames Fleischer and Frieda Zames's study *The Disability Rights Movement: From Charity to Confrontation* (2001) is a notable exception.

The English professor John Rogers's class on Milton, available online through Yale University's Open Courses program, provides a powerful introduction to Milton's work, and oriented me to Milton's various writings on blindness. There are centuries of writings on Milton, but I especially appreciated the work of two blind scholars: M. Leona Godin's *There Plant Eyes* (2021) and Eleanor Gertrude Brown's *Milton's Blindness* (1934). The quotation from Milton here comes from *Complete Poems and Major Prose*, edited by Merritt Y. Hughes (1957), from Milton's "Second Defense of the People of England."

"See it feelingly" is from *King Lear*, but I recalled the line only when I encountered it as the title and epigraph to Ralph James Savarese's 2018 book about reading literature with autistic people.

3: BLINDED BY DEFINITION

I first heard the story of Heinrich Küchler and the history of the eye chart in a talk given by NYU professor Mara Mills at "Touch This Page! A Symposium on Ability, Access, and the Archive" at Northeastern and Harvard Universities in April 2019.

The story of James Holman, the eighteenth-century blind explorer, is exceedingly well told in Jason Roberts's *A Sense of the World: How a Blind Man Became History's Greatest Traveler* (2006).

For more on the construction of legal (or "economic") blindness as a criterion for federal benefits beginning in the US in the 1930s, see Frances Koestler's *The Unseen Minority*.

The line about being "blinded by definition" is by Lloyd Greenwood, in a column called "Shots in the Dark" that appeared in the *BVA Bulletin*, the publication of the Blinded Veterans Association, in 1949.

A recent survey of doctors' negative views of disabled people's quality of life can be found in "Physicians' Perceptions of People with Disability and Their Health Care," Iezzoni Li et al., in *Health Affairs Journal* 40, no. 2 (February 2021). Numerous studies over the years have placed blindness near the top of the list of most-feared disabilities; for an overview, as well as the results of a survey of more than two thousand Americans on their attitudes toward vision loss, see Scott et al., "Public Attitudes About Eye and Vision Health," *JAMA Ophthalmology* 134, no. 10 (August 2016).

Historical material about the analogies between Jews and blind people in medieval France comes from Edward Wheatley's *Stumbling Blocks Before the Blind: Medieval Constructions of a Disability* (2010).

The Aktion T4 program is documented in Henry Friedlander's *The Origins of Nazi Genocide: From Euthanasia to the Final Solution* (1995), as well as in Tamara Zwick's "First Victims at Last: Disability and Memorial Culture in Holocaust Studies," which looks at the way in which recognition of disabled victims has been an "afterthought" in Holocaust memorials. (Zwick's article is collected in *The Disability Studies Reader*, edited by Lennard Davis [Sixth Edition, 2021]—an excellent introduction to the field.)

The quote from Jonathan Sterne appears in *Diminished Faculties: A Political Phenomenology of Impairment* (2021). My understanding of the relationship between Jewishness and disease was enriched by Masha Gessen's *Blood Matters: From Inherited Illness to Designer Babies, How the World and I Found Ourselves in the Future of the Gene* (2008). (My thanks also to Rebecca Saletan for steering me toward this material.)

4: THE MALE GAZE

I am hardly the first blind writer to observe the powerful semiotic force that the white cane has in blasting apart clumps of tourists; Jim Knipfel, in his immensely entertaining RP memoir *Slackjaw* (1999), notes that with his cane, "everybody parts in front of me like the fucking Red Sea, that's for damn sure."

Robert Hine's memoir is called *Second Sight* (1993).

I refer to Kate Tunstall's translation of Denis Diderot's "Letter on the Blind for the Use of Those Who Can See" (1749), which appears as an appendix to Tunstall's *Blindness and Enlightenment: An Essay* (2011).

Gili Hammer's study is called *Blindness Through the Looking Glass: The Performance of Blindness, Gender, and the Sensory Body* (2019).

For more on the British columnist who questioned Emily Brothers's gender identity because of her blindness, see Roy Greenslade, "The Sun Censured by Ipso for Rod Liddle's Discriminatory Column," *The Guardian*, May 28, 2015.

For more on Bill Cosby's blindness defense, see: Karen Brill, "Bill Cosby's Lawyers Say He Is Registered as Legally Blind, Unable to Recognize His Accusers," Vulture.com, October 28, 2016; Emily Smith,

"Bill Cosby Is 'Completely Blind' and Homebound," Pagesix.com, July 18, 2016; and "Bill Cosby Has Nothing to Teach," letter to the editor, *The Washington Post*, June 26, 2017.

For more on Steve Wynn's blindness defense, see Nicole Raz, "Steve Wynn Sues for Defamation, Claims 'Leering' Accusations False," *Las Vegas Review-Journal*, April 5, 2018.

The NFB hired a law firm to conduct an investigation of the widespread sexual misconduct allegations within the organization; see *Special Committee Final Report on Sexual Misconduct and the NFB's Response*, published on the NFB's website in November 2021, alongside an interim report published earlier that year.

The lines quoted here from Ovid's *Metamorphoses* are translated by Allen Mandelbaum (1993).

The foundational work on the social stigma of disability (including an extended discussion of blindness) is Erving Goffman's book *Stigma: Notes on the Management of Spoiled Identity* (1963).

Ellen Samuels provides a useful analysis of the intersections (and divergences) between queer and disabled identity in her essay "My Body, My Closet: Invisible Disability and the Limits of Coming Out" (2003, reprinted in *The Disability Studies Reader*; my thanks to Maren Linett for suggesting I read it).

5: CAMERA OBSCURA

To supplement my interview with Emilie Gossiaux, I also consulted Manny Fernandez's "Hit by a Truck and Given Up for Dead, a Woman Fights Back," *The New York Times*, December 21, 2010, as well as a segment on *Radiolab*, "Finding Emilie," from January 25, 2011. I first learned about Gossiaux's work from a profile by Emily Watlington, published in the January 2020 issue of *Art in America*.

Details about Monet and Cézanne come from Patrick Trevor-Roper's *The World Through Blunted Sight: An Inquiry into the Influence of Defective Vision on Art and Character* (1970).

"How a Blind Man Saw the International Exhibition" was published in *Temple Bar* 7 (January 1863), pp. 227–37. I first learned about this remarkable essay reading Vanessa Warne's chapter on blindness in *A Cultural History of Disability in the Long Nineteenth Century* (2022); Warne's lucid readings of the *Temple Bar* text surely influenced mine.

The quotations from Georgina Kleege in this chapter are from *More Than Meets the Eye: What Blindness Brings to Art* (2018). John Lee Clark's are from his essay "Tactile Art," published in *Poetry* magazine's October 2019 issue.

My understanding of blind culture has been immeasurably enriched by conversations with Chancey Fleet, but her quotations in this chapter come from her appearance on the *InEx* podcast, season one, episode two, published June 19, 2022.

The "Saturday Morning Cartoons" episode of the *Say My Meme* podcast was published on July 13, 2021.

Roland Barthes's theory of the *punctum* appears in *Camera Lucida: Reflections on Photography*, in Richard Howard's translation (1981).

The quotation from Gregory Frazier is from Robert Mcg. Thomas Jr.'s *New York Times* obituary, "Gregory T. Frazier, 58; Helped Blind See Movies with Their Ears," published July 17, 1996. Joel Snyder's book *The Visual Made Verbal: A Comprehensive Training Manual and Guide to the*

History and Applications of Audio Description (2014) is a thorough road map to the field. I've also benefited from work done on AD by thinkers including Thomas Reid (whose podcast, *Reid My Mind Radio*, is mandatory listening for anyone interested in cultural issues relating to blindness), Serena Gilbert, Robert Kingett, Bojana Coklyat, and Shannon Finnegan. I also want to acknowledge the experimental AD work of artists like Alice Sheppard, whose collaborations with Georgina Kleege, Eli Clare, Dylan Keefe, and others to produce multisensory access to her dance performances are breaking new artistic ground in the field.

Quotations on audio description from the NFB in this chapter are from Chris Danielsen's article "Federal Appeals Court Rules against Mandated Described TV," published in the *Braille Monitor*, April 2003, and the NFB's brief in the DC Circuit US Court of Appeals, November 8, 2002, No. 01-1149: *Motion Picture Association of America, Inc., et al., v. Federal Communications Commission and United States of America.*

Hector Chevigny's 1946 blindness memoir has a superbly weird title: *My Eyes Have a Cold Nose.*

6: THE LIBRARY OF BABEL

The story of Joyce's dictation to Beckett is from Richard Ellmann's biography *James Joyce* (1959). Ellmann's source for this anecdote is a 1954 interview with Beckett, though the story may be apocryphal. (Joyce did, however, dictate to amanuenses.) See Peter Chrisp, "Samuel Beckett Takes Dictation," *From Swerve of Shore to Bend of Bay* (blog), January 28, 2014. I'm also indebted to Maren Tova Linett, whose *Bodies of Modernism: Physical Disability in Transatlantic Modernist Literature*

(2016) helped orient me to figures of blindness in Joyce (and elsewhere), as did M. Leona Godin's *There Plant Eyes* and late-in-the-game conversations with Cleo Hanaway-Oakley, who is currently finishing a book called *James Joyce and Non-Normative Vision*.

I gleaned the etymology of Joyce's invented hundred-letter word from William York Tindall's *A Reader's Guide to Finnegans Wake* (1969).

Beckett's line about Joyce as "synthesizer" is from *Beckett Remembering/Remembering Beckett: A Centenary Celebration* (2006), edited by James and Elizabeth Knowlson, and his line about *Finnegans Wake* as "that something itself" is from "Dante . . . Bruno. Vico . . . Joyce," in *Our Exagmination Round His Factification for Incamination of Work in Progress: James Joyce / Finnegans Wake: A Symposium* (1929). (I encountered the latter quotation in Namwali Serpell's *Seven Modes of Uncertainty* [2014].)

Rodney Evans's excellent 2019 documentary *Vision Portraits*, distributed by New Day Films, is available on numerous online streaming platforms, including Kanopy, where viewers can also find an audio-described version.

I first came to the rich histories of reading technology for the blind through the work of Mara Mills, whose intellectual generosity has been a tremendous boon and inspiration from the moment I encountered her. I'm also grateful to Sari Altschuler and David Weimer, whose "Touch This Page!" exhibition (online at touchthispage.com) and conference at Northeastern and Harvard Universities provided me with numerous generative encounters. They also led me to Jen Hale and Jennifer Arnott at the Perkins School for the Blind, who shared crucial resources and information from the Perkins archive.

For details on the history of reading systems for the blind, I relied on conversations with Mike Hudson at the American Printing House for the Blind, as well as Frances Koestler's *The Unseen Minority*; Zina Weygand's *The Blind in French Society from the Middle Ages to the Century of Louis Braille*; and Philippa Campsie's "Charles Barbier: A hidden story," published in *Disability Studies Quarterly* 41, no. 2 (Spring 2021).

The study I cite on the activation of the visual cortex when listening to a text versus reading it in braille is H. Burton and D. G. McLaren's "Visual Cortex Activation in Late-Onset, Braille Naive Blind Individuals: An fMRI Study during Semantic and Phonological Tasks with Heard Words," *Neuroscience Letters* (2006).

The story about reading braille in the cold is from Elizabeth Cameron's translation of the autobiography of Jacques Lusseyran, *And There Was Light* (1963). The story of the gentleman who reads braille with his fingers and print with his nose came from Robert Englebretson's address at a panel titled "Can the Science of Reading Fix Everything?" at the 2022 OSEP Leadership and Project Directors' Conference on July 19, 2022 (available on YouTube).

"Poem of the Gifts" appears in Jorge Luis Borges's *Poems of the Night* (2010), and was translated by Alastair Reid. "Borges and I" appears in his *Collected Fictions* (1998), translated by Andrew Hurley. Both quotations appear here with the permission of Penguin Books.

7: THE MAKERS

The full title of Aimi Hamraie's book is *Building Access: Universal Design and the Politics of Disability* (2017). As Hamraie shows, the curb cut's status as the prevailing emblem of universal design dates back at least to 1946 (see chapter 4, "Curb Cuts, Critical Frictions, and Disability [Maker] Cultures"). The specific phrase "curb-cut effect," however, was probably first coined by the civil rights activist Angela Glover Blackwell in her article of the same name, published in the Winter 2017 issue of the *Stanford Social Innovation Review.*

Much of my thinking about disability and design in this chapter is indebted to the work of Sara Hendren, which is distilled and articulated in her 2020 book *What Can a Body Do? How We Meet the Built World.*

All of my knowledge of phone phreaks comes from Phil Lapsley's entertaining and authoritative *Exploding the Phone: The Untold Story of the Teenagers and Outlaws Who Hacked Ma Bell* (2013); Rachael Morrison's documentary on Joybubbles is still in production as of this writing.

I've heard numerous disabled people describe "life-hacking" as a specifically disabled skill; the earliest published reference I can find is Liz Jackson's *New York Times* op-ed, "We Are the Original Lifehackers," May 30, 2018.

Eric Dibner's oral history is available through the Online Archive of California in volume III of *Builders and Sustainers of the Independent Living Movement in Berkeley.*

For more on the EPUB format's roots in blindness, see George Kerscher, "Structured Text, the Key to Information Now and in the Future," presented to the IFLA Conference (Copenhagen), August 28, 1997, http://kerscher.montana.com/ifla97.htm.

For this chapter, I also consulted Bess Williamson's "The People's Sidewalks" in *Boom California* 2, no. 1 (Spring 2012); Joseph P. Shapiro, *No Pity: People with Disabilities Forging a New Civil Rights Movement*

(1993); Martyn Lyons, *The Typewriter Century: A Cultural History of Writing Practices* (2021); Matthew Rubery, *The Untold Story of the Talking Book* (2016); Mara Mills and Jonathan Sterne, "Aural Speed-Reading: Some Historical Bookmarks," from *PMLA* 135, no. 2 (2020); Mara Mills, "Optophones and Musical Print," from the *Sounding Out!* blog, January 5, 2015; Tiffany Chan, Mara Mills, and Jentery Sayers, "Optophonic Reading, Prototyping Optophones" in *Amodern* 8: Translation–Machination, January 2018; Ray Kurzweil, *The Age of Spiritual Machines* (1999); Elizabeth R. Petrick, *Making Computers Accessible: Disability Rights and Digital Technology* (2015); and April Kilcrease, "10 Questions with . . . Chris Downey," *Interior Design*, June 6, 2016.

In addition to my conversations with Josh Miele, I consulted Wendell Jamieson, "The Crime of His Childhood," *The New York Times*, March 2, 2013; Isabella Cueto, "'Where the Bats Hung Out': How a Basement Hideaway at UC Berkeley Nurtured a Generation of Blind Innovators," in *STAT*, March 28, 2022; Bill Gerrey, *Smith-Kettlewell Technical File* (archived at ski.org); and Miele's own essay, "The Making of a Blind Maker," in *Future Reflections* 35, no. 2 (2016).

The quote from the NFB leader on guide dogs here is from Scott LaBarre's "The True Nature of Self-Confidence," which appeared in a special issue of the *Braille Monitor* devoted to the guide dog debates (vol. 38, no. 9, October 1995).

Rod Michalko's book is *The Two-in-One: Walking with Smokie, Walking with Blindness* (1999).

The quotes from Mia Mingus are taken from "Access Intimacy, Interdependence and Disability Justice," published on her *Leaving Evidence* blog, April 12, 2017. I first encountered Mingus's work, along with that of so many other disabled writers, artists, activists, and thinkers, through Alice Wong's indispensable podcast, *Disability Visibility*, along with her anthology of the same name, published in 2020.

8: AGAINST BLINDNESS

Lynda Charters's "Targeting Human Retinal Progenitor Cell Injections for Retinitis Pigmentosa" in *Ophthalmology Times Europe* 17, no. 8 (October 2021), provided a useful overview of recent stem cell treatment for RP.

The quotes about the risks of the Argus II are from Finn et al., "Argus II Retinal Prosthesis System: A Review of Patient Selection Criteria, Surgical Considerations, and Post-operative Outcomes," *Clinical Ophthalmology* 12 (2018). Eliza Strickland and Mark Harris's investigative report on the Argus II, "Their Bionic Eyes Are Now Obsolete and Unsupported," appeared in *IEEE Spectrum*, February 15, 2022.

Dr. Sheila Nirenberg's quotes about her Bionic Eye technology are drawn from NBC News, "Cracking the Code to Treat Blindness," November 30, 2018.

The quotation from Alison Kafer is drawn from her 2013 book, *Feminist, Queer, Crip.*

9: LADY JUSTICE

Osagie K. Obasogie's *Blinded by Sight: Seeing Race Through the Eyes of the Blind* (2014) was foundational to my understanding of the doctrine of legal color blindness, and his research on blind people's conceptions of race was useful in grounding my own impressions of racial consciousness among blind people. It's also where I first encountered Langston Hughes's "Justice" (Obasogie's epigraph), which was first published in *Scottsboro Limited: Four Poems and a Play in Verse* (1932).

Jacobus tenBroek's "The Right to Live in the World: The Disabled in the Law of Torts" was published in *California Law Review* 54, no. 2 (May 1966).

My research for this chapter was immensely enriched by Angela Frederick and Dara Shifrer's "Race and Disability: From Analogy to Intersectionality," in *Sociology of Race and Ethnicity* 5, no. 2 (April 2019).

The Judy Heumann interview I heard while washing dishes appeared in *On the Media*, "The Summer Camp That Inspired the Disability Rights Movement," on WNYC, July 24, 2020.

The quotation about intellectually disabled minors receiving electric shocks to correct their behavior comes from the DC Circuit Court of Appeals decision of July 6, 2021, between the Judge Rotenberg Educational Center in Canton, Massachusetts, and the FDA. See Lydia X. Z. Brown's comprehensive "Bearing Witness, Demanding Freedom: Judge Rotenberg Center Living Archive" at autistichoya.net/judge-rotenberg-center/.

Judy Heumann's memoir was cowritten with Kristen Joiner, and published as *Being Heumann: An Unrepentant Memoir of a Disability Rights Activist* (2020).

Douglas Baynton's "Disability and the Justification of Inequality in American History" appears in *The New Disability History: American Perspectives*, edited by Paul K. Longmore and Lauri Umansky (2001). (Thanks to Cathy Kudlick for steering me toward it.)

In addition to Heumann's memoir, for details on the 504 sit-in, I consulted Susan Schweik's "Lomax's Matrix: Disability, Solidarity, and the Black Power of 504" in *Disability Studies Quarterly* 31, no. 1 (2011), and Steve Rose, "Dennis Billups: He Helped Lead a Long, Fiery Sit-in—and Changed Disabled Lives," *The Guardian*, September 16, 2021.

Encountering Ann Lage's 2007 interview with Adrienne Asch, available online through UC Berkeley's *Disability Rights and Independent Living Movement Oral History Project*, radically altered the course of this chapter, and perhaps my life. I'll always be grateful to Robert Englebretson for pushing me toward Asch's work.

The second edition of Sins Invalid's disability justice primer, *Skin, Tooth, and Bone: The Basis of Movement Is Our People* (2019), is available for purchase through their website, sinsinvalid.org.

Details of the NFB's involvement with the passage of the ADA are drawn from the National Council on Disability's publication *Equality of Opportunity: The Making of the Americans with Disabilities Act* (1997); Kenneth Jernigan, "Reflections on the Americans with Disabilities Act," *Braille Monitor* 33, no. 2 (February 1990); and James Gashel's contribution to *Building the Lives We Want*.

Justice Shorter's comments about emergency management and disability outreach are drawn from her presentation to the Bill Anderson Fund Fellows' Fall Webinar, posted to YouTube in December 2020, and linked from her website, justiceshorter.com.

The statistics on crime and disability here come from Dr. Erika Harrell's US Department of Justice report, "Crime Against Persons with Disabilities, 2009–2014—Statistical Tables," November 2016, NCJ 250200.

Laura Wolk's childhood essay quoted here was published as "What Freedom Means to Me" in *Future Reflections* (Spring 2002).

Adrienne Asch coedited *Prenatal Testing and Disability Rights* in 2000 with Erik Parens.

Dorothy Roberts's remembrance was published as "Adrienne Asch (1946–2013)" in *Nature* 504, no. 377 (2013).

10: HALF SMILING

My understanding of the "structured discovery" approach to blindness rehabilitation and training—and its history—was deeply informed by James H. Omvig's *Freedom for the Blind: The Secret Is Empowerment* (2002). I'm grateful to Bryan Bashin for pointing me toward this work.

The full title of Robert Scott's book is *The Making of Blind Men: A Study of Adult Socialization* (1969).

Kenneth Jernigan's reaction to Thomas Carroll can be found in his seminal NFB banquet speech "Blindness: Handicap or Characteristic?," widely reprinted (sometimes under an alternative title, "Blindness: A Living or a Dying?"). See the NFB-produced compilation *Kenneth Jernigan: The Master, the Mission, the Movement* (1999).

The *Colorado Sun*'s investigation of sexual misconduct at CCB was published as "They Came to the Colorado Center for the Blind Seeking Confidence. They Left Traumatized," written by David Gilbert, published November 18, 2021. This article also links to the full text of the "Open Letter on Sexual Misconduct and Abuse Experienced through Programs of the National Federation of the Blind and National Blindness Professionals Certification Board." For more on sexual misconduct at NFB training centers, see Kaylee Poche's reporting on the Louisiana Center: "Months after National Federation of the Blind's Abuse Scandal, Survivors Want Accountability," New Orleans *Gambit*, July 5, 2021. Jonathan Mosen's July 8, 2022, interview with NFB president Mark Riccobono offered excellent insight into the NFB's position two years after the sexual misconduct investigations began. See the *Mosen at Large* podcast, episode 191.

Bryan Bashin's remarks on the Zen of blindness appear in Lee Kumutat's article "Bryan Bashin Marks 10 Years as LightHouse CEO" on the *LightHouse* blog, April 9, 2020.

Charles Baudelaire's lines are from his poem "The Blind," from *Flowers of Evil*, translated by James McGowan (1993).

The interview where I first learned about the half smile was Harsha Menon's "A So-Called Artist: An Interview with Helen Mirra," in *Buddhistdoor Global*, June 27, 2019. Mirra offers further citations, from Thích Nhất Hạnh and others, in a PDF devoted to her "Half-Smiler" project on her website, hmirra.net.

CONCLUSION: ENDGAME

I first encountered the idea of blindness as a kind of liberatory slapstick in an interview between the blind writers Jim Knipfel and Ryan Knighton (both of whom have RP), published in *The Believer* magazine, in a weird coincidence, since I worked there at the time, though I was years away from buying my first white cane, in October 2007. I'm also indebted to their RP memoirs—Knipfel's *Slackjaw* (1999), and Knighton's *Cockeyed* (2006) and *C'mon Papa* (2010), books that I treasure for the absurdist humor they find in the experience of vision loss.

William Loughborough's unpublished book, "Blindless" (1997), is available on his website at w3.gorge.net/love26/book.htm. I learned about Loughborough and the notion of "blindlessness" from a comment Matt May made on *InEx*, his podcast on "inclusive design," in an interview with Chancey Fleet (season 1, ep. 2, June 19, 2022).

Georgina Kleege's quotation in this chapter is from "Blind Rage: An Open Letter to Helen Keller," in *Southwest Review* 83, no. 1 (1998); she later expanded this work of creative nonfiction into a book of the same title.

The quotations from John Lee Clark are from his essay "Of Masks and Blindfolds," which will appear in his forthcoming collection of essays, to be published by W. W. Norton in late 2023.

Stanley Cavell's remark about Beckett's knack for glazing calm onto terror comes from "Ending the Waiting Game: A Reading of Beckett's *Endgame*," in *Must We Mean What We Say? A Book of Essays* (1969).

The notion of a sighted person lacking object permanence when it comes to blind people emerged out of a conversation I had with PJ Vogt and Alex Goldman, in a never-aired follow-up to my anonymous appearance on *Reply All*'s first call-in episode.

Image Descriptions

A dozen or so figures are scattered around the front of the dust jacket, surrounding the book's title and the author's name. The figures are illustrated by Ilya Milstein in a colorful, graphic-novelistic style. With a few exceptions, all of the figures have either white canes or guide dogs in harnesses. A few (a little girl; a pair of roller skaters) are accompanied by sighted guides, but the majority are going about their business independently, many of them carrying bags of groceries, rolling suitcases, backpacks, and cell phones. Some stand, some walk, and one rides a skateboard with his cane extended in front of him. The figures have a wide range of skin tones and visual styles: one wears a headscarf, another wears a baby strapped to her chest, the skateboarder has a man bun. They also have diverse abilities: a bearded Black man holds a walker, his ball-tipped cane at his side, and a white woman sits in a manual wheelchair (with a braille book on her lap, and a cell phone in her hand), her cane leaning against the chair's back. At the center of the jacket, a preppily dressed man in sunglasses holds a white cane—a possible stand-in for the author—and stands with a slight smile on his face, gazing into the distance. The author photo, which appears on the inside back flap of the dust jacket, shows me, a faintly chubby, not-bad-looking middle-aged white man with short black hair and rectangular glasses, smiling and looking at the camera. I'm sitting on a wooden bench on my back porch, framed by bright green tree leaves and the table before me.

Index

Index

Index

Index

Index

Index

Index

Index

Index

Index

Index

Index

Index